Palgrave Studies in European Union Politics

Series Editors
Michelle Egan
American University
Washington, DC, USA

Neill Nugent
Manchester Metropolitan University
Manchester, UK

William E. Paterson
Aston University
Birmingham, UK

Following on the sustained success of the acclaimed European Union Series, which essentially publishes research-based textbooks, Palgrave Studies in European Union Politics publishes cutting edge research-driven monographs. The remit of the series is broadly defined, both in terms of subject and academic discipline. All topics of significance concerning the nature and operation of the European Union potentially fall within the scope of the series. The series is multidisciplinary to reflect the growing importance of the EU as a political, economic and social phenomenon.

More information about this series at
http://www.springer.com/series/14629

Nathalie Brack

Opposing Europe in the European Parliament

Rebels and Radicals in the Chamber

Nathalie Brack
Université Libre de Bruxelles
Bruxelles, Belgium

Palgrave Studies in European Union Politics
ISBN 978-1-137-60199-5   ISBN 978-1-137-60201-5   (eBook)
https://doi.org/10.1057/978-1-137-60201-5

Library of Congress Control Number: 2017947170

This Palgrave Macmillan imprint is published by Springer Nature
The registered company is Macmillan Publishers Ltd.
The registered company address is: The Campus, 4 Crinan Street, London, N1 9XW,
United Kingdom

PREFACE AND ACKNOWLEDGEMENTS

These are challenging times for the EU. The term "crisis" has often been used to describe European integration as the EU is a political system in a state of quasi-permanent crisis. But the term crisis seems to have become truly meaningful in the last couple of years. Indeed, the EU is facing a "polymorphic crisis". Since 2009, the ongoing economic crisis has called into question one of the central pillars of the European project's legitimacy, i.e. the economic prosperity it is supposed to bring to its citizens. More recently, the migration crisis evidences the division of European leaders and their inability to solve urgent issues, feeding the arguments of sovereigntist parties for closed borders and returning to the nation state. The EU is also facing a value crisis with governments in some countries calling liberal democracy into question and the rise of radical right parties in several Member states. And of course, Brexit attests to the rejection of the European project by a (small) majority of British citizens. As one Member state has decided, by referendum, to leave, the EU is now facing an existential crisis.

Such a period provides fertile ground for the galvanization of opposition to Europe. And it is not surprising that the 2014 EP elections saw the unprecedented success of Eurosceptic parties. Euroscepticism has become a stable of European politics but with the complex crisis, the integration process has entered a new phase characterized by the mainstreaming of Euroscepticism: anti-EU rhetoric and arguments stressing the need for major reforms have become commonplace across the continent, including among mainstream political parties.

Against this backdrop, these are not only challenging times for the EU but also very interesting times to be an EU-scholar, especially if one is interested in opposition to Europe. This research was initiated partly out of academic interest but mostly out of personal curiosity. I was surprised by the fact that people opposing the European Union would want to seat in the European Parliament. This seemed to me to be a paradox: Why are there Eurosceptics in the European chamber? I also was curious as to how they see their job. How do they deal with the tension between the Eurosceptic platform they ran on and the tasks and expectations arising from the representative mandate? What are their strategies once inside the institution? Rather than focusing on the sources of Euroscepticism, I wanted to understand and explain the behaviours of Eurosceptics in the EP.

Gathering data and meeting more than a hundred Eurosceptic MEPs were quite time-consuming. But it is, I believe, the best way to fully grasp the paradoxical situation of these actors. This research provides a detailed picture of the strategies of Eurosceptics in the EP and the motivation behind their behaviour. But it also provides food for thought on the implications of their presence at the heart of the EU and on what these actors can bring to the table to contribute to alleviating the EU's democratic deficit.

The research and writing process can sometimes be a lonely path. But I was lucky to be able to count on the help and support of colleagues and friends. Over the course of this project, I have received many useful suggestions that have helped me improve the analysis and arguments presented in the chapters of this book. I would like to extend a special thanks to Olivier Costa, Jean-Benoit Pilet, Jean-Michel De Waele, Kris Deschouwer and Simon Usherwood who provided insightful comments on various parts of this research. This research would not have been possible without the help of many MEPs, parliamentary assistants and EP civil servants, who I would like to thank.

This project, at an early stage, was presented during my stay at the St Antony's College at the University of Oxford. I would like to thank the participants of the seminar for their comments and especially Kalypso Nicolaïdis for her support and useful suggestions.

I would also like to express my gratitude to the series editors for their careful reading of the manuscript and their many useful suggestions as well as to Imogen Gordon Clark, Steven Kennedy and the Palgrave team for their help, patience and work on this book.

I gratefully acknowledge the financial assistance of the Université libre de Bruxelles which made this research and its publication possible.

Finally, my friends have been a considerable source of encouragement, notably Katya who I especially thank for her careful reading and helpful advice as well as Karel, Corinne and Lou for their love and support.

Bruxelles, Belgium   Nathalie Brack

CONTENTS

ABBREVIATIONS

AFCO	Constitutional Affairs Committee
ALDE	Alliance of Liberals and Democrats for Europe
AT	Austria
BE	Belgium
CY	Cyprus
CZ	The Czech Republic
DE	Germany
DK	Denmark
ECR	European Conservatives and Reformists
EFD	Europe of Freedom and Democracy
EFDD	Europe of Freedom and Direct Democracy
ENF	Europe of Nations and Freedom
EP	European Parliament
EPP	European's People Party
ES	Spain
EU	European Union
EUL/NGL	European United Left/Nordic Green Left
FI	Finland
FN	Front National
FR	France
GR	Greece
Greens/EFA	Greens/European Free Alliance
HR	Croatia
HU	Hungary
IND/DEM	Independence/Democracy
IRL	Ireland

IT	Italy
ITS	Identity, Tradition, Sovereignty
LIBE	Civil liberties, Justice and Home affairs committee
LU	Luxemburg
MEPs	Members of the European Parliament
NA	Non-attached members
NL	The Netherlands
PES	Party of European Socialists
PL	Poland
PT	Portugal
PVV	Party for Freedom
RoP	Rules of Procedure
S&D	Socialists and Democrats
SE	Sweden
UEN	Union for Europe of the Nations
UK	United Kingdom
UKIP	UK Independence Party

LIST OF FIGURES

LIST OF TABLES

CHAPTER 1

Introduction

The European Union (EU) is once again in the midst of a storm. After two decades of treaty revisions which transformed the European project into a political system, the EU is now facing a new and multifaceted crisis. The ongoing economic crisis, the migration crisis and the Brexit have reopened debates and provoked tensions on the nature and "raison d'être" of European integration. With the economic and financial crisis, it seems that the EU is no longer able to deliver one of the key promises of the integration process, i.e. prosperity. But more than that, the EU's scope of intervention as well as its legitimacy is increasingly challenged. These crises, combined to the current context of democratic malaise, provide fertile ground for the success of radical, populist and Eurosceptic parties. In the 2014 European parliament elections, parties such as the UK Independence Party, the National Front in France, the Alternative For Germany Party, the Five Star movement in Italy and Syriza in Greece had an unprecedented electoral success (Brack and Startin 2015; Hobolt 2015, Hobolt and De Vries 2016). More importantly, the integration has reached a critical point as it has been fundamentally called into question with the Brexit referendum on the 23rd of June 2016. As a small majority of British citizens voted to leave the EU, they signalled their rejection of the European project and contributed to a partial disintegration of the EU. Although it is too soon to fully evaluate the consequences of this vote, it undeniably reflects the growing discontent of citizens towards the EU and will maintain a momentum for the Eurosceptic agenda in the coming years.[1]

© The Author(s) 2018
N. Brack, *Opposing Europe in the European Parliament*,
Palgrave Studies in European Union Politics,
https://doi.org/10.1057/978-1-137-60201-5_1

This opposition to the European project is far from new. European integration has always been a contested undertaking that has given rise to fears and oppositions within public opinions and among political elites (De Wilde 2010; Katz 2008). While these oppositions have long been seen as marginal or temporary, today there is a wide consensus that Euroscepticism has become a stable and persistent phenomenon across Europe (Usherwood and Startin 2013). Indeed, almost every party system has at least one Eurosceptic party competing in elections, and Europe has become an issue, if not a divider, in most European political arenas (Harmsen 2005, p. 79). These oppositions to the EU soon became evident in the European parliament (EP). Indeed, if the EP is often presented as a bastion of Europhiles, there have been Eurosceptic MEPs since the 1970s who have used it as a forum to actively defend and promote their points of view. Initially dominated by socialists, Christian-democrats and liberals who are universally in favour of European integration, the EP came to include new political groups representing the opposition of an increasing number of segments of the population. The pro-/anti-Europe axis quickly became particularly salient and remains even more so today (Hix et al. 2007; Otjes et al. 2016).

Eurosceptics face an interesting paradox: they achieve their greatest electoral success in European elections, but once elected, they must operate within an institution and, more generally, a polity they strongly criticize or even simply oppose (Benedetto 2008). This situation creates tensions not only for these actors but also for the parliament and the EU. Their presence inside the EU's institutions can trigger existential questions as to how they should carry out their representative mandate. In addition, the existence of these dissenting voices has implications for the EP and raises the issue of their impact on the institution, its functioning and its image. More broadly, the reality of Eurosceptic MEPs questions the place of political conflict within the EU as a political system which relies on consensual interactions. One may wonder the extent to which the persistent presence of Eurosceptics at the heart of the Union is an asset or a threat to its democratic legitimacy.

Surprisingly, only limited attention has been paid to Euroscepticism within the EP. Since Taggart's seminal article (1998), the study of Euroscepticism has become a well-established interdisciplinary subfield within European studies (Flood 2002b). This literature seeks, first and foremost, to understand the nature of the policy positions of political actors and the factors underlying them. Scholars have highlighted the heterogeneity and complexity of attitudes towards the European project and the influence of institutional, cultural, ideological and strategic factors (Hooghe and Marks 2007; Leconte 2010; Mudde 2011; Szczerbiak and Taggart 2008). Generally, however, they have neglected the analysis of these actors once elected to parliament (Jensen and Spoon 2010), and the field of research remains the national political arena. Apart from a few recent exceptions (Brack 2013; Brack and Costa 2012; Katz 2008; Lynch et al. 2012; Whitaker and Lynch 2014), scholars ignore the supranational level, while EP specialists tend to overlook Eurosceptic MEPs who are considered to be a weak minority with very limited opportunities within the EU institutional system (Neunreither 1998). As a result, studies of the strategies of Eurosceptic MEPs' are still comparatively scarce. In other words, Eurosceptic actors are frequently dismissed from the analysis because they are not numerous, organized or sufficiently integrated in the EP to really influence its deliberation. Their attitudes, motivations and strategies at the supranational level remain largely understudied.

This book aims to address this gap. Rather than investigating the source of Euroscepticism, it seeks to understand and explain how Eurosceptics, once elected to the EP, conceive and carry out their mandate. More specifically, the ambition of this study is to determine how these actors cope with the tension between the Eurosceptic platform on the basis of which they were elected and the tasks and expectations arising from their European representative mandate. It stresses that the interaction between the institutional context and individual preferences is a key to understand these anti-system actors. In addition, this book also analyses how the institution has managed them. Doing so, it offers a more general reflexion on the impact of the presence of Eurosceptic MEPs for the EU and its democratic legitimacy.

1   An Analysis of Eurosceptic Members of the European Parliament: What for?

Eurosceptics have constituted a persistent minority in the EP for more than 40 years and, until recently, did not seem to have had a major impact on European integration. The EU has a remarkable integrationist track record: it has faced multiple crises, has weathered them and continued to integrate (Fossum 2015). The institutions, though in persistent turmoil, are still standing; integration has widened as a result of several enlargements and deepened through successive treaty reforms which have considerably empowered the EP. Although so far Eurosceptics have not been able to stop the integration process, they can claim victory with the results of the June 2016 referendum in the UK which will lead to the first exit of a country from the EU. In the short run, the Brexit caused a surge in support for the EU and the values of integration. But it is likely to have tremendous and more negative consequences in the longer term. As noted by Usherwood (2016), the Brexit will act as an icebreaker for Eurosceptic movements: leaving the EU is no longer a purely theoretical option but can be presented as a real possibility on the basis of the Brexit.

If the Brexit is the first obvious and direct victory of Eurosceptics, it should actually be seen as the result of a more gradual and latent process. Eurosceptic actors have played a significant role as agenda-setters on European issues and have progressively contributed to the mainstreaming of their views. Through their success in national but mostly in EU elections, these parties have gained legitimacy, visibility and the means to pressure governmental parties, notably to demand the organization of referenda in relation to the EU but also a shift in other parties' stances on European integration. The long duration and complexity of the crises have led to the blossoming of contestation against the EU and have reinforced the power of Eurosceptics in many Member states. While in the past, the solutions to crisis were framed between the status quo and more Europe, in contemporary debates, less Europe has emerged as a real option (Young 2016, p. 5). Euroscepticism is no longer a fringe phenomenon, and with its mainstreaming, we are witnessing a slowing down of the integration process (Brack and Startin 2015; Taggart and Sczerbiak 2013; Usherwood and Startin 2013). Against this backdrop, it is essential to understand Euroscepticism, not only at the national but also at the supranational level. More particularly, an analysis of Eurosceptic MEPs' strategies marks a contribution on two fundamental issues.

First, this research adds to the still limited literature on anti-system opposition within democratic institutions by providing a framework for the analysis of this type of actors (Berger 1979). This framework can be applied to other dissenting actors in other parliaments, such as regionalists within the national parliaments of several European countries. The EP is considered here as a convenient laboratory for the study of the strategies of anti-system actors. It is the only directly elected institution of a political system in a state of quasi-permanent crisis, where the tensions regarding the nature and the *finalité* of the EU are reflected. As noted by Mény (2012, p. 159), in the absence of a shared vision of what the EU could or should be, a permanent tension results from the persistent uncertainty about the nature of the European beast. The EU is a specific case of a deeply contested polity whose legitimacy remains questioned and in which constitutional issues are numerous, recurring and perceived as problematic (Neunreither 1998, p. 428). This is not a unique situation as several nation states also face strong contestations such as Belgium, Spain and the UK. However, the EU is a magnified example of a political system whose very existence is frequently challenged and in which the debate not only deals with the choice of preferred policies but also with how and at which territorial level decisions are to be made. In other words, the European project is underpinned by a fundamental conflict over how politics should be organized in Europe (Hooghe and Marks 1997, p. 7). This struggle is reflected in the EP as it provides one of the few channels of expression for oppositional actors. It is precisely around that matter that Euroscepticism is situated. Indeed, this book suggests that Euroscepticism should be understood not as an opposition to European policies but as a systemic opposition to European integration and its results (i.e. the EU and its institutions). It is located outside "normal politics" (Magnette and Papadopoulos 2008; Trenz and De Wilde 2009), differs from classical opposition directed at public policies and reflects an opposition to the constitutive dimension of the EU. Eurosceptic MEPs are therefore a case of principled opposition or anti-system actors (Sartori 1966) who challenge the European polity, its legitimacy and its basic principles. Thus, this book concentrates on these actors in order to understand how they operate, once elected, within the system they oppose and, by doing so, provides a framework for scholars of anti-system opposition in other parliamentary settings.

Second, the actor-centred approach adopted in this research addresses, in a fresh and innovative way, the issue of the EU's democratic and legitimacy deficit. By focusing on Eurosceptic MEPs, this book outlines the consequences of their presence for the EP and for the legitimacy of the EU. Indeed, while political opposition is central to democracy, the EU lacks an institutionalized site for its expression. It missed the third milestone in the path towards democratic institutions, i.e. the possibility for an organized opposition to appeal for votes against the government (Dahl 1966). More precisely, while citizens enjoy the right to participate in EU elections and to be represented in the EP, "we emphatically lack the right to organize opposition within the system. We lack the capacity to do so, and, above all, we lack an arena in which to do it" (Mair 2007, p. 7). This leads to the transformation of political opposition, from a classical opposition directed towards policies and the government to a principled opposition directed against the regime, i.e. Euroscepticism. And, as rightly pointed out by Mair (2007, p. 7), "once we cannot organize opposition *in* the EU, we are then almost forced to organize opposition *to* the EU". The role of Eurosceptic MEPs is then fundamental in that respect. They raise the issue of the limits of the integration process. And, they also cast light on the key question of the role of opposition in a political system like that of the EU, which relies on relatively depoliticized and consensual interactions (Leconte 2010). Through an analysis of Eurosceptic MEPs' strategies, the idea is also to assess whether their presence could paradoxically be an asset for the EU and the EP or, as some scholars argue, if it contributes to the delegitimization of the EP and the EU or indirectly hinders the pursuit of the integration process (Diez Medrano 2012; Schmidt 2015).

2   Research Design

The goal of this book is to understand the strategies of Eurosceptic MEPs in parliament and to explore their impact on the EP's decision-making as well as on the EU's legitimacy.

In order to do so, this analysis connects EU studies, legislative studies and comparative politics. Indeed, along with other recent studies, this research relies on the assumption that the EU can be effectively studied with tools provided by comparative politics. More precisely, it is argued that, even if it is important to take into account the specific nature of political representation at the supranational level, MEPs are first and foremost representatives, facing similar constraints and driven by similar motivations as those of their national counterparts (Costa 2001; Kreppel 2012). In accordance with this view, this book connects legislative studies to EU studies in order to examine the particular situation of Eurosceptic MEPs in a comparative way. Drawing on the literature on political representation, it relies on role theory which has been central to legislative studies and, more specifically, the neo-institutional approach of roles (Searing 1994; Strøm 1997, 2012).

The motivational approach developed by Searing in his study of the House of Commons provides a conceptual framework for understanding the multidimensionality of the representative mandate while taking into account the subjective dimension of the representative process. Defined as a "dynamic configuration of interrelated objectives, attitudes and behaviours that are characteristic of people in a particular position" (Searing 1994, p. 18), the concept of role encompasses cognitive, normative and behavioural components. This approach emphasizes the content of roles in order to comprehend how, but also why, elected representatives act in one way rather than another. In the particular case of Eurosceptics, this approach enables to go beyond the apparent heterogeneity of their individual behaviours in order to highlight the interrelatedness of their motivations, attitudes and behaviours and determine the roles they play. It is complemented by the insights of studies on MEPs as well as on role orientations (Strøm 1997). As a result, this research is structured along two research questions. First, how can one categorize the roles played by Eurosceptic MEPs? Second, how can one best explain the diversity of their roles? In other words, the objective is to analyse and explain how and why Eurosceptics understand and carry out their representative mandate.

The empirical analysis is divided into two phases. The first aims at determining the roles played by Eurosceptic MEPs. Relying on a qualitative methodology and an inductive and interpretative approach, a typology of roles is proposed in order to demonstrate how these actors operate within the institution, outline their priorities and motivations and explain their emphasis on certain aspects of their representative mandate over others. This typology shows that, beyond the apparent homogeneity of their positions on Europe, Eurosceptic MEPs develop heterogeneous strategies within the institution. They carry out their mandate in different ways and have contrasting views of their job, their duties and their relations to citizens. These actors do not all adopt an outsider position, some are relatively well integrated into the parliamentary game.

The second phase of the analysis aims at explaining the actors' choice of role. Thereby, it contributes to the intellectual debate on the factors expounding the choice of a role. The hypothesis, which is tested here, assumes that the roles played by Eurosceptics result from the interaction between institutional and individual factors. Indeed, the roles adopted by actors are embedded in particular institutions; therefore, the institutional framework influences the scope of opportunities available to actors (Searing 1994). But individual factors also matter.

In the case of Eurosceptics, the *central hypothesis* is that the role played by a Eurosceptic MEP depends on the interaction between his/her preferences regarding European integration and the EU's institutions, on the one hand, and the formal and informal rules of the EP, on the other hand. The research thus examines a combination of macro-level (institutional rules) and micro-level factors (individual preferences).

3   DATA AND METHODS

By mobilizing multiple sources of data, this book combines both qualitative and quantitative methods to test whether the role of an MEP results from the combination of institutional- and individual-level factors. It emphasizes an actor-centred perspective—the actor and his subjectivity being at the core of the analysis—and relies on the comparison between Eurosceptic MEPs from 18 Member States and 38 national parties (for an overview, see Chap. 3).

An inductive and interpretative approach is used to identify and categorize the roles played by Eurosceptics. The roles are not dictated by a priori constructs but reflect the actors' universe of meaning (Searing 2012). In other words, rather than testing pre-established typologies, the focus here is on the way MEPs conceive their role as elected representatives and on their motivations to develop the typology of roles. The aim is to understand how they consider and carry out their mandate and why they do it in one way rather than another. To this end, interviews were carried out with more than 100 Eurosceptic MEPs, their assistants and EP officials. In addition, their parliamentary activities were analysed to determine their priorities, their use of time and resources and their involvement in parliamentary work. Additionally, data regarding their responsibilities within the EP (presidency or vice-presidency of a group, committee or delegation) were also collected to examine their level of integration in the parliamentary structure. The content of their parliamentary questions over the course of two years has also been analysed to understand the subject matter of their questions and their territorial focus (electoral district, national interest, broader European interest or third countries/international relations). Their voting behaviour during the same two-year period has been also evaluated to ascertain if they evolve according to the topic. Finally, the meetings of two Eurosceptic parliamentary groups (EUL/NGL and EFD) were observed during a six-month period to establish their priorities, working dynamics and to study the behaviour of, and interactions between, Eurosceptic MEPs more directly.

The typology is not the result of just one element but rather of the combination of these data. Indeed, as role perception and actual behaviour form a coherent and dynamic whole, it's only through the use of different data that one can reconstruct the typology of roles developed by Eurosceptic MEPs.

The second phase aims at providing an explanation for why we observe a variation within the typology of roles. The analysis is based on a mixed-method and a deductive approach. In order to test the central hypothesis of this research, the evolution of the formal and informal rules of the EP is analysed through a study of Rules of Procedures reforms. The aim is to systematically identify the constraints and resources derived from the institutional framework which could influence Eurosceptics' room for manoeuver as well as their perception of the institutional reality. I then examine qualitatively and quantitatively the extent to which the roles played by Eurosceptics are influenced by three main factors: their attitudes towards European integration and the EU; socio-biographical aspects; and the electoral system. The use of both qualitative and quantitative methods helps to identify general mechanisms explaining the choice of a strategy by these anti-system parliamentarians.

4   STRUCTURE OF THE BOOK

The book is comprised of eight chapters. After this introduction, Chap. 2 presents the theoretical foundation of the book. It offers a critical review of three strands of literature: political representation, legislative studies and EU studies. First, it describes how, for a long time, research focused on the "descriptive" or symbolic side of representation, on trying to assess the representativeness of the EP. It is only recently that scholars have studied the substantive aspect of political representation at the supranational level, with a more recent and limited strand of literature concentrating on role orientations. Like these recent studies, this research considers that political representation should be seen as a dynamic process in which it matters less to know who the representatives are than to know how they understand and carry out their mandate. Therefore, the second part of the chapter discusses the role theory and more particularly, the motivational approach which is used here to study representation in the EP.

Chapter 3 presents an up-to-date literature review on Euroscepticism. First, it describes the evolution of the phenomenon and the parallel development of scholarly work trying to unpack these oppositions to Europe. The main characterisations and categorizations of Euroscepticism are briefly exposed as well as the debates within the literature on the relative influence of ideological, strategic and institutional factors on the positions of political parties towards Europe. On the basis of this literature as well as on work on political opposition, it is argued that Euroscepticism should be seen as an anti-system opposition.

Chapter 4 provides an in-depth analysis of how Eurosceptics conceive and carry out their representative mandate. It proposes a typology of roles played by Eurosceptics in the EP. The analysis demonstrates that these actors play four ideal-types of roles: the Absentee, the Public Orator, the Pragmatist and the Participant. It shows that, despite the apparent homogeneity of their attitudes towards the EU, they develop heterogeneous strategies within the institution.

The next two chapters (five and six) test the central hypothesis of the research, i.e. the role played by a Eurosceptic MEP results from the combination of institutional- and individual-level factors.

Chapter 5 focuses on the institutional context. Drawing on the insights of legislative studies, the main argument there is that the rules of the game have an impact on the way parliamentarians understand and carry out their mandate. In this chapter, a systematic analysis of the formal and informal rules of the EP is carried out to determine the extent to which they affect the roles played by Eurosceptic MEPs. The first section is dedicated to the formal rules, i.e. the rules of procedure of the chamber, while the second section concentrates on the informal rules. Both sections show that the institutional context is a key to understand the roles played by Eurosceptics. Although the rules of the game are the same for all MEPs, they have a specific impact on the room for manoeuvre of Eurosceptic members and determine the range of strategies available to them.

Chapter 6 focuses on individual-level factors. Whereas attitudes and preferences are usually used in the literature as "an explanatory complement" to other factors, the claim here is that the preferences of MEPs are keys to explaining their roles. This chapter examines the extent to which their roles are influenced by their attitudes towards European integration and the EU in general. It also tests an alternative hypothesis related to the impact of the electoral system, political affiliation, seniority and previous political experiences.

The Conclusion summarizes briefly the main arguments and empirical findings. It then examines the consequences of the presence of Eurosceptic MEPs for the EP and the EU. It discusses the issues of the institution's representativeness and the EU's democratic legitimacy. On the basis of the empirical results, the Conclusion claims that, rather than endangering European integration, the presence of Eurosceptics in the EP and the roles they play might be an asset for the EP's and the EU's legitimacy.

NOTE

1. On the impact of the Brexit on Euroscepticism, see for instance Usherwood, S., "The UK referendum's impact on British and European euroscepticism", paper presented at the conference "Euroscepticism and the Eurocrisis", ULB, Brussels, 1st of December 2016.

REFERENCES

Benedetto, G. (2008). Explaining the failure of Euroscepticism in the European parliament. In P. Taggart & A. Szczerbiak (Eds.), *Opposing Europe? The comparative party politics of Euroscepticism* (pp. 127–150). Oxford: Oxford University Press.

Berger, S. (1979). Politics and antipolitics in Western Europe in the seventies. *Daedalus*, 27–50.

Brack, N. (2013). Euroscepticism at the supranational level: The case of the 'untidy right' in the European parliament. *Journal of Common Market Studies, 51*(1), 85–104.

Brack, N., & Costa, O. (2012). *Euroscepticism within EU institutions: Diverging views of Europe*. London: Routledge.

Brack, N., & Startin, N. (2015). Euroscepticism: From the margins to the mainstream. *International Political Science Review, 36*(3), 239–249.

Costa, O. (2001). *Le Parlement européen, assemblée délibérante*. Brussels: Editions de l'Université de Bruxelles.

Dahl, R. (1966). *Political oppositions in Western democracies*. New Haven: Yale University Press.

De Wilde, P. (2010). *Under what conditions does Euroscepticism flourish? An evaluation of different approaches and empirical findings*. Oslo: Trial Lecture.

Diez Medrano, J. (2012). The limits of European integration. *Journal of European Integration, 34*(2), 191–204.

Flood, C. (2002a). Euroscepticism: A problematic concept. *Communication for the UACES 32nd annual conference and 7th research conference*. Belfast: Queen's University.

Flood, C. (2002b). The challenge of Euroscepticism. In J. Gower (Ed.), *The European Union handbook* (pp. 73–84). London: Fitzroy Dearborn.

Fossum, J. E. (2015). *Competing European stories? Integration, disintegration and accommodation*. Paper Presented at the CES Conference, Paris.

Harmsen, R. (2005). L'Europe et les partis politiques nationaux: les leçons d'un non-clivage. *Revue internationale de politique comparée, 12*(1), 77–94.

Hix, S., Noury, A., & Roland, G. (2007). *Democratic politics in the European parliament*. Cambridge: Cambridge University Press.

Hobolt, S. (2015). The 2014 European elections: Divided in unity? *Journal of Common Market Studies, 53*(S1), 6–21.

Hobolt, S. B., & De Vries, C. (2016). Turning against the union? The impact of the crisis on the Eurosceptic vote in the 2014 European parliament elections. *Electoral Studies, 44,* 504–514.

Hooghe, L., & Marks, G. (1997). The making of a polity: The Struggle over European integration. *European Integration Online Papers, 1/004.*

Hooghe, L., & Marks, G. (2007). Sources of Euroscepticism. *Acta Politica, 42*(2–3), 119–127.

Jensen, C., & Spoon, J.-J. (2010). Thinking locally, acting supranationally: Niche party behavior in the European parliament. *European Journal of PoliticalResearch, 4*(2), 174–201.

Katz, R. (2008). Euroscepticism in parliament: A comparative analysis of the European parliament and national parliaments. In P. Taggart & A. Szczerbiak (Eds.), *Opposing Europe? The comparative party politics of Euroscepticism: Volume 2* (pp. 151–180). Oxford: Oxford University Press.

Kreppel, A. (2012). The normalization of the European Union. *Journal of European Public Policy, 19*(5), 635–645.

Leconte, C. (2010). *Understanding Euroscepticism*. Basingstoke: Palgrave MacMillan.

Lynch, P., Whitaker, R., & Loomes, G. (2012). The UK Independence Party: Understanding a niche party's strategy, candidates and supporters. *Parliamentary Affairs, 65*(4), 733–757.

Magnette, P., & Papadopoulos, Y. (2008). *On the politicization of the European consociation: A middle-way between Hix and Bartolini* (p. C0801). Eurogov: European Governance Papers.

Mair, P. (2007). Political opposition and the European Union. *Government and Opposition, 42*(1), 1–17.

Mény, Y. (2012). Conclusion: A voyage to the unknown. *Journal of Common Market Studies, 50*(S1), 154–164.

Mudde, C. (2011). Sussex v. North Carolina: The comparative study of party-based Euroscepticism. *SEI Working Paper, 121,* 1–32.

Neunreither, K. (1998). Governance without opposition: The case of the European Union. *Government and Opposition, 33*(4), 435–438.

Otjes, S., & van Der Veer, H. (2016). The Eurozone crisis and the European parliament's changing lines of conflict. *European Union Politics, 17*(2), 242–261.

Sartori, G. (1966). Opposition and control problems and Prospects. *Government and Opposition, 1*(1), 149–154.

Schmidt, V. (2015). *The Eurozone Crisis of Democratic Legitimacy: Can the EU Rebuild Public Trust and Support for European Economic Integration?* Discussion paper 015.

Searing, D. (1994). *Westminster's world understanding political roles.* Cambridge: Harvard University Press.

Searing, D. (2012). Foreword. In M. Blomgren & O. Rozenberg (Eds.), *Parliamentary roles in modern legislatures* (pp. xxi–xxvii). London: Routledge.

Strøm, K. (1997). Rules, reasons and routines: Legislative roles in parliamentary democracies. In W. C. Müller & T. Saalfeld (Eds.), *Members of parliament in Western Europe: Roles and behaviour* (pp. 155–174). London: Frank Cass.

Strøm, K. (2012). Roles as strategies: Towards a logic of legislative behavior. In M. Blomgren & O. Rozenberg (Eds.), *Parliamentary roles in modern legislatures* (pp. 85–100). London: Routlege/ECPR studies in European Political Science.

Szczerbiak, A., & Taggart, P. (2008). *Opposing Europe? The comparative party politics of Euroscepticism.* Oxford: Oxford University Press.

Taggart, P. (1998). A touchstone of dissent: Euroscepticism in contemporary western political systems. *European Journal of Political Research, 33*(3), 363–388.

Taggart, P., & Szczerbiak, A. (2013). Coming in from the cold? Euroscepticism, government participation and party positions on Europe. *Journal of Common Market Studies, 51*(1), 17–37.

Trenz, H.-J., & De Wilde, P. (2009). Denouncing European integration, Euroscepticism as reactive identity formation. *Arena Working Paper, 14.*

Usherwood, S. (2016). *The UK referendum's impact on British and European euroscepticism.* Paper presented at the conference 'Euroscepticism and the Eurocrisis', ULB, Brussels, 1 December 2016.

Usherwood, S., & Startin, N. (2013). Euroscepticism as a persistent phenomenon. *Journal of Common Market Studies, 51*(1), 1–16.

Whitaker, R., & Lynch, P. (2014). Understanding the formation and actions of eurosceptic groups in the European parliament: Pragmatism, principles and publicity. *Government and Opposition, 49*(2), 232–263.

Young, A. R. (2016). An inflection point in European Union studies? *Journal of European Public Policy, 23*(8), 1109–1117.

CHAPTER 2

Political Representation Beyond the Nation State

Representation is one of the most fundamental political concepts. It is at the core of modern democracies. But as a complex phenomenon, it can be studied from a number of different angles. Both political theory and legislative studies have provided numerous studies on political representation. For long, these studies were confined to the national political arena as there was no representative democracy beyond the nation state. Even with the creation of the European Communities in the 1950s, the European assembly did not attract much attention from scholars, especially not in terms of political representation. The institution was mostly a talking shop, without real power and seemed the least interesting or original part of the newly established supranational political system. Specialists of European integration rather turned to the Commission and the Council, which also fitted the dominant theoretical frameworks at the time—i.e. neofunctionalism and intergovernmentalism (see Costa and Rozenberg 2008).

It is only with the gradual empowerment of the EP and its direct election that the situation evolved. The parliamentarization of the EU has triggered research on the supranational assembly. Scholars have provided numerous analyses of the EP's powers, internal decision-making but also on EU elections and the emergence of politics outside the framework of the state (Blondel et al. 1998; Judge and Earnshaw 1994; Tsebelis 1994). From the 1990s onwards, a shift occurred as European studies evolved along with the EU, which started to resemble a normal, state-like political system. As a result, European studies

© The Author(s) 2018   15
N. Brack, *Opposing Europe in the European Parliament*,
Palgrave Studies in European Union Politics,
https://doi.org/10.1057/978-1-137-60201-5_2

have undergone a process of "normalization": specialists in comparative politics and legislative studies started studying the EU with concepts developed in the framework of the nation state (Keeler 2005; Kreppel 2012; Young 2016). The literature on the EP has expanded and become increasingly diversified. Scholars have been drawing on the insights of approaches and theoretical tools usually used to analyse national chambers, especially the US Congress, to examine the internal organization of the EP and the development of a supranational party system (Bendjaballah 2016; Hix et al. 2007; Kreppel 2002; Yordanova 2011).

But these studies tend to neglect older and more fundamental questions related to representative democracy beyond the nation state. By concentrating on the institution and its inner workings, they leave aside the analysis of the elected representatives at the individual level whereas the performance of a system is to a large degree dependent on the personnel acting within it (Katz and Wessels 1999, p. 11). It's only recently, notably with "the representative turn" in EU studies (Kröger and Friedrich 2013), that a burgeoning literature on political representation at the supranational level has developed. It emphasizes individual MEPs, their attitudes, career paths and representative practices. And it has showed that an in-depth analysis of MEPs' identity and behaviour is a promising avenue to understand the EU but also to re-examine concepts such as political representation, legitimacy and democracy (Costa and Rozenberg 2008, p. 251). Yet, the current knowledge of how MEPs understand their role as individual representatives remains limited, and there is much more we should know about how they perform their representative function (Busby 2013; Farrell and Scully 2007; Priestley 2008).

Building on these studies, this research aims at investigating parliamentary representation at the supranational level and its role in the democratic legitimization of the EU. It is argued that even if it is important to take into account the specific nature of political representation at the EU level, MEPs are first and foremost elected representatives, facing similar constraints as their national counterparts and driven by similar motivations (Bale and Taggart 2006; Kreppel 2012).

The ambition here is to concentrate on a specific group of elected representatives who have been neglected so far—Eurosceptic MEPs—to analyse how they conceive of and carry out their representative mandate. Indeed, once elected, they have to operate within an institution and a political system they strongly criticize or oppose. This situation is likely to trigger existential questions and tensions for these actors.

This research seeks therefore to determine how they cope with these issues and how they view their mandate. By shifting the focus from the institutional to the individual level (Jenson and Mérand 2010), the aim is to put the emphasis on opponents to the European political system in order to reflect on their role in the legitimization challenges the EU is currently facing.

To do so, this chapter presents the theoretical foundation of this book. It offers first a critical review of the relevant literature on political representation which can be conceptualized and studied in a range of different ways. It briefly explains studies devoted to the "descriptive" or symbolic side of representation, trying to assess the social and political representativeness of the EP. A second part then turns to the "substantive" approach to representation. It discusses research devoted to the relationships between MEPs, political parties, EP groups and constituents as well as the limited research on roles within the EP. Along with these recent studies on roles, political representation is considered here as a dynamic process in which it matters less to know the backgrounds of elected representatives than to know how they conceive of and carry out their mandate. The last sections concentrate therefore on role theory. The concept of role as understood by the motivational approach is central in this research: this analytical tool takes into account the subjective dimension of representation and helps understand how Eurosceptics conceive of and carry out their parliamentary mandate in the EP. This book is structured along two research questions: How can one categorize the roles played by Eurosceptic MEPs? And how can one best explain the variation between them? The central hypothesis states that the roles are the result of the interaction between the institutional context and individual preferences.

1   A "Descriptive Approach" to Representation

Political representation is a complex and multifaceted phenomenon, at the heart of modern democracies (Sartori 1987). It usually refers to the process by which a community is made present in a parliamentary assembly (Deschouwer 2005, pp. 85–86).[1] As a delegation mechanism, the notion essentially refers to a relationship between a representative and those represented by him or her (Walczak and van der Brug 2013). But despite this broad definition, political representation can be studied from various angles (Farrell and Scully 2007, p. 41).

A first way to analyse it is to adopt a so-called descriptive approach (Pitkin 1967) and investigate the representativeness of the assembly. The idea is to analyse the characteristics and identities of the representatives and to compare them to the represented, the quality of representation being measured by the proximity between the two (Best and Cotta 2000; Esaiasson and Holmberg 1996). Among this approach, two strands of literature can be distinguished. The first concentrates on the social representativeness of the parliament and studies the characteristics of its members. The second focuses on the political representativeness of the assembly by measuring the congruence between voters and elected representatives.

1.1   Social Representativeness of MEPs: An Elite like Any Other?

The issue of social representativeness of parliaments has been central to the literature on democracy and the theory of representation. The extent to which the composition of the legislature reflects that of the electorate from which it is drawn matters for at least two reasons. On the one hand, the social representativeness of the parliament plays a role in the legitimacy of the political regime if the people identify themselves to the elite. Norris (1999, p. 88) highlighted in that regard that "legislative bodies which fails to reflect society may be perceived as symbolically less legitimate". On the other hand, the legitimacy of elected representatives to stand for the represented is at stake. One of the assumptions of this approach in terms of "mirror-representation" is indeed that the social background of members of parliament has an impact on their behaviour, attitudes, priorities and role perceptions (Norris and Franklin 1997, pp. 185–186). The composition of the assembly will determine, at least partially, its policies and priorities (Clinchamps 2006; Pitkin 1967). Applied to the EP, the aim is to determine to what extent the assembly is an accurate reflection or a mirror of European society. These studies aim therefore to investigate who MEPs are in order to understand what they do (Beauvallet and Michon 2007, p. 9). This symbolic challenge related to the EP's composition is significant in the EU because its legitimacy is frequently questioned. Scholars have therefore analysed the selection process of MEPs, their profiles and careers as well as their social backgrounds to evaluate to what extent the EP is a microcosm of the European people (Costa and Rozenberg 2008; Scarrow 1997).

These studies demonstrated that MEPs are not representative of their electorate in terms of their social backgrounds (Mather 2001). The social background of MEPs is more similar to those of political elites in general with a majority of well-educated middle-aged men, belonging to higher social-professional categories, with an underrepresentation of people from the farming or working classes. Second, the characteristics of MEPs have evolved over time. Whereas for a long time the status of MEPs may have been perceived as of second order, the situation changed: in many countries nowadays, MEPs are elected after a tough political competition and are often identified as specialists in EU matters (Costa and Rozenberg 2008, p. 121). There has been a process of professionalization of MEPs over time, and their profiles are close to those of their national counterparts. (Daniel 2015; Kauppi 2005; Marrell and Payre 2006).

These findings have generated a series of works on the emergence of a supranational elite, understood as a relatively homogenous political class, independent from the national level (Cotta 1984; Verzichelli and Edinger 2005). This political class is argued to be composed of "professionals living from and for Europe, accumulating political and symbolic resources allowing them to claim leadership positions in the EP" (Beauvallet and Michon 2009). Overall, European integration did not lead to the emergence of an autonomous political class because of the multilevel structure of the EU (Kauppi 1996, 2005). Careers and profiles of MEPs are still deeply embedded in national political cultures.

Even if the EP does not mirror European society and cannot claim a form of symbolic legitimacy derived from its social representativeness, the institution can still bring legitimacy to the European political regime. Indeed, since the 1990s, the EP has been a stepping stone for politicians who are marginalized at the national level such as women or representatives from small and fringe parties. One of the unintended consequences of the presence of both federalists and Eurosceptics in the EP is to increase the democratic legitimacy of the EP (Kauppi 2005, p. 97). However, this literature tends to concentrate on the development of a transnational elite and to overlook fringe actors such as Eurosceptics.

1.2   Political Representativeness: The Issue of Congruence Between Citizens and MEPs

Drawing on the work of Miller and Stokes on the US Congress (1963), scholars have tried to determine to what extent the preferences of citizens are reflected by their parliamentarians. In that approach, we can speak of democratic representation if there is a policy congruence between the views of citizens and the actions and preferences of representatives in the chamber (Powell 2004).

In order to apply this perspective to the EP, the majority of authors base their work on the Responsible Party Model of representation which focuses on the electoral process as a delegation mechanism. It assumes that for elections to work as instruments that link citizens' policy preferences with the positions of elected representatives, two main conditions need to be met. First, political parties need to offer a range of choices to the electorate in terms of policy proposals. Second, voters have to vote according to their policy preference and choose the party whose positions represent their preferences best. If both conditions are met, the electoral process will lead to policy congruence between a party and its voters (Costello et al. 2012; Katz 1997; McEvoy 2012; Thomassen 1994).

European elections are thus supposed to link citizens' and representatives' policy preferences. The EP, as institution, should then increase the transparency of the European decision-making process and translate citizens' preferences into legislation (Yordanova 2011). The aim is then to evaluate to what extent voters' positions are reflected by the positions of MEPs to determine if European elections are an efficient instrument for political representation at the supranational level (Thomassen and Schmidt 1997).

A series of works have analysed the voters–MEPs congruence on a scope of policy issues ranging from employment and the euro to border control and European integration. They found that the congruence between voters and MEPs' preferences is rather high for issues related to the left-right cleavage but moderate or even weak for matters regarding the process of integration as well as cultural issues (Dalton 1985; Marsh and Wessels 1997). Indeed, there is a gap between political elites and the electorate on cultural issues and on issues related to European integration. This could explain the success of populist and Eurosceptic parties across Europe since they mobilize voters on those very issues (Costello et al. 2012; Mattila and Raunio 2006; Van der Eijk and Franklin 2004). Schmitt and Thomassen (2000, p. 320) noted for instance that "if it comes to the specifics of European Union policy-making, the congruence between voters and their representatives is remarkably poor. Political elites are much more European-minded than their voters regarding questions such as the abolition of border controls or the elimination of national currencies in favour of a new European currency". Similarly, recent studies demonstrated that parties do not represent their voters adequately on European issues, and this disjuncture seems to worsen over time (Lefkofridi and Casado-Asensio 2013; Lefkofridi and Katsanidou 2014; Mattila and Raunio 2012).

Because of the second-order nature of European elections, political representation at the EU level may be compromised. Citizens' lack of knowledge of (or interest in) European politics leads to a weak turnout at EU elections and a vote based on national rather than European issues. Moreover, parties do not offer voters a wide enough range of different positions on European issues and "European elections fail as an instrument of democracy at the European level in that they fail to express the will of the European people on European issues" (Mair and Thomassen 2010, p. 21). In order for the EP to be more representative, one option would be for MEPs to be less Europhile (Marsh and Wessels 1997, p. 238; Thomassen 2012). But as studies on socialization show, the EP is a bastion of Europhiles because of a (auto-) selection process. In sum, candidates in EU elections tend to be politicians interested in and favourable to Europe (Katz 1997; Kerr 1973). In order words, MEPs do not go native in the EP and Eurosceptics do not become more pro-European as a result of their experience at the supranational level (Scully 2005). The gap between the electorate and MEPs feeds the disconnection between the EP and European voters and contributes to the success of Eurosceptics' arguments.

In a nutshell, the EP is not a perfect mirror of European societies. MEPs can hardly claim to embody the European people or draw some legitimacy from their resemblance with the electorate. But, they are not that different from their national counterparts: MEPs are not a coherent elite, cut off from national realities and going native in the EP. Contrary to national assemblies though, the weak representativeness of the EP could be problematic as its very legitimacy is called into question by a significant minority of its members (Farrell and Scully 2007, p. 95). If several studies mention that the increasing presence of Eurosceptics could have an impact on the institution, they do not provide any in-depth reflections on that subject. Moreover, these studies tend to present a frozen picture of representation, rather than a dynamic process and where the elected representative is often presented as being "passive" rather than as an actor (Pitkin 1967, pp. 90–113).

This is why this research turns to a more dynamic approach of political representation in order to understand Eurosceptic MEPs' strategies, how they interact with their environment and their impact on the EP and the EU.

2   A Substantive Approach to Political Representation

The other main angle of study of political representation is the so-called substantive approach which focuses on what elected representatives do, rather than on their resemblance to their electorate (Nay 2002; Pitkin 1967). Representation is seen here as a dynamic process with, at its core, a relation between represented and representative. According to this approach, we should examine what the representatives do with their mandate, their room for manoeuvre, their objectives and attitudes in order to understand political representation.

Political representation at the supranational level is hybrid and ambiguous. It is not clear whom MEPs are supposed to represent, because of the absence of a uniform electoral system and of a transnational constituency for EU elections as well as the weakness of the electoral connexion between citizens and EU decision-makers (Brack and Costa 2013; Costa 2001; Costa and Navarro 2003; Niedermayer and Sinnott 1995; Reif and Schmitt 1980; Schmitt 2005).

But despite the particular nature of representation at the EU level, MEPs are similar to any other elected representatives (Bale and Taggart 2006). Legislative studies' scholars have therefore applied concepts and methods from the literature on the US Congress and to a lesser extent on European national chambers to the study of MEPs' behaviour. They have showed how fruitful such approach can be to understand the European representative mandate.

2.1   MEPs as Agents with Two Principals

Numerous studies seek to understand how elected representatives deal with their multiple allegiances, their relations to their principals and whether they are independent of them or bound by a mandate from their principals. Because of the weakness of the electoral connexion at the supranational level, most of the work in EU studies concentrates on the relation between the MEPs, their national political party and EP group, while some recent researches have examined the linkage between MEPs and their constituents.

Drawing on the literature on electoral behaviour in American politics, a series of studies have analysed MEPs' behaviour through the lens of the "principal-agent" approach (Hix 2002; Hix et al. 2007; Mühlböck 2012). This approach conceives the individual MEP as an agent of two principals: his/her national party and his/her EP political group. Each principal pushes the agent to adopt its position during votes. But as the agent is driven by three main objectives (vote-, office-, and policy-seeking), each principal has an influence on the agent, depending on the hierarchy of his/her goals. European elections are in fact organized by national political parties at the national level, and the national party remains the gatekeeper for the MEP's re-election as well as for his/her career at the national level. But the EP group controls the resources within the chamber, i.e. offices as well as policy influence (Bowler and Farrell 1995; Coman 2009; Faas 2003; Lindstädt et al. 2012). Scholars have therefore examined the tripartite relationship between individual MEPs, the national party and the EP group through roll-call vote analysis. Through roll-call vote analysis, they demonstrate that in case of conflict between the positions of the two principals, MEPs tend to follow the voting instructions of the national party, as their first objective is to get re-elected. But at the same time, they have shown that political groups have been increasingly cohesive and that political competition in the EP is structured more by two ideological dimensions (the left/right cleavage and the pro-/anti-integration axis) than by nationality (Hix and Noury 2009).

Following a rigorous methodology, these studies greatly contributed to our understanding of the determinants of MEPs' behaviour and of the way the EP works. But they also triggered controversies regarding their extensive use of roll-call votes,[2] the normative implications of their findings and their narrow view of the European representative mandate.

The normative implications of their findings in particular triggered criticism, as Hix and his colleagues argue that their findings indicate a "normalization" of the EP. They noted that "politics in the European Parliament is very much like politics in other democratic parliaments, dominated by left-right positions and driven by traditional party families of domestic European politics", which is "an optimistic conclusion about the accountability and stability of EU governance" (Hix et al. 2007, p. 181). Other scholars consider that such conclusion overlooks the hybrid nature of political representation in the EU (Costa and Saint Martin 2011), but also the fact that multiple dimensions structure political debates in the chamber and that variable coalitions occur in the EP depending on the issue, the period and the legislative procedure under study (Crespy and Gajewska 2010). Recent studies (Otjes and van Der Veer 2016) also demonstrate that the pro-/anti-EU divide is increasingly salient in the EP with the ongoing crisis, which could overshadow the left-right cleavage on specific policy issues. Settembri and Neuhold (2009) also refuted the idea of a normalization of the EP, showing that its functioning remains in line with consociationalism as political conflict in the chamber is rare.

The theoretical foundations of these studies have also been criticized as scholars consider that they rest on a narrow and simplistic view of the representative mandate. MEPs are reduced to the status of an agent of two principals, mostly motivated by his/her desire for re-election, and the mandate is reduced to the votes in plenary. The scope of MEPs' incentives is in fact broader than assumed in these studies (Navarro 2009). Not all MEPs seek re-election, and the hierarchy of their priorities might differ from one individual to another. Eurosceptics for instance might be more driven by policy-seeking objectives to satisfy their party and voters (Faas 2003). Strategies of MEPs might vary depending on their attitudes towards European integration, the size of their EP group or the status of their party at the national level (Hausemer 2006; Kaeding 2004). And because these studies exclusively analyse the voting behaviour of MEPs, they do not take into account the multidimensionality of the representative mandate. Whereas MEPs are involved in all kinds of activities, we still know little about how they perform their representative functions beyond roll-call voting (Priestley 2008).

2.2   Subjective Dimension of Representation: Role Theory

If the literature on how MEPs understand their role as representatives has been distinctly limited, recent studies have started to fill in this gap by analysing a broader range of political behaviour (see a.o. Benedetto 2005; Høyland 2006; Whitaker 2011) As elected representatives, MEPs face potentially infinite possibilities with a finite quantity of time, resources and energy; they must make choices and prioritize their activities. But they are relatively free to determine their own priorities. As a result, "parliamentarians differ considerably in the priorities they select and the models of representation they follow" (Farrell and Scully 2007, p. 94).

In order to understand how and why MEPs make these trade-offs, scholars have drawn on the insights of role theory, which emphasizes not only parliamentary behaviour but also the views of elected representatives on their duties and responsibilities. The concept of role has proved to be a useful theoretical tool to grasp the strategies of elected representatives, including in the EP. After falling out of fashion for two decades, this concept reappeared on the scientific agenda with the neo-institutional turn in political science. Although it has not been the main driver of research on the EP so far, it has made a discrete return in EU studies and provided scholars with a useful concept to understand the multiple facets of the European representative mandate through an actor-centred approach (Bale and Taggart 2006; Blomgren and Rozenberg 2012; Farrell and Scully 2003; Katz 1997; Navarro 2009).

The concept of role is central to this book: it is at the heart of the theoretical and methodological framework of this research. Indeed, following Blomgren and Rozenberg (2012, p. 9), my argument is that analysing roles enables us to open the "black box" of legislatures and to study some of the more complex aspects of political representation. It allows us to articulate parliamentary behaviours and parliamentarian perceptions of their mandate and to explain why they act the way they do within the institution.

After briefly outlining the fluctuating success of role theory, the two main neo-institutional perspectives on roles will be presented and the theoretical approach of this research will be explained.

2.2.1 The Fluctuating Success of the Concept of Role in Political Science

For a long period of time, the study of role was central to legislative studies, before falling out of fashion due to flaws and shortcomings of the two main approaches from which role analysis takes its legacy: functionalism and interactionism.

Functionalism assumes that understanding a political system requires analysing its functions, and the concept of role is a means to link MPs' behaviour to the functions of the legislature. The pioneering study for role theory is undoubtedly the volume by Wahlke, Eulau, Buchanan and Ferguson, titled The Legislative System: explorations in legislative behaviour (1962). Their study aimed at mapping the roles of members of four American state legislatures (California, Ohio, Tennessee and New Jersey) in order to uncover the underlying political processes and informal channels within institutions. Roles were closely connected to institutional positions and behaviour and were defined as a coherent set of norms of behaviour (Wahlke et al. 1962, p. 552). Their work resulted in an abundant literature on legislative and political roles in democratic institutions (Aberbach and Rockman 1988; Cayrol et al. 1973; Clarke and Price 1981; Converse and Pierce 1986; Gross 1978; Rush 2001). But the impact of their study is mainly related to one specific core role: the so-called representational role. It refers to the relationship between elected representatives and their voters. Wahlke and his colleagues distinguished the focus of representation (i.e. whether a representative should represent a specific, territorial interest or the general interest) and the style of representation (i.e. whether MPs consider themselves as bound by the instructions of those they represent or as free agents). Regarding the style of representation, they developed three categories: the delegate (bound by a mandate from voters), the trustee (does not follow instructions but rather his own judgement) and the politico (trustee or delegate, depending on the circumstances). There has been considerable research applying these concepts and categories to MPs, especially on the US Congress (Eulau et al. 1959; see Jewell 1983 for an overview of this literature). In the framework of the EP, many studies on role orientations are based on these categories and seek to determine who MEPs feel they represent, how they solve conflicts between various principals, what their main duties are and how they set their priorities (Brack and Costa 2013; Hagger and Wing 1979; Katz 1999; Scully and Farrell 2003; Wessels 2005).

As a counterpoint, the interactionist approach emphasizes the theatrical metaphor: roles are taken and played by actors, according to the institutional context and their interlocutors (i.e. the framework of interaction). These scholars insist on the role taking: how politicians learn, negotiate and cultivate their roles in actual situations. The most influential study in this approach is the work of Fenno (1978) on the home style of Congressmen. He followed the activities of 18 members of the US House of Representatives in their district over a period of almost eight years to observe how they related to their constituents. He showed how the activities in their districts were connected to their actions in Washington but also that the two are different worlds and the roles and strategies of elected representatives in their district change over time. Wodak's study of the EP (2009) draws on this approach as she seeks to understand the various discourses MEPs deploy depending on their audience. The interactionist approach focuses on the creation of roles in various social interactions, emphasizing the individual meaning that is given to them. It has the merit of highlighting the facts that individual elected representatives participate in defining their roles and that social situations shape roles. But the idea that parliamentarians are in a permanent state of representation, changing roles according to the audience is quite unrealistic. The professionalization and institutional socialization of MPs tend to generate a certain degree of role internalization, being a tool to reduce uncertainty for political actors (Costa and Kerrouche 2007, p. 185). As noted by Strøm (2012, p. 85), roles in politics as in any other aspects of our life exist to reduce uncertainty about effective and appropriate behaviour and help others develop plausible expectations about the ways in which we are likely to behave.

More generally, the inconclusive and contradictory results of the both interactionist and functionalist perspectives have gradually contributed to discrediting role theory. As noted by Jewell (1985, pp. 103–104), "most research on legislative roles have simply classified legislators according to their role orientations and little effort has been made to identify the variables explaining role orientations and even less to identify behavioural consequences". Also, the meaning of the concept itself is rather vague, and the conceptual pluralism in role theory has created confusion rather than clarification (Biddle 1986; Searing 1994). While some authors consider that there exists a consensus around the concept and that therefore there is no need to define it, others retain only one dimension of the role—mostly the trustee/delegate/politico categories—reducing roles to a bare minimum. As those roles do not exist in the minds of politicians and seem to describe academic ways of conceptualizing parliamentary representation rather than cohesive patterns of norms and behaviour, they appear meaningless (Price 1985, p. 169). This fragmented conceptualization explains the discrepancy often found between role orientations and behaviour, contributing to the discredit of the very concept of role (Navarro 2005; Price 1985). As Blomgren and Rozenberg (2012, p. 18) appropriately remark that "inconclusive results, conceptual confusion, empirical costs, and parochialism all contributed to a substantial decline in the use of the role concept in legislative research during most of the 1980s and 1990s". Even though the concept continued to be used in multiple studies, there were no theoretical or methodological developments in role theory until the "neo-institutionalist turning point" (Vom Beyme 2006).

2.2.2 Rediscovering Roles: The Neo-Institutionalist Approach

The neo-institutionalist turning point in political science has generated a renewed interest in role analysis. Two authors in particular have had an important impact on the reappearance of role theory in legislative studies: Kaare Strøm and Donald Searing. Each is associated with a variant of neo-institutionalism: Strøm outlined a strategic perspective while Searing proposed a motivational approach.

Both these approaches have made great theoretical contributions to legislative studies and role theory. They are presented as contradictory to each other, whereas they in fact share a number of similarities. They agree on one of the basic tenets of methodological individualism, i.e. that human action is the key to explaining social phenomena. They also agree on saying that the concept of role is a relevant analytical tool to make sense of the behaviour of elected representatives and that beyond individual interpretations of the role, each representative predominantly plays one single role. And they consider that roles are the results of the interaction between the institutional context and individual preferences. The strategic and motivational approaches should therefore be seen as degrees on a continuum of new institutionalism rather than as irreconcilable positions (Aspinwall and Schneider 2009; Lowndes and Roberts 2013; Peters 2011).

Strøm's strategic approach

This approach provides a conceptual framework inspired by rational choice theory to understand parliamentary behaviour. The concept of role is defined as "strategies for the employment of scare resources towards specific goals" (Strøm 1997, p. 155).

According to Strøm (1997, p. 163, 2012, pp. 87–88), roles are routinized strategies induced by the representatives' pursuit of their political objectives, constrained by the institutional environment in which they operate. Parliamentarians have four kinds of goals relative to their legislative service: reselection, re-election, party office and legislative office. In order to maximize their likelihood of achieving their preferences and objectives, they develop strategies or game plans to allocate their scarce resources most efficiently, i.e. political roles. Role differentiation results from the various ways in which parliamentarians allocate such scarce resources. But these strategies are not only driven by MPs' goals but also constrained by the institutional setting in which they operate. Institutions define the range of behaviours available to parliamentarians by shaping the incentives they face.

As parliamentarians' strategies are prescriptions and not directly observable, one must infer them from the patterned behaviour displayed by these representatives. Furthermore, one should systematically identify the institutions which affect the ability of parliamentarians to achieve their goals. Each goal is connected to a particular institutional constraint: the selection procedure (reselection), the electoral system (re-election), the member's position within the party (party office) and his or her position within parliament (legislative office).

This approach has been quite influential. Several studies have shown how the clarity of the concept and the parsimonious nature of the model proposed are particularly suited for comparative studies. One of the strengths of the strategic approach lies in the systematic analysis of the actors' resources as well as of the institutional constraints leading to the selection of a role (Blomgren and Rozenberg 2012; Zittel 2012; Zittel and Gschwend 2008). But the strategic approach has also been criticized on two elements: its view on actors' motivations and rationality on the one hand and its definition of role as strategy on the other hand. Its view on rationality has been considered rather restrictive. Portraying representatives as utility maximizers, i.e. able to rank priorities on a scale of static and exogenous preferences, this approach considers parliamentarians as motivated by an instrumental rationality (Aspinwall and Schneider 2000, p. 10). Their actions are based on cost/benefit analysis to determine the most efficient strategy to maximize their gains (Esaisson and Holmberg 1996, p. 59). Yet, political action cannot be reduced to strategic calculations to achieve a rational interest (Brubaker 1984, pp. 49–51; see also March and Olsen 2005; Navarro 2007). Politicians are not always calculating their expected utilities: "political behaviour, like other behaviour, can be described in terms of duties, obligations, rules and roles. Actions are not solely based on calculations of the return expected from alternative choices" (March and Olsen 1984, p. 744). And preferences are not purely exogenous: institutions are not a neutral framework for the strategies of elected representatives but frame, enable and constrain their actions' repertoire and preferences (Aspinwall and Schneider 2000; Giddens 1984; March and Olsen 1984). In addition to that, the definition of the role by the strategic approach triggered some questions. Roles are considered as routinized strategies[3] enabling actors to rationalize a complicated environment characterized by constant arbitrations. As such, it concentrates on patterns of behaviour, leaving aside any normative elements. However, preferences and normative incentives are generally considered an integral part of roles. One could then wonder if the concept does not become superfluous if one can talk of strategies only (Rozenberg and Blomgren 2012, p. 28). As argued by Searing (2012, p. xxii), the parsimony of the strategic approach in defining roles as strategic behaviour may be so parsimonious that its constructs are no longer recognizable as roles and is not well suited for in-depth analysis of case studies such as a supranational parliament (Searing 1991, 1994, 2012).

Searing's motivational approach

Inspired by the new institutionalism of March and Olsen (1989) and Powell and DiMaggio (1991), Searing developed a conceptual framework for the analysis of roles. He seeks to incorporate the insights from both sociological (functional and interactional) and strategic traditions. He believes that the previously disappointing results of role theories are not due to the concept itself but to the way it was used and defined. Through a study of the members of the House of Commons, he proposed a motivational approach to roles (Searing 1994). His main claim is that roles should be studied on the basis of how MPs view them. Politicians are purposive actors, but they are embedded in an institutional context.

Roles are defined here as "particular patterns of interrelated goals, attitudes and behaviors that are characteristic of people in particular situations" (Searing 1994, p. 18). It is composed of a motivational core (career goals and emotional incentives) and secondary components—characteristic attitudes and behaviours. But emotional incentives are the principal energizing forces in all parliamentary roles, rooted in the personality of the MP. The role here is not dictated by predetermined theoretical models but is the result of an inductive and interpretive approach so that the role reflects how the actor understands it.

In order to understand elected representatives' behaviour, the motivational approach pays particular attention to their perceptions and visions of their mandate, as indicators of the motivations underlying their behaviour. Indeed, seeking to describe the roles from the actor's point of view, this approach examines what actors do, how they do it and why they think it is appropriate to act this way rather than another (Searing 1994, p. 351). But this motivational core, composed of beliefs, goals and desires, is closely related to attitudes and behaviour: "in studying purposive roles, the motivational approach seeks to reconstruct characteristic clusters of desires, beliefs and behaviours that are inherently intertwined. These are the roles and the behaviour is part of the role" (Searing 1994, p. 380). The roles are established if there is a correspondence between the motivational core and attitudes and behaviour.

According to the motivational approach, roles are "the place where individual choices meet institutional constraints" (Searing 1994, p. x). This means that MPs are rational actors, motivated by career goals and emotional incentives and constrained by the formal and informal rules of the institution. Roles are embedded in institutional contexts: elected representatives enter parliament with their own motivations and preferences, but once in the institution, these preferences and goals can change to adapt to the situation.

Two steps are involved in the analysis of roles according to the motivational approach (Searing 1991, p. 1255). The first one is a mapping operation, in order to identify the major roles. The idea is to understand political roles from the players' point of view but to go beyond individual interpretations of the role to reconstruct, with sufficient generality, composite patterns of beliefs, attitudes and behaviours. The second is to explain, through an interpretive approach, the connections between the components of the roles, examine their origins and consequences, and illuminate their institutional contexts (Searing 1994, p. 22).

This approach is not without drawbacks. Mapping the roles relies on an inductive process, which is inherently subjective as well as time-consuming given the large numbers of interviews needed. This process complicates cross-national comparisons and is better suited for in-depth case studies or international institutions, but it also makes it difficult to replicate and poses a challenge in terms of generalizability (Searing 2012, p. xxii).

However, several studies have shown that the conceptual framework of the motivational approach and its inductive complexity are its greatest strengths. Wood and Yoon (1998) have demonstrated that the preference roles identified by Searing withstood the test of time and are still played today by members of the House of Commons. Others have shown that the motivational approach and its emphasis on emotional incentives enable scholars to grasp particular behaviour which could not be explained by the strategic approach (Rozenberg 2005). Navarro's work (2009, 2012) reveals the relevance of the motivational approach in the case of the EP and its members. Offering a middle way between sociological and strategic perspectives, it is particularly suited for the specific situation of MEPs. Indeed, the uncertainties surrounding the nature of the European representative mandate, the weak electoral connection at the EU level and the multitude of tasks and demands MEPs face give them a significant degree of freedom in the way they carry out their mandate. They are relatively free to set their own priorities. In addition to that, the motivational approach takes into account the impact of the formal and informal rules of the institution on elected representatives' behaviour and preferences. This is crucial in the context of the EP. While most research on political roles tend to underestimate the interplay between rules and preferences, or use simplified understandings of rationality, the motivational approach considers that politicians' preferences are both endogenous and exogenous. In other words, political actors define their goals and motivations in an ongoing dialogue with the rules that structure their environment (Searing 1991, 1994). Their behaviour is seen as rational, that is to say, oriented towards certain ends, but it is never entirely strategic. As Hooghe argues (1998, p. 8), politicians "are neither puppets on a string nor 'thick' rationalists calculating utilities of particular strategies to achieve given ends".

For all these reasons, this approach provides the best conceptual and methodological framework to understand how Eurosceptic MEPs conceive of and carry out their mandate.

3   A Motivational Approach to Study the Roles of Eurosceptic MEPs

The aim of this research is to analyse how Eurosceptic MEPs conceive of and carry out their representative mandate. To do so, it relies on the concept of role as defined by the motivational approach and is structured around two research questions: (1) How can one categorize the roles played by Eurosceptic MEPs? (2) How can one best explain the variation between their roles?

The concept of role will enable to overcome the apparent heterogeneity of their behaviour taken individually and to highlight the way in which motivations, attitudes and behaviour are articulated. More precisely, the research follows a two-step structure. A first one seeks to identify through an inductive method the roles played by Eurosceptic MEPs and to propose a typology of roles. The second step uses this typology as the dependent variable and examines the factors which explain the variations of roles among Eurosceptics.

3.1   Mapping the Roles Played by Eurosceptic MEPs

MEPs tend to resort to familiar patterns to achieve their goals, and their choice of a course of action depends on their interpretation of the situation rather than on a purely utilitarian calculation. Therefore, these familiar patterns—the roles—cannot be reduced to a rational strategy but also include a subjective dimension that should be taken into account to understand their behaviour.

Roles are thus understood here as dynamic patterns of interrelated goals, attitudes and behaviours that are characteristics of people in particular situations. The first step in the research is to reconstruct the roles played by Eurosceptic MEPs by identifying their main components (motivations, characteristic attitudes and behaviour). Emphasis will be put on the motivational core of the role, that is the goals and emotional incentives of the MEP and the way they perceive their mandate. But characteristic behaviour will also be taken into account.

However, because of the particular nature of the population studied (a minority of anti-system actors), the motivational approach will be amended on one aspect. Roles here will be closer to ideal types than to categories that live in the minds of politicians. The EP is not as institutionalized as the British House of Commons; it is a relatively young institution, with a high turnover, and whose powers and organization are in constant evolution and where multiple national parliamentary traditions coexist. Therefore, the roles of Eurosceptic MEPs reconstructed here rely on the perceptions, attitudes and behaviour of Eurosceptic MEPs, but in order to go beyond their individual interpretation of the role and identify the contrasts between roles, the characteristics of each have been emphasized. Each MEP was then categorized according to the role he/she was the most similar to.[4]

3.2   Explaining Role Choice

The second challenge of role theory is to determine why an elected representative plays one role rather than another. The roles identified during the first step become the dependent variable, with the aim to explain the variation among them.

The central hypothesis derived from the motivational approach postulates that roles result from the interaction between individual preferences and institutional rules. However, while Searing's approach provides a detailed and thorough analysis of the roles, it does not offer the same level of sophistication when it comes to explaining why elected representatives play one role rather than another. He proposes an interpretative explanation, i.e. explaining "the roles by identifying and describing the relevant sets of characteristic desires, beliefs and behaviours and their interconnection" (Searing 1994, p. 22). As this remains rather descriptive, this research turns to the literature on legislative studies, and more particularly on parliamentary behaviour in EU studies, to clarify the central hypothesis of this research. Studies on MEPs' role orientations identified three alternative sources of variance.

A first source comes from institutional variables. On the one hand, the formal and informal rules of the institution have an impact on the roles of elected representatives (Strøm 2012, p. 97). But these constraints and resources are not the same for all as they depend on the representative's position within the institution (March and Olsen 2005; Searing 1994). In the framework of the EP, Bowler and Farrell notice that the institutional context does in fact affect parliamentary behaviour: "it is all too easy—especially when comparing across different nations—to forget factors which affect the behaviour of parliamentarians that are more related to the legislature in which they work" (Bowler and Farrell 1993, pp. 48–49). It has been shown elsewhere that the formal and informal rules of the EP influence the way radical right MEPs conceive of and carry out their mandate (Brack 2012). On the other hand, institutional factors also refer to the electoral system. Indeed, there have been debates within legislative studies on the impact of the electoral system on parliamentary behaviour. While some scholars show that it has a significant impact on the strategies of elected representatives (André and Depauw 2013; Cain et al. 1987; Carey and Shugart 1995; Norton 2002; Thomassen and Esaiasson 2006), others nuanced this statement and offered alternative explanations (Bogdanor 1985; Davidson 1969; Desposato 2006; Thames 2005). On the basis of these studies, scholars have examined the relationship between the electoral system and MEPs' behaviour and view of representation (Bowler and Farrell 1993). Scully and Farrell (2003, 2007) examined role orientations of MEPs, i.e. the way they see the people they represent and the most important aspects of their mandate. They highlight two explanatory variables: district magnitude and ballot structure. Smaller districts and an open ballot structure tend to incentivize MEPs to cultivate a personal vote as they might be rewarded for their efforts towards the constituency. "As the electoral system becomes more open, greater emphasis is placed on individual politicians, who in turn, it can be hypothesised, place greater emphasis on the representation of individual constituents and on personal vote chasing" (Farrell and Scully 2010, p. 8). This analysis reveals a relation between electoral system design and the representative style of MEPs. But this impact remains moderate due to the relative homogeneity of the electoral system for EP elections. In other words, electoral system effects do not fully account for MEPs' attitudes and behaviour (Scully and Farrell 2007, p. 122; Scully and Farrell 2010). On the basis of those works, the aim will be therefore to systematically identify the constraints and resources originating from the institutional framework which affect how Eurosceptic MEPs perceive and carry out their role. In that respect, it can be hypothesized that there is a relation between the (formal and informal) rules of the EP as well as the electoral system (more particularly the ballot structure) and the roles played by Eurosceptics.

The second source of variance refers to cultural factors. General cultural differences across countries in the expectations and demands placed upon elected representatives are essential to understand parliamentary behaviour. Katz (1997, 1999) in particular argues that the constituency orientation of British MEPs is not due to the electoral system, since they are elected on closed lists but is the result of the national culture. Yet, he observed that MEPs' attitudes towards Europe also influence significantly the way they perceive their roles (Katz 1999). Other research also tends to confirm the (moderate) impact of nationality on the way MEPs see their mandate (Costa 2001; Wessels 1999).

A third source of variance is related to individual factors. Political sociology has emphasized the impact of the individual background, especially career paths and political experience (Beauvallet and Michon 2010; Georgakakis 2002, 2012). Bale and Taggart (2006) argue that political roles cannot be explained by nationality or political affiliation and that research should investigate individual-level variables. More particularly, they consider that professional training, seniority and political experience impact the way MEPs respond to their environment whereas variables related to social background variables offer little to explain legislative role-taking. Many studies also mention individual preferences, as an additional variable, alongside cultural and institutional factors. The studies by Hagger and Wing (1979) as well as by Katz (1999) underline the influence of MEPs' attitudes towards European integration and the institutional architecture of the EU on role orientations. Similarly,

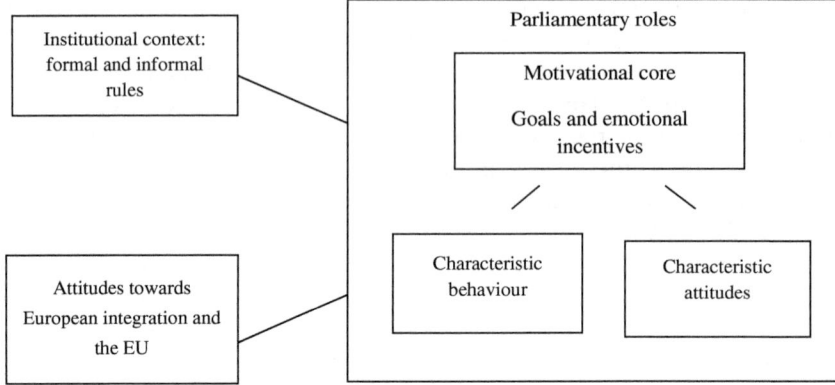

Fig. 2.1 Roles—components and explanatory model

Scully and Farrell (2003, 2007) reveal that MEPs' perception of their mandate depends in part on their vision of the EP. As the effect of the electoral system seems moderate, they suggest research needs to move on to an individual-level approach and take into account more subjective elements. Navarro (2009) for his part argues that normative considerations are central to understand MEPs' roles. In his study of MEPs, he shows that neither social background variables nor seniority can explain the variance of their roles. Although he fails to analyse Eurosceptic MEPs, his analysis shows that the choice of a role depends not only on MEPs' career goals but also on their views of European integration and democracy (Navarro 2009, p. 255).

Combining these studies with the motivational approach, the general hypothesis of this research states that the variance of roles results from the interaction between institutional factors and individual preferences. Figure 2.1 summarizes the theoretical framework used here: the roles played by Eurosceptic MEPs depends on the institutional context and members' preferences with regard to European integration and the EU.

4   Data and Method

This approach takes an actor-centred and interpretative perspective to understand how Eurosceptic MEPs conceive of and carry out their mandate. Individual actors and their subjectivity are at the centre of the analysis (Searing 1994). Most of the research relies on a qualitative method in order to grasp the meaning MEPs give to their actions and to understand the motivations underlying their behaviour (Della Porta and Keating 2008, p. 26). But quantitative methods will also be combined to the qualitative methodology as this blend is more likely to provide a better understanding of the variation in the roles played by Eurosceptic MEPs.

4.1   An Inductive Method to Identify Parliamentary Roles Played by Eurosceptic MEPs

An inductive method was used to identify the roles played by Eurosceptic MEPs. Because the literature on Eurosceptic MEPs is particularly limited, such a method is useful to analyse the behaviour and attitudes of these actors without losing information. Indeed, it is particularly suited for the purpose of this research because of its bottom-up perspective Morse et al. (2002). Such an inductive approach takes into account the complexity of the parliamentary mandate by seeking to reconstruct the roles from the actors' point of view, focusing on their meanings and motivations (Searing 2012).

First, priority is given to the way Eurosceptics conceive of their role as MEP. Semi-structured interviews were conducted with a sample of 101 Eurosceptic MEPs as well as with 32 parliamentary assistants, civil servants and non-Eurosceptic MEPs. The answers they gave during the interviews served as indicators to determine how they perceive their role and what their motivations and priorities are. In addition to that, the observation of group meetings (EFD and EUL/NGL) and the interviews with non-Eurosceptic MEPs provide information on the broader context of the group and on the interactions among MEPs. Data on MEPs' parliamentary behaviour were also collected and served as indicators for the identification of roles given that, according to the motivational approach, the perception of role and behaviour forms a coherent and dynamic whole. Indeed, their parliamentary activities were analysed to determine their priorities and establish how they use their time and resources. These data also allow to determine to what extent they are involved in parliamentary work and to which activities they devote more resources and energy. Moreover, including behaviour in the analysis tests whether there is a correspondence between what Eurosceptics say and what they actually do. Finally, data regarding their responsibilities within the EP were also examined to assess their level of integration in the parliamentary structure. Rather than rely on a single indicator, these elements were combined to develop the typology of roles (see annex on the operationalization of the concept of role). Following Martin (2011), this approach combines observational studies, self-presentations during interviews and behavioural analysis in order to account for how elected representatives conceive of and carry out their mandate.

Each Eurosceptic MEP is more or less close to one role. To categorize him or her, priority was given to his or her role conception and motivations (the motivational core) as well as to the overall consistency between the perception of the mandate and the parliamentary activities of the MEP.

4.2   Testing the Hypothesis: Qualitative and Quantitative Methods

The second central question of this research addresses the variation between roles. Why does an actor play a parliamentary role rather than another?

The hypothesis argues that roles are the result of the interaction between the institutional framework and individual preferences relative to European integration and the EU. The analysis will therefore seek to identify in a systematic way the constraints and resources derived from the institutional framework which could influence the room for manoeuvre of Eurosceptic MEPs and their perception of the institutional reality. This entails not only analysing the evolution of the formal rules of the EP through an analysis of its rules of procedure but also examining the informal rules. Then, the influence of MEPs' preferences regarding European integration on the roles they play will be examined. To do so, the analysis is based on data from the interviews pertaining to MEPs' positions vis-à-vis European integration and the European institutions. The combination of qualitative and a quantitative analysis will enable me to determine whether there is a relation between MEPs' Euroscepticism and the role they play.[5]

5   CONCLUSION

The EP is by now at the heart of a very rich body of literature, essentially because of its role in the debates on the democratic deficit of the EU. Parliamentary representation is the core of modern democracies. With the parliamentarization of the European political system, people hope to increase the EU's legitimacy and to develop a democratic European polity. Many studies have therefore been devoted to the role of the EP in the integration process and the democratic legitimacy of the EU. For long, this literature has concentrated on the institution's powers and organization, but as the EU evolved towards a more "state-like" political regime, scholars started examining the issue of political representation at the supranational level. They showed how the EP could be used as a laboratory to test hypothesis on legislators' behaviour derived from comparative politics and legislative studies. Indeed, they revealed that despite the hybrid nature of the EP, MEPs are elected representatives like any other, facing similar constraints and driven by similar motivations as national parliamentarians. These studies greatly contribute to our understanding of the EP internal decision-making process as well as of the relationship between its members, its political groups and national parties. But they tend to provide a partial account of the representative mandate as they focus almost exclusively on voting behaviour. There is a need to move to an individual-level approach to enrich these quantitative roll-call analyses with qualitative and longitudinal methods. As Farrell and Scully note (2010, p. 37), "representation is a dynamic process and to understand it, we need to move beyond a macro perspective on institution and aggregate outcomes towards a more micro-level analysis of individuals. We need to consider how these elected representatives interpret and seek to carry out their role as representatives".

This is precisely the aim of this research to analyse, through an actor-centred approach, how Eurosceptics operate once elected in the EP. Recent studies have shown that MEPs are still in an "experimental phase" in the sense that there is no consensus on the best way to carry out the European mandate (Costa and Navarro 2003, p. 132). As a result, they display very divergent views and behaviours. In the specific case of the Eurosceptics, research on UKIP reveals that if representation in the EP provides resources for these actors, it also poses awkward questions about the extent to which they should engage with the EU, leading to some variation in the way Eurosceptics approach their role (Lynch et al. 2012).

Role theory, in its motivational variant, was used in this chapter to understand Eurosceptics' strategies. This was particularly suited to understanding how Eurosceptic MEPs conceive of and carry out their representative mandate. It provides a comprehensive conceptual framework that takes into account the subjective dimension of political representation and enables one to make sense of the behaviour of elected representatives. Through the use of role theory, this research will contribute to filling in the gap in the literature on Euroscepticism at the supranational level. More generally, through an in-depth analysis of Eurosceptic MEPs' strategies, it will provide a better understanding of representative democracy at the supranational level, by making sense of the behaviour of (a group of) representatives of the people.

NOTES

1. There is an extensive literature on representation in comparative politics, EU studies, philosophy, political theory and sociology. This chapter will only concentrate on EU studies and comparative politics/legislative studies, and the reader is referred to these works for alternative perspectives: Mansbridge (2003), Przeworski et al. (1999), Rehfeld (2011), Saward (2010), Urbinati and Warren (2008).
2. On this issue, see Carrubba et al. (2006, 2008), Høyland (2010).
3. Some scholars also pointed out the tension between routine and strategy in the definition of the roles by the strategic approach. See Searing (2012).
4. For a similar approach, see Navarro (2009), Costa and Kerrouche (2007).
5. To test the robustness of the analysis, alternative explanatory factors such as seniority, the electoral system and MEPs' previous political experiences will also be tested.

REFERENCES

Aberbach, J. D., & Rockman, B. A. (1988). Image IV revisited: Executive and political roles. *Governance, 1*(1), 1–25.

André, A., & Depauw, S. (2013). District magnitude and home styles of representation in European democracies. *West European Politics, 36*(5), 986–1006.

Aspinwall, M., & Schneider, G. (2000). Same menu, seperate tables: The institutionalist turn in political science and the study of European integration. *European Journal of Political Research, 38*(1), 1–36.

Aspinwall, M., & Schneider, G. (2009). Un menu commun pour des tables séparées. Le tournant institutionnaliste de la science politique et les études sur l'intégration européenne. In M. Delori, D. Deschaux-Beaumes, & S. Saurugger (Eds.), *Le choix rationnel en science politique : débats critiques* (pp. 103–140). Rennes: Presses universitaires de Rennes.

Bale, T., & Taggart, P. (2006). First-timers yes, virgins no: The roles and background of new MEPs. *SEI working papers*, 89.

Beauvallet, W., & Michon, S. (2007). Eurodéputés et représentation des territoires. *Les cahiers du CRESS, 7*.

Beauvallet, W., & Michon, S. (2009). Les transformations sociologiques des parlementaires européens. *Revue Politique et Parlementaire, 1052*, 83–89.

Beauvallet, W., & Michon, S. (2010). L'institutionnalisation inachevée du Parlement européen. Hétérogénéité nationale, spécialisation du recrutement et autonomisation. *Politix, 23*(8), 147–172.

Bendjaballah, S. (2016). Des illusions perdues? Du compromis au consensus au Parlement européen et à la Chambre des représentants américaine. Brussels: Editions de l'Université de Bruxelles.

Benedetto, G. (2005). Rapporteurs as legislative entrepreneurs: the dynamics of the codecision procedure in Europe's Parliament. *Journal of European Public Policy, 12*(1), 67–88.

Best, H., & Cotta, M. (2000). *Parliamentary representatives in Europe 1848–2000: Legislative recruitement and careers in eleven European countries.* Oxford: Oxford University Press.

Biddle, B. J. (1986). Recent developments in role theory. *Annual Review of Sociology, 12*, 67–92.

Blomgren, M., & Rozenberg, O. (2012). *Parliamentary Roles in Modern Legislatures.* London: ECPR Press, Routledge.

Blondel, J., Sinnott, R., & Svensson, P. (1998). *People and parliament in the European Union: Participation democracy and legitimacy.* Oxford: Clarendon Press.

Bogdanor, V. (1985). *Representatives of the People? Parliamentarians and constituents in Western democracies.* Aldershot: Gower.

Bowler, S., & Farrell, D. (1993). Legislator shirking and voter monitoring: Impacts of European parliament electoral systems upon legislator–voter relationships. *Journal of Common Market Studies, 31*(1), 45–69.

Bowler, S., & Farrell, D. M. (1995). The organizing of the European Parliament: committees, specialization and coordination. *British Journal of Political Science, 25*(2), 219–243.

Brack, N. (2012). Eurosceptics in the European Parliament: Exit or voice? *Journal of European Integration, 34*(2), 151–168.

Brack, N., & Costa, O. (2013). The challenges of territorial representation at the supranational level: The case of French MEPs. *French Politics, 11*(1), 1–23.

Brubaker, R. (1984). *The limits of rationality. An essay on the social and moral thought of Max Weber.* London: George Allen & Unwin.

Busby, A. (2013). 'Normal Parliament': Exploring the organisation of everyday political life in an MEP's office. *Journal of Contemporary European Research, 9*(1), 94–115.

Cain, B. E., Ferejohn, J. A., & Fiorina, M. P. (1987). *The personal vote: Constituency service and electoral independence.* Cambridge: Harvard University Press.

Carey, J. M., & Shugart, M. S. (1995). Incentives to cultivate a personal vote: A rank ordering of electoral formulas. *Electoral Studies, 14*(4), 417–439.

Carrubba, C. J., Gabel, M., Lacey, M., Clough, R., Montgomery, E., & Schambach, R. (2006). Off the record: Unrecorded legislative votes, selection bias and roll-call vote analysis. *British Journal of Political Science, 36*(4), 691–704.

Carrubba, C., Gabel, M., & Hug, S. (2008). Legislative voting behavior: Seen and unseen: A theory of roll-call vote selection. *Legislative Studies Quarterly, 33*(4), 543–572.

Cayrol, R., Parodi, J.-L., & Ysmal, C. (1973). *Le député français*. Paris: Armand Colin.

Clarke, H. D., & Price, R. G. (1981). Parliamentary experience and representational role orientations in Canada. *Legislative Studies Quarterly*, 373–390.

Clinchamps, N. (2006). *Parlement européen et droit parlementaire. Essai sur la naissance du droit parlementaire de l'Union européenne*. Paris: LGDJ.

Coman, E. (2009). Reassessing the influence of party groups on individual MEPs. *West European Politics, 32*(6), 1099–1117.

Converse, P. E., & Pierce, R. (1986). *Political representation in France*. Cambridge: Harvard University Press.

Costa, O. (2001). *Le Parlement européen, assemblée délibérante*. Brussels, Editions de l'Université de Bruxelles.

Costa, O., & Kerrouche, E. (2007). *Qui sont les députés français?* Paris: Presses de Sciences Po.

Costa, O., & Navarro, J. (2003). La représentation au Parlement européen. Qui représentent les parlementaires européens? In S. Saurugger (Ed.), *Les modes de représentation dans l'Union européenne* (pp. 123–152). Paris: L'Harmattan.

Costa, O., & Rozenberg, O. (2008). Parlementarisme. In C. Belot, P. Magnette, & S. Saurugger (Eds.), *Science politique de l'Union européenne, Economica* (pp. 249–283). Paris: Economica.

Costa, O., Roger, A., & Saurruger, S. (2008). Les remises en cause de l'intégration européenne. Introduction. *Revue Internationale de Politique Comparée, 15*(4), 533–539.

Costa, O., & Saint Martin, F. (2011). *Le Parlement européen* (2nd ed.). Paris: La Documentation française.

Costello, R., Thomassen, J., & Rosema, M. (2012). European parliament elections and political representation: Policy congruence between voters and parties. *West European Politics, 35*(6), 1226–1248.

Cotta, M. (1984). Direct elections of the European Parliament: A Supranational political elite in the making? In K. Reif (Ed.), *European elections 1979–1984. Conclusions and perspectives from empirical research* (pp. 122–126). Berlin: Quorum.

Crespy, A., & Gajewska, K. (2010). New parliament, New cleavages after the Eastern enlargement? The conflict over the services directive as an opposition between the Liberals and the Regulators. *Journal of Common Market Studies, 48*(5), 1185–1208.

Dalton, R. (1985). Political parties and political representation: Party supporters and party elites in nine nations. *Comparative Political Studies, 18*, 267–299.

Daniel, W. T. (2015). *Career behaviour and the European parliament: All roads lead through Brussels?* Oxford: Oxford University Press.

Davidson, R. H. (1969). *The Role of the Congressman.* New York: Pegasus.

Della Porta, D., & Keating, M. (2008). *Approaches and Methodologies in the social sciences. A pluralist perspective.* Cambridge: Cambridge University Press.

Deschouwer, K. (2005). Pinball Wizards: Political Parties and Democratic Representation in the Changing institutional Architecture of European Politics. In E. Römmele, D. Farrell, & P. Ignazi (Eds.), *Political parties and political systems. The concept of linkage revisited* (pp. 81–99). Westport: Praeger.

Desposato, S. W. (2006). The impact of electoral rules on legislative parties: Lessons from the Brazilian senate and chamber of deputies. *Journal of Politics, 68*(4), 1018–1030.

DiMaggio, P. J., & Powell, W. W. (Eds.). (1991). *The new institutionalism in organizational analysis.* Chicago: University of Chicago Press.

Esaiasson, P. E., & Holmberg, S. (1996). *Representation from above. Members of parliament and representative democracy in Sweden.* Aldershot: Darmouth Publishing Company.

Eulau, H., Wahlke, J. C., Buchanan, W., & Ferguson, L. (1959). The role of the representative: Some empirical observations on the theory of Edmund Burke. *The American Political Science Review, 53*(3), 742–756.

Faas, T. (2003). To defect or not to defect? National, institutional and party group pressures on MEPs and their consequences for party cohesion in the European Parliament. *European Journal of Political Research, 42*(6), 841–866.

Farrell, D., & Scully, R. (2007). *Representing Europe's citizens? Electoral institutions and the failure of parliamentary representation.* Oxford: Oxford University Press.

Farrell, D., & Scully, R. (2010). The European parliament: one parliament, several modes of political representation on the ground? *Journal of European Public Policy, 17*(1), 36–54.

Fenno, R. (1978). *Home style: House members in their districts.* Boston: Little Brown.

Georgakakis, D. (2002). *Les métiers de l'Europe politique.* Strasbourg, PUS: Acteurs et professionnalisation de l'Union européenne.

Georgakakis, D. (Ed.). (2012). *Le champ de l'Eurocratie. Une sociologie politique du personnel de l'UE.* Economica: Paris.

Giddens, A. (1984). *La constitution de la société: Elements de la théorie de la structuration*. Paris: PUF.

Gross, D. A. (1978). Representative styles and legislative behavior. *Western Political Quarterly, 31*, 359–371.

Hagger, M., & Wing, M. (1979). Legislative roles and clientele orientations in the European parliament. *Legislative studies quarterly, 4*(2), 165–196.

Hausemer, P. (2006). Participation and political competition in committee report allocation under what conditions do MEPs represent their constituents? *European Union Politics, 7*(4), 505–530.

Hix, S. (2002). Parliamentary behavior with two principals: Preferences, parties and voting in the European Parliament. *American Journal of Political Science, 46*(3), 688–698.

Hix, S, & Noury, A. (2009). After enlargement: Voting patterns in the sixth European Parliament. *Legislative Studies Quarterly, 34*(2), 159–174.

Hix, S., Noury, A., & Roland, G. (2007). *Democratic politics in the European parliament*. Cambridge: Cambridge University Press.

Hooghe, L. (1998). Serving Europe. Political Orientations of Senior Commission Officials. *EIOP working paper, 1*(8).

Høyland, B. (2006). Allocation of co-decision reports in the fifth European Parliament. *European Union Politics, 7*(1), 30–50.

Høyland, B. (2010). Procedural and party effects in European parliament roll-call votes. *European Union Politics, 4*(4), 597–613.

Jenson, J., & Mérand, F. (2010). Sociology, institutionalism and the European Union. *Comparative European Politics, 8*(1), 74–92.

Jewell, M. E. (1983). Legislator-constituency relations and the representative process. *Legislative Studies Quarterly, 8*, 303–337.

Jewell, M. E. (1985). Legislators and constituents in the representative process. *Handbook of legislative research*, 97–131.

Judge, D., & Earnshaw, D. (1994). Weak parliament influence? A study of the Environment Committee of the European parliament. *Government and opposition, 29*(2), 262–276.

Kaeding, M. (2004). Rapporteurship allocation in the European parliament. *European Union Politics, 5*(3), 353–371.

Katz, R. (1997). Representational roles. *European Journal of Political Research, 32*(2), 211–226.

Katz, R. (1999). Role orientations in parliaments. In R. Katz & B. Wessels, *The European parliament, the national parliaments, and European integration* (pp. 61–85). Oxford: Oxford University Press.

Katz, R., & Wessels, B. (1999). *The European parliament, the national parliaments, and European integration*. Oxford: Oxford University Press.

Kauppi, N. (1996). European Union institutions and French political careers. *Scandinavian Political Studies, 19*(1), 1–24.

Kauppi, N. (2005). *Political power in the European parliament.* Manchester: Manchester University Press.

Keeler, J. (2005). Mapping EU studies: The evolution from boutique to boom field 1960–2001. *Journal of Common Market Studies, 43*(3), 551–582.

Kerr, H. (1973). Changing attitudes through international participation: European parliamentarians and integration. *International Organization, 27*(1), 45–83.

Kreppel, A. (2002). *The European parliament and supranational party system: A study in institutional development.* New York: Cambridge University Press.

Kreppel, A. (2012). The normalization of the European Union. *Journal of European Public Policy, 19*(5), 635–645.

Kröger, S., & Friedrich, D. (2013). Introduction: The representative turn in EU studies. *Journal of European Public Policy, 20*(2), 155–170.

Lefkofridi, Z., & Casado-Asensio, J. (2013). European vox radicis: Representation and policy congruence on the extremes. *Comparative European Politics, 11*(1), 93–118.

Lefkofridi, Z., & Katsanidou, A. (2014). Multilevel representation in the European parliament. *European Union Politics, 15*(1), 108–131.

Lindstädt, R., Slapin, J. B., & Wielen, R. J. V. (2012). Adaptive behaviour in the European Parliament: Learning to balance competing demands. *European Union Politics, 13*(4), 465–486.

Lowndes, V., & Roberts, M. (2013). *Why institutions matter: The new institutionalism in political science.* Basingstoke: Palgrave Macmillan.

Lynch, P., Whitaker, R., & Loomes, G. (2012). The UK Independence Party: Understanding a Niche Party's strategy, candidates and supporters. *Parliamentary Affairs, 65*(4), 733–757.

Mair, P., & Thomassen, J. (2010). Political representation and government in the European Union. *Journal of European Public Policy, 17*(1), 20–35.

Mansbridge, J. (2003). Rethinking Representation. *American Political Science Review, 97*(4), 515–527.

March, J. G., & Olsen, J. P. (1984). The new institutionalism: Organizational factors in political life. *American Political Science Review, 78*(3), 734–749.

March, J. G., & Olsen, J. P. (1989). *Rediscovering institutions. The organizational basis of politics.* New York: The Free Press.

March, J. G., & Olsen, J. P. (2005). Elaborating the New Institutionalism. *Arena working paper,* 11.

Marrell, G., & Payre, R. (2006). Des carrières au Parlement: Longévité des euro-députés et institutionnalisation de l'arène parlementaire. *Politique européenne,* (18), 69–104.

Marsh, M., & Wessels, B. (1997). Territorial representation. *European Journal of Political Research, 32*(2), 227–241.

Martin, S. (2011). Using parliamentary questions to measure constituency focus: An application to the Irish case. *Political Studies, 59*(2), 472–488.

Mather, J. (2001). The European parliament: a model of representative democracy? *West European Politics, 24*(1), 181–201.

Mattila, M., & Raunio, T. (2006). Cautious voters—supportive parties: Opinion congruence between voters and parties on the EU dimension. *European Union Politics, 7*(4), 427–449.

Mattila, M., & Raunio, T. (2012). Drifting Further Apart: National Parties and their Electorates on the EU dimension. *West European Politics, 35*(3), 589–606.

McEvoy, C. (2012). Unequal representation in the European Union: A multi-level analysis of voter-party congruence in EP elections. *Representation, 48*(1), 83–99.

Morse, J., Barrett, M., Mayan, M., Olson, K., & Spiers, J. (2002). Verification strategies for establishing reliability and validity in qualitative research. *International Journal of Qualitative Methods, 1*(2), 13–22.

Mühlböck, M. (2012). National versus European: Party control over members of the European Parliament. *West European Politics, 35*(3), 607–631.

Navarro, J. (2005). Comparer les rôles de représentation : bilans et perspectives de recherche. communication présentée au séminaire Le comparatisme dans tous ses états organisé par le CERVL, Sciences Po Bordeaux, le 7 mars.

Navarro, J. (2007). Comment le Parlement européen socialise-t-il les députés européens? *Revue française de science politique, 57*(1), 94–97.

Navarro, J. (2009). *Les députés européens et leur rôle. Sociologie interprétative des pratiques parlementaires*, Brussels, Editions de l'Université de Bruxelles.

Nay, O. (2002). Le jeu du compromis. Les élus régionaux entre territoire et pratiques d'assemblée. In O. Nay & A. Smith (Eds.), *Le gouvernement du compromis, courtiers et généralistes de l'action politique* (pp. 47–86). Paris: Economica.

Neuhold, C., & Settembri, P. (2009). Achieving consensus through committees: Does the European parliament manage? *Journal of Common Market Studies, 47*(1), 127–151.

Niedermayer, O., & Sinnott, R. (1995). *Public opinion and internationalized governance*. Oxford: Oxford University Press.

Norris, P. (1999). Recruitment into the European parliament. In R. Katz & B. Wessels (Eds.), *The European parliament, national parliaments and European integration* (pp. 86–102). Oxford: Oxford University Press.

Norris, P., & Franklin, M. (1997). Social representation. *European Journal of Political Research, 32*(2), 185–210.

Norton, P. (2002). The United Kingdom: Building the Link between constituent and MP. In P. Norton (Ed.), *Parliaments and citizens in Western Europe* (pp. 19–42). London: Frank Cass.

Otjes, S., & van Der Veer, H. (2016). The Eurozone crisis and the European parliament's changing lines of conflict. *European Union Politics, 17*(2), 242–261.

Peters, B. G. (2011). *Institutional theory in political science: The new institutionalism.* New York: Bloomsbury Publishing.

Pitkin, H. (1967). *The concept of representation.* Berkeley: University of California Press.

Powell, G. B., Jr. (2004). Political representation in comparative politics. *Annual Review of Political Science, 7,* 273–296.

Price, K. C. (1985). Instability in representational role orientation in a state legislature: A research note. *Western Political Quarterly, 38*(1), 162–171.

Priestley, J. (2008). *Six battles that shaped Europe's parliament.* London: John Harper Publishing.

Przeworski, A., Stokes, S., & Manin, B. (1999). *Democracy, accountability, and representation, 2.* Cambridge: Cambridge University Press.

Rehfeld, A. (2011). The concepts of representation. *American Political Science Review, 105*(3), 631–641.

Reif, K., & Schmitt, H. (1980). Nine second order national elections: A conceptual framework for the analysis of European election results. *European Journal of Political Research, 8*(1), 3–44.

Rozenberg, O. (2005). *Le Parlement français et l'Union européenne (1993–2005): l'Europe saisie par les rôles parlementaires,* PhD thesis, Institut d'Etudes Politiques de Paris.

Rush, M. (2001). *The role of the Member of Parliament since 1868: From gentlemen to players.* Oxford: Oxford University Press.

Sartori, G. (1987). *The Theory of Democracy Revisited.* Chatham: NJ, Chatham House.

Saward, M. (2010). *The Representative Claim.* Oxford, Oxford University Press.

Scarrow, S. (1997). Political career paths and the European parliament. *Legislative Studies Quarterly, 22*(2), 253–262.

Schmitt, H. (2005). The European Parliament elections of June 2004: Still second order? *West European Politics, 28*(3), 650–679.

Schmitt, H., & Thomassen, J. (2000). Dynamic representation. The case of European integration. *European Union Politics, 1*(3), 318–339.

Scully, R. M. (2005). *Becoming Europeans. Attitudes, behaviour, and socialization in the European parliament.* Oxford: Oxford University Press.

Scully, R., & Farrell, D. (2003). MEPs as representatives: Individual and institutional roles. *Journal of Common Market Studies, 41*(2), 269–288.

Searing, D. (1991). Roles, rules and rationality in the new institutionalism. *The American political science review, 85*(4), 1239–1260.

Searing, D. (1994). *Westminster's world. Understanding political roles.* Cambridge: Harvard University Press.

Searing, D. (2012). Foreword. In M. Blomgren & O. Rozenberg (Eds.), *Parliamentary roles in modern legislatures* (pp. xxi–xxvii). London: Routledge.

Strøm, K. (1997). Rules, reasons and routines: Legislative roles in parliamentary democracies. In W. C. Müller & T. Saalfeld (Eds.), *Members of parliament in Western Europe: Roles and behaviour* (pp. 155–174). London: Frank Cass.

Strøm, K. (2012). Roles as Strategies: Towards a logic of legislative behavior. In M. Blomgren & O. Rozenberg (Eds.), *Parliamentary roles in modern legislatures* (pp. 85–100). London: Routlege/ECPR studies in European Political Science.

Thames, F. C. (2005). A house divided: Party strength and the mandate divide in Hungary, Russia, and Ukraine. *Comparative Political Studies, 38*(3), 282–303.

Thomassen, J. (1994). Empirical research into political representation: Failing democracy or failing models? In M. K. Jennings & T. E. Mann (Eds.), *Elections at Home and Abroad, Essays in Honor of Warren E. Miller* (pp. 237–264). Ann Arbor: University of Michigan Press.

Thomassen, J. (2012). The blind corner of political representation. *Representation, 48*(1), 13–27.

Thomassen, J., & Esaiassen, P. (2006). Role orientations of members of parliament. *Acta Politica, 41*(3), 217–231.

Thomassen, J., & Schmitt, H. (1997). Policy representation. *European Journal of Political Research, 32*(2), 165–184.

Tsebelis, G. (1994). The power of the European parliament as a conditional agenda-setter. *American Political Science Review, 88* (1), 128 142

Urbinati, C., & Warren, M. (2008). The Concept of Representation in Contemporary Democratic Theory. *Annual Review of Political Science, 11*, 387–412.

Van der Eijk, C., & Franklin, M. (2004). Potential for contestation on European matters at national elections in Europe. In G. Marks & M. R. Steenbergen (Eds.), *European Integration and Political Conflict* (pp. 32–50). Cambridge: Cambridge University Press.

Verzichelli, L., & Edinger, M. (2005). A critical juncture? The 2004 European elections and the making of a supranational elite. *Journal of Legislative Studies, 11*(2), 254–274.

Vom Beyme, K. (2006). Political institutions—Old and new. In S. A. Binder, R. A. W. Rhodes, & B. A. Rockman (Eds.), *Oxford handbook of political institutions* (pp. 743–757). Oxford: Oxford University Press.

Wahlke, J., Eulau, H., Buchanan, W. & Ferguson, L. (1962). *The legislative system. Explorations in legislative behavior.* New York: Wiley.

Walczak, A., & Van der Brug, W. (2013). Representation in the European Parliament: Factors affecting the attitude congruence of voters and candidates in the EP elections. *European Union Politics, 14*(1), 3–22.

Wessels, B. (1999). Whom to represent? Role orientations of Legislators in Europe. In H. Schmitt & J. Thomassen (Eds.), *Political Representation and Legitimacy in the European Union* (pp. 209–234). Oxford: Oxford University Press.

Whitaker, R. (2011). *The European Parliament's Committees: National party influence and legislative empowerment.* London: Routledge.

Wood, D.M. & Yoon, J.B. (1998). Role Orientations of junior MPs: A Test of Searing's categories with emphasis on constituency activities. *Journal of Legislative studies, 4*(3), 51–71.

Yordanova, N. (2011). The European parliament: In need of a theory. *European Union Politics, 12*(4), 597–617.

Young, A. R. (2016). An inflection point in European Union studies? *Journal of European Public Policy, 23*(8), 1109–1117.

Zittel, T. (2012). Legislators and their representational roles. Strategic choices or habits of the heart? In M. Blomgren & O. Rozenberg (Eds.), *Parliamentary roles in modern legislatures* (pp 101–120). London: ECPR Press Routledge.

Zittel, T., & Gschwend, T. (2008). Individualised constituency campaigns in mixed-member electoral systems: Candidates in the 2005 German elections. *West European Politics, 31*(5), 978–1003.

CHAPTER 3

Euroscepticism in the European Parliament

The development of anti-EU sentiment is one of the most important features of the integration process over the last two decades (Usherwood 2007a). The ongoing economic, political and migration crisis has provided fertile ground for the galvanization of oppositions to the EU. Euroscepticism has progressively become embedded at the national and supranational levels and is now part of the mainstream. Indeed, with the migration crisis, populist and Eurosceptic discourses have flourished, assimilating migrants, terrorism, and the free movement of persons and blaming the EU for the lack of border controls. The duration of the economic crisis has also provoked a blossoming of contestation against the EU (Conti 2016), presented either as an "alien" power imposing austerity measures on national democracies or as incapable of providing efficient solutions in times of financial and economic turmoil.

As a result, Euroscepticism has generated a great wealth of scientific studies. Since the late 1990s, the study of Euroscepticism has gradually become an established sub-discipline of European studies (Flood 2009; Mudde 2011). Scholars have sought to understand the complex nature of this phenomenon. They have proposed various typologies and classifications and examined the main factors explaining these oppositions to Europe. The literature has significantly enriched our knowledge of Euroscepticism and its determinants, notably through the analysis of the impact of ideological, strategic, institutional and contextual factors on attitudes towards European integration. However, it suffers from two shortcomings. Firstly, most studies focus on taxonomic issues,

© The Author(s) 2018   51
N. Brack, *Opposing Europe in the European Parliament*,
Palgrave Studies in European Union Politics,
https://doi.org/10.1057/978-1-137-60201-5_3

defining and categorizing parties according to their position vis-à-vis the European project (Harmsen 2010, p. 339). They overlook the behaviour of Eurosceptics once elected to parliamentary assemblies (Jensen and Spoon 2010). Secondly, with some recent exceptions, these studies focus on national parties and the national level with little consideration for the European level. While Euroscepticism is not a new phenomenon and the EP has served as a forum of expression for dissenting voices, Eurosceptic MEPs' attitudes, motivations and strategies have been understudied so far.

This research seeks to address this gap. To do so, this chapter aims to define the concept of Euroscepticism such as it is understood here and to identify the Eurosceptics elected to the EP during the period under study (2004–2016). After placing Euroscepticism within a broader historical context, the next section will review the main conceptualizations and their shortcomings before explaining how Euroscepticism is defined in the framework of this book. Going back to the core idea behind Taggart's first definition of the phenomenon and drawing on research on political opposition, Euroscepticism is seen here as an anti-system opposition. Such a definition allows for a connection between research on Euroscepticism on the one hand and on political opposition and the study of anti-system actors on the other. The final section empirically identifies the Eurosceptic MEPs since 2004.

1   Unpacking Oppositions to the EU: A Complex and Evolving Phenomenon

Euroscepticism is often presented as a relatively new phenomenon which emerged in the early 1990s and marked the end of the permissive consensus (Vasilopoulou 2013). Yet while the term is relatively new, the attitudes to which it refers, namely opposition to the European project, are as old as the project itself (Katz 2008). European integration has always been inherently controversial, and the EU has been shaped by disagreements between political actors on how to organize politics in Europe (Crespy and Verschueren 2009; Hooghe and Marks 1997). Indeed, the history of European integration, far from being linear and consensual, has gone through various crises, revealing the existence of diverging visions of the European project (Brack and Costa 2012; Giacone and Olivi 2007; Ross 2011).

1.1   The First Decades of Integration: The Golden Age of Permissive Consensus?

In the early 1950s, there was relatively widespread reticence among Western political elites to the establishment of a supranational institutional system. Similarly, one can consider that it is not so much out of conviction but out of interest that national leaders rallied around the idea of the European project. This was facilitated by the ambiguity surrounding the objectives of European integration. From the 1960s to the mid-1980s, Euroscepticism was somewhat stifled: the absence of major treaty revisions, market regulation and integration through the Europeanization of national legislation made the impact of the European Communities relatively unremarkable within national territories (Leconte 2010, pp. 100–101). Tacit approval prevailed in national public opinion. Attitudes towards the EU and integration were generally favourable but unstructured and largely marked by a follow-the-leader attitude (conceptualized as "permissive consensus") (Lindberg and Scheingold 1970). Objections by political elites towards the European project remained peripheral—confined to the margins of the political system; temporary—such as the empty chair crisis in 1965; or sectoral—such as trade union opposition to specific policies. In the early days of European integration, members were appointed directly by their national parliaments; hence, there was an overrepresentation of large parties and representatives favourable to European integration, especially with the refusal of the French and Italian Communists to send representatives (Mény 2009, p. 35). But since the 1970s, the EP has provided a platform for parties critical of the integration process and, since then, the assembly is divided along two main dimensions: left/right and pro/anti-integration (Hix et al. 2007). During this first period, as opposition remained marginal and temporary, it attracted little interest from the academic world and, while early studies provided very detailed analyses of specific cases, they did not produce a theoretical framework with major explanatory value.

An initial rupture occurred within the context of the adoption of the Single European Act and the programme on the internal market. The apparent consensus among political elites as to both the economic and political benefits of integration was shattered by the emergence of a debate on the transformation of the European Economic Community and the regulation of the internal market (Usherwood 2007).

In response to Jacques Delors' ambitions to strengthen European economic and political cooperation, Margaret Thatcher's speech in Bruges in 1988 revealed competing visions of the European project. From the mid-1980s, the development of the Communities provoked a debate on how the market should be regulated and organized: the programme on the internal market became then the starting point for the argument over the institutional configuration of the European system (Hooghe and Marks 1997, p. 6).

1.2   *The Critical Turning Point in European Integration*

It is the Maastricht Treaty however which undeniably marked a qualitative break. Although the thesis of a permissive consensus must be nuanced, there is no denying that this treaty's negotiation and ratification campaigns constituted a "critical turn" for European integration, as opposition became more visible and diversified (Lacroix and Coman 2007). Symbolically, the treaty transformed the community into a Union and introduced European citizenship, triggering fears within public opinion about the erosion of national identity. Moreover, by transferring competencies such as currency and foreign policy to the EU, the treaty provoked opposition given the challenges which these transfers pose to national sovereignty and the implications on national redistribution policies of the economic prescriptions contained in the treaty (Verney 2011). It was also a key moment in the debate surrounding the development of the EU. Boundaries between what is national and what is supranational became increasingly blurred, and the forms of opposition were increasingly diversified. European citizens also became more aware of the scale and nature of European integration, marking the beginning of the politicization of Europe (Franklin et al. 1994). European issues are increasingly becoming "normal" political discussions, subject to debate in national political arenas and polarizing opinions. While studies have shown that the level of public support towards integration nowadays is quite similar to what it was in the 1970s, there is, however, a greater differentiation of attitudes towards Europe and a greater visibility of opposition within public opinion (Down and Wilson 2008). Hooghe and Marks (2009, p. 5) believe, therefore, that one can speak of a "constraining dissensus": the politicization of European issues has revealed the gap between citizens and elites, and the latter should now take a more reluctant public into account.

Previously a marginal phenomenon, Euroscepticism became more complex as it spread across the continent and the political landscape. It has since become a stable and embedded phenomenon in a majority of Member states (Harmsen 2005, p. 79). European elections since 1994 and the successive enlargements have broadened the spectrum of partisan positions towards the European project and consolidated the ranks of Eurosceptics within the EP. In parallel, the process of constitutionalization has generated a public debate on the nature and future of the EU, facilitating the mobilization of Eurosceptic actors (Trenz and De Wilde 2009). Since the pioneering article by Taggart (1998), literature seeking to understand Euroscepticism has grown exponentially (Flood 2009). There are, in that respect, ongoing debates and controversies regarding the respective importance of ideology and strategy and, to a lesser extent, of cultural and institutional factors.

A first approach relies on Lipset and Rokkan's cleavage theory to examine the relationship between ideological positions and attitudes towards the EU. The traditional cleavages can then be seen as prisms through which the parties respond to integration (Hooghe and Marks 2007; Marks and Wilson 2000; Marks et al. 2002). These studies demonstrate that the political family, combining historical divisions, provides a reliable and effective indicator of party position on integration (Marks and Wilson 2000). Specifically, two major dimensions structure party competition and help explain actors' positions on European issues: the left/right economic cleavage and the GAL/TAN (Green-Alternative-Libertarian/Traditional-Authoritarian-Nationalist) dimension on non-economic issues such as the environment, lifestyle and values (Bartolini et al. 2012). Parties on the GAL side of the axis, such as the Greens, tend to be more pro-EU whereas parties on the TAN side, such as radical right, tend to be Eurosceptic (Marks et al. 2009).

Conversely, the authors of the "Sussex School" believe it is not so much ideology but strategy that explains parties' positions on European integration. Euroscepticism is seen as the result of strategic calculations in the national competition. In other words, there is no linear relationship between the ideological position on the left/right cleavage and the party's attitude towards European integration: "a party's ideological position does not provide sufficient information to deduce its position on the EU" (Taggart 1998, p. 377). Several elements are then highlighted as explanatory factors: the characteristics of the national context and constraints arising from national institutions (Lees 2002; Usherwood 2007); the parties' objectives (office-seeking, vote-seeking, policy-seeking) (Raunio 2007; Sitter 2001); the type of parties and their position in the party system (Taggart and Szczerbiak 2002, 2008); and the dynamics of partisan competition (Batory and Sitter 2008). Euroscepticism, according to this approach, is mainly found among opposition parties as well as protest-based actors as a strategic resource in the party competition.

Other studies have attempted to go beyond this debate between ideological and strategic considerations by emphasizing not only institutional factors and political culture, national history, but also the perceptions of politicians and public opinion. The analysis of resistance to Europe is inseparable from the analysis of the political culture in which it operates (Lacroix and Coman 2007). Some authors have thus emphasized the influence of the history, context and identity of the nation state in which Euroscepticism has its roots (see a.o. Emanuele et al. 2016). Recent research has investigated the relationship between partisan positioning and the level of Euroscepticism in public opinion, demonstrating that this influence is reciprocal. Parties not only shape public opinion but also respond to the attitudes of citizens (Gifford 2008; Harmsen 2010; De Vries and Edwards 2009; Steenbergen et al. 2007).

Finally, researchers have recently emphasized the role played by the supranational context and the attitudes of European elites. The uncertain nature of the European project and the process of the EU's constitutionalization provide fertile ground for the galvanization of opposition to the EU (De Wilde 2010). Moreover, the reluctance so far of European elites to engage in a debate with Eurosceptics is damaging to the EU's legitimacy, especially since this position contradicts the EU's ambition to become a democratic polity, attentive to its audience (citizens) (Usherwood and Startin 2013). European elites have not developed arguments to justify and discuss their positions towards European integration and therefore are not responsive to the normative challenge posed by Eurosceptics (Morgan 2005; Nivet 2016). Finally, the EU's democratic deficit and lack of institutional structure for the expression of conflicting views not only strengthen Eurosceptic arguments but also harden their position.

1.3   Economic Crisis and Galvanization of Opposition

The window for institutional reform was just barely closed with the adoption of the Lisbon Treaty (2009) when the economic and Eurozone crises reopened the debate on European integration and on the capacity and legitimacy of EU intervention in economic governance (Emanuele et al. 2016; Serrichio et al. 2013). The unpopular bailouts increased the Union's visibility in the public sphere (Mudde 2014), leading to the emergence or resurgence of opposition to Europe in several Member states. Interest in Euroscepticism grew again although most works concentrate on electoral results analysis or propose an assessment of the potential dangers Eurosceptic parties could constitute (for instance Dye 2015; Ivaldi 2014; Harris 2014). There is a consensus to consider that European integration has now entered a new and more difficult phase of its existence, characterized by mass Euroscepticism, the rise of radical and populist parties and the mainstreaming of anti-EU rhetoric (Vasilopoulou 2013; Verney 2015). The European elections of May 2014 and the UK referendum on EU membership attest to these trends. Claims on the non-democratic nature of the EU and on the need for major reforms have become commonplace among mainstream parties (Abbarno and Zypruanova 2013) while we are also witnessing "a changing and more challenging media discourse with regards to portrayals of the EU" (Brack and Startin 2015). This context has provided particularly fertile ground for Eurosceptic actors over the last few years. Eurosceptic and anti-establishment parties, both left and right, experienced unprecedented success in the 2014 EP elections (Hobolt 2015), leading some commentators to speak of a "Eurosceptic storm in Brussels" (FT 26 May 2014). The radical right has never won so many seats in the EP, particularly with the victory of the Front National in France and the Danish People's Party. These elections also saw the entry of neo-Nazi parties such as the German NDP and Golden Dawn in the EP. Furthermore, in 2015, for the first time since the short-lived "Identity, Tradition, Sovereignty" group (2007), a radical right group was formed in the EP (called Europe of Nations and Freedom). The crisis context was also favourable to the radical left, particularly in Southern European countries which were most affected by the economic crisis. Podemos in Spain and Syriza in Greece have been particularly

successful at the national and European levels. In the EP, the group of
the radical left has increased from 35 to 52 MEPs. Against this backdrop, it is therefore more important than ever to analyse these dissenting
voices within supranational institutions.

2   A PROBLEMATIC CONCEPTUALIZATION

The diversification of negative reactions to European construction poses
a real challenge to conceptualization; the term tends to be used as a
generic concept that encompasses a disparate set of attitudes of opposition, reluctance and doubts towards European integration and the EU
(Mudde 2011; Szczerbiak and Taggart 2008). Sometimes it is used to
describe any form of opposition to or critique of the process of European
integration, whereas on other occasions, it implies an ideological position that structures parties' stances on other issues. Like other concepts
in political science such as populism, there is no commonly accepted definition but rather a series of different interpretations within the academic
community.

The most influential conceptualization is undoubtedly the one proposed by Taggart (1998), which he refined with his colleague Szczerbiak
(2000). This categorization distinguishes between two forms of
Euroscepticism: soft and hard. Soft Euroscepticism covers cases where
there is no principled objection to European integration or EU membership but where actors' concerns towards one or more policy areas
lead to the expression of qualified opposition to the EU (political
Euroscepticism). It also covers cases where there is a perception that
national interest is at odds with the trajectory of the EU (national interest Euroscepticism). Hard Euroscepticism refers to a principled opposition to the EU and European integration, which can therefore be
observed among parties which believe their country should leave the EU
or whose positions towards the EU can be equated with opposition to
the entire project of European integration (Taggart 1998; Taggart and
Szczerbiak 2002).

Mudde and Kopecky (2002) believe that the overly inclusive definition of soft Euroscepticism may incorporate any disagreement with
specific or general EU policies and that the boundary between these
two forms of Euroscepticism is not easily identifiable. They propose
therefore two different axes. The first relates to attitudes towards the
general principles of integration that underpin the EU. This axis

opposes Europhiles who support the ideas of European integration (institutionalized cooperation on the basis of pooled sovereignty and an integrated liberal market economy) and Europhobes who do not support or are opposed to one or more of these ideas. The second axis relates to attitudes towards the EU as political system. On the one hand, it separates EU-optimists who support the EU as it is and as it is developing (although they may be critical of some EU policies) and, on the other hand, EU-pessimists who do not support the EU as it is, are pessimistic about the direction of its development or believe that it does not match their idea of integration. Four categories result from these axes: Euro-enthusiast (Europhile and EU-optimist); Euro-pragmatic (Europhobe and EU-optimist); Eurosceptic (Europhobe and EU-pessimist) and Euro-reject (Europhobe and EU-pessimist).

These two main conceptualizations have attracted a number of criticisms. Both have been characterized as imprecise and failing to take into consideration the complex and dynamic nature of Euroscepticism (Krouwel and Abts 2007). Flood and Usherwood (2007) consider that both conceptualizations suffer from the same type of shortcomings: they propose a binary and simplistic opposition between Europhilia and Europhobia vis-à-vis an ideal of European integration, without taking into account the diverging visions of the integration process. Furthermore, if Taggart and Szczerbiak use the same label for parties holding very different views on the EU and European integration, Mudde and Kopecky use the term "Euroscepticism" to describe a single category, leading to some ambiguity. Mudde and Kopecky's "Euro-pragmatic" has also been considered to be unrealistic and a priori contradictory while their "Euro-enthusiast" category has been criticized for being overly inclusive.

Despite an extensive literature, Euroscepticism remains an elusive and poorly defined concept which has become increasingly difficult to mobilize and operationalize (Harmsen 2010). The border between reformism and Euroscepticism is often blurry and difficult to draw precisely. If one accepts an overly inclusive definition, any actor might be perceived as being Eurosceptic from the moment they do not accept the EU unconditionally and want their preferences to be taken into consideration more (Usherwood 2005b). Moreover, while the concept remains marked by its roots in the post-Maastricht period and therefore takes on a radical dimension related to nationalism, much of the discourse is now more about qualified criticisms than the desirability of

European integration (Harmsen and Spiering 2004). Another difficulty is that the term contains a strong normative charge, serving in some contexts to disqualify certain actors or political adversaries (Neumayer 2008; Ward 1996). Finally, not only do several conceptualizations coexist and come with their own labels,[1] but a series of researchers, dissatisfied with the term, have created neologisms better suited to their object of study, be it euro-indifference for neutral positions (Delmotte 2007), euro-realism in the framework of the CEEC (Neumayer 2008), euro-cynicism, euro-ambivalence or euro-alienation for public opinion (Krouwel and Abts 2007; Van Ingelgom 2014) or even, resistances to cover a broader set of actors (Crespy and Verschueren 2009; Lacroix and Coman 2007). As noted by Roger (2007, p. 31), "the literature on reactions to European integration is facing a proliferation of ad hoc concepts, which follow from semantic confusion and poor categorizations".

3   EUROSCEPTICISM AS POLITICAL OPPOSITION

In order to define Euroscepticism as it is understood here, it is essential to return to what constitutes the essence of the phenomenon: a posture of opposition. Indeed, as noted by Taggart (1998, p. 366), Euroscepticism is an opposition, whether qualified or principled, to the existing institutional reality.

Considering Euroscepticism not as an attitude of doubt, reluctance or an expression of critical reformism but as a form of political opposition against the status quo, that is to say, the European project, such as it is, makes it possible to delineate the contours of the studied population more precisely. But it also allows us to go beyond the "artificially maintained dichotomy between political science and European studies understood as an independent sub-specialty" (Costa et al. 2008, p. 533). Indeed, the concept of political opposition has been the subject of major theories in both comparative politics and political theory. Through their work, authors such as Dahl (1971), Kircheimer (1964), Sartori (1966), Schapiro (1965), Madariaga and Ionescu (1968) as well as Berger (1979) have contributed to a better understanding of political opposition, particularly parliamentary opposition in democratic regimes. Despite the normative biases and evolutionary perspectives of this literature, it has the merit of having promoted a binary distinction between so-called normal opposition and its deviant counterpart

(Brack and Weinblum 2011). Thus, Kircheimer drew a distinction between classical or loyal opposition, which offers alternative political choices while recognizing the government's right to be in power, and, on the other hand, opposition on principle, opposition not only to the government and its policies, but also to its legitimacy and the very foundation of the governance system. Similarly, Sartori distinguishes normal constitutional opposition from its anti-system form by affirming that "true opposition presupposes consent on the essentials, namely, the foundations of the community and the regime".

However, this understanding of political opposition, as theorized by these authors, is not fully applicable to the EU. The existence of political opposition in the traditional sense of the term is essentially based on the identification of an executive against which this opposition is directed. But, the traditional pattern between majority and opposition is not easily identifiable at the European level (Helms 2008). The EU is one of those political systems where, according to Dahl (1999), "it is difficult to determine those who govern and those who oppose". In addition, the EU lacks a fixed and institutionalized place from where opposition might be expressed. As a result of the absence of an executive with partisan coherence and the support of a majority of elected representatives, the EP is not structured by a permanent divide between majority and minority but rather by a juxtaposition of cleavages and a tendency to resort to the large majorities therein (Costa 2001; Neuhold and Settembri 2009). The structures and procedures of the EP do not allow the institution to play its role as a "site of opposition" in the classic sense of the term.

This work draws inspiration from the binary typologies outlined by the literature and suggests that Euroscepticism is a "deviant" form of political opposition, namely an anti-system opposition or principled opposition, directed against the system and the polity. Indeed, Euroscepticism is different from "normal politics", from the classic opposition to public policy and denotes rather an opposition to the constitutive dimension of the EU (Magnette and Papadopoulos 2008; De Wilde and Trenz 2012). As noted by Neunreither (1998), the EU is different in this respect from the majority of its Member states: in the latter, the regime's existence is no longer questioned, and the opposition tends to focus on public policy issues.[2] Indeed, although the nation state no longer benefits from an undisputed status, the overall political structure is generally not questioned and the opposition focuses on policy choices, government priorities and certain constitutional issues.

Contrarily, at the supranational level, systemic and constitutional issues are numerous and recurring, especially now with the existential crisis the EU is facing. These issues are, moreover, seen as essential and problematic, particularly because of the lack of political *finalité* shared by a large majority of actors (Neunreither 1998). The EU's lack of legitimacy, the uncertainties regarding its nature and the absence of channels for the expression of opposition are all sources of tension and conflict (Mény 2012). In the EU, the debate is not only about the type of fiscal, social, industrial or monetary policy but also about the territorial level where these policies are elaborated and the way in which decisions are made. In other words, "the conflict that underlies European integration concerns nothing less than the manner in which Europe should be organized politically" (Hooghe and Marks 1997, p. 7), and it is precisely on this dispute over the constitutive dimension that Euroscepticism is located. As noted by Hix and his colleagues (Hix et al. 2007), two main dimensions of conflict structure the EP debates: the traditional left/right axis and the pro/anti-EU divide. The latter cleavage is even becoming more salient since the Eurozone crisis (Otjes and van der Veer 2016). The EP resembles some national parliaments which have experienced situations of internal opposition to the regime. For instance, under the Fourth Republic, the French National Assembly was divided by a pro/anti-regime split comparable to the pro/anti-integration split in the EP.[3] Euroscepticism should not be understood as opposition to implemented policies or in reference to the left/right axis, but as a systemic opposition aimed at the integration process and the resulting political system.

Based on this literature, the concept of Euroscepticism will be used here to describe the attitudes of opposition to the European regime, its institutions, its legitimacy and the very foundations of the system of governance. MEPs who are opposed to European (political and economic) integration and/or to the EU as it is currently will be considered to be Eurosceptic. However, as a result of the heterogeneity and complexity of Euroscepticism, it becomes necessary to differentiate it both in nature and in degree. Combining the conceptualization of Taggart and Szczerbiak with the work of Mudde and Kopecky, Euroscepticism should be seen as a continuum ranging from a soft, or reformist, position to a hard, or principled, opposition (Fig. 3.1). We should bear in mind that this distinction is based not only on the degree of opposition but also on the target of this opposition. Relying on Mudde and Kopecky's conceptualization, it is essential to distinguish actors opposed to the integration

Soft Euroscepticism ◄—————————————————► Hard Euroscepticism

Fig. 3.1 Euroscepticism as an axis of opposition

process and the general (political and economic) ideas and values underlying it[4] on the one hand and to the EU as a polity on the other hand.

This definition has three major implications. Firstly, it relies on a more restrictive definition of Euroscepticism and to assume its radical nature, referring only to an opposition to integration and the EU and excluding any attitude of doubt, reticence or criticism towards EU policies. The aim is to distinguish Euroscepticism as an opposition to integration and/or the EU from other reactions that may be seen as the result of a normal politicization of European issues in a multi-level system (as traditional and normal opposition). Secondly, this definition allows for the inclusion of the study of Euroscepticism into the broader scope of research on opposition and in particular on anti-system actors found in other political systems. Finally, such a definition leaves aside any a priori regarding the motivations of parties who adopt a Eurosceptic attitude. Unlike the research of the schools of Sussex and North Carolina, this study does not examine the impact of the type of party or its position in the political arena on the degree of Euroscepticism, nor does it ambition to determine how ideology affects the actor's position on the axis of integration. Here, the differentiation between actors is based on the degree and target of their opposition, without integrating the actor's motivations for adopting a Eurosceptic attitude.

4   WHO ARE THE EUROSCEPTIC MEPS?

In order to apply this conceptualization and determine who the Eurosceptics were during the time frame of this research, several indicators are used. First, the voting behaviour of MEPs on key texts concerning the European project is analysed. The selection was then refined on the basis of their party affiliation and their discourse. Because there was no major report on European integration during the 7th and 8th parliamentary terms (respectively, 2009–2014 and 2014–2019), other elements, i.e. party affiliation, interviews with MEPs and the literature on Euroscepticism, were mobilized as well to identify Eurosceptic elected representatives.

4.1   A Two-Step Approach to Identifying Eurosceptic MEPs (2004–2016)

First, an exploratory analysis of the voting behaviour of all MEPs on key texts on the EU's future and the European integration process was carried out to identify the Eurosceptics. Indeed, the voting behaviour is not only one of the most visible aspects of parliamentary activities but also the best way for MEPs to publicly and definitively express their positions (Scully 1999, 2005). Contrary to national party programmes, expert surveys, survey responses or media statements (Proksch and Lo 2012), voting is a real behaviour which publicly engages the MEPs. Moreover, these votes deal with particularly symbolic texts. These addressed the state and future of both the EU and European integration, the principles of this process and their implementation.[5] A recurring opposition to this kind of text is thus a good indicator of Euroscepticism (Bouillaud 2008).

During the 6th legislature (2004–2009), there were eight such texts: the EP resolution on the ratification procedures of the treaty establishing a Constitution for Europe and the communication strategy around it[6]; the Corbett/Mendez de Vigo report on a constitution for Europe[7]; the resolution on the future of Europe sixty years after World War II[8]; the Duff/Voggenhuber report on the period of reflection: structure, themes and framework of evaluation[9]; the EP resolution on the next steps for the period of reflection and analysis of the future of Europe[10]; the Baron Crespo/Brok report on the continuation of the constitutional process[11]; the Leinen report on the convening of the Intergovernmental Conference[12]; and the Corbett/Mendez de Vigo report on the Treaty of Lisbon.[13]

A principal component analysis was first conducted on the eight votes to determine if one could speak of only one dimension. Indeed, one could have considered that these texts are not all of the same nature but the results of this analysis show that a single dimension is detectable throughout these votes and that this dimension explains 81.5% of the variance. The component matrix and the Cattell scree test show that a single component can be extracted from the data: the eight votes refer to a single dimension and each vote is highly correlated with the extracted dimension. All of these votes represent thus a single dimension, interpreted as attitude towards EU integration.

For each of the texts mentioned above, the voting behaviour of each MEP was then encoded as follows: vote in favour (0), vote against (1), absent (missing value),[14] abstention (0.5).[15] The scores of each MEP were totalled to obtain an opposition scale ranging from 0 to 8. Any MEP who opposed at least half of these texts, or with a score of at least 4, was considered to be a Eurosceptic (see Fig. 3.2). This resulted in a group of 151 individuals during the sixth parliament.[16] MEPs who were absent more than half the time (163 individuals) were excluded from this initial selection and have been treated on a case-by-case basis depending on three factors: their voting behaviour when they were present and took a position, party affiliation and, if they took the floor, their discourse during the debate on the texts submitted to a vote. Twenty-one additional MEPs were added to the initial selection and were also considered Eurosceptics as a result of their negative attitude regarding these texts through their voting and party affiliation. In total, there were 165 Eurosceptic MEPs (out of 862 individuals)[17] in the European parliament during the sixth legislature, which is consistent with estimates by other researchers according to which Eurosceptics represented approximately 20% of the EP (Bouillaud 2008; Leconte 2010) (Fig. 3.2, Table 3.1).

The 2009 and 2014 European elections changed the composition of the assembly considerably, especially within the Eurosceptic population. Indeed, some parties, such as the June List (Sweden) and "Europa transparent" (The Netherlands), lost all parliamentary representation

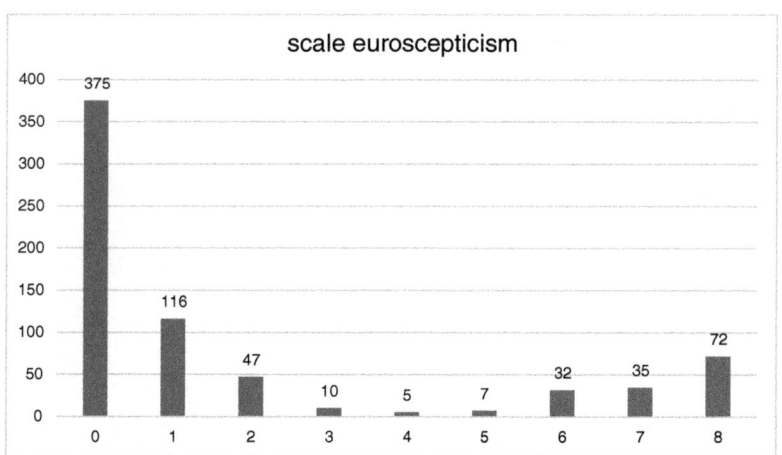

Fig. 3.2   Scale of Euroscepticism

Table 3.1 Eurosceptic MEPs—6th legislature (2004–2009, opening session)

	EUL/NGL	Greens/ALE	PES	ALDE	EPP-ED	UEN	IND/DEM	NA	TOTAL
Belgium								3	3
Bulgaria								3	3
Czech Rep.	6				9		1	1	17
Denmark	2					1	2		5
Germany	6								6
Estonia									0
Ireland	1						1		2
Greece	4						2		6
Spain	1	2							3
France	4						3	7	14
Italy	7					5	1	2	15
Cyprus	2								2
Latvia									0
Lithuania									0
Luxembourg									0
Hungary									0
Malta									0
Netherlands	2	1					2		5
Austria								2	2
Poland						19	4	2	25
Portugal	3								3
Romania									0
Slovenia									0
Slovakia					1				1
Finland	1								1
Sweden	3	1			1		2		7
UK	1	3			26		10	5	45
Total	43	7	0	0	37	25	28	25	165
									19,14%

Source European Parliament

while new parties like the Dutch Freedom Party (Partij voor de Vrijheid), the Finns (Perussuomalaiset—Finland), the Five Star Movement (Movimento 5 Stelle - Italy) and Alternative for Germany (AfD—Germany) made their appearance in the EP. In the absence of votes similar to those of the 6th legislature, party affiliation, more precisely EP group membership, was used as an indicator. Although the choice of a group in the EP is sometimes dictated by domestic considerations and the founding charters often lack detail, even this lowest common denominator can give us information as to the stance of MEPs towards the EU. Indeed, MEPs adhere to the principles of their group's charter and programme, and their parties choose to sit in groups whose political platform is closest to their programme, at least on the most salient issues (McElroy and Benoit 2010). Membership in group also helps to determine the MEP's capacity for compromise on the issue of integration, some sitting in Europhile groups and others preferring to belong to a smaller but Eurosceptic group (Benedetto 2008). On the basis of an analysis of the EP groups' platforms, MEPs belonging to EUL/NGL, EFD, EFDD, ECR as well as non-attached MEP from radical right parties and anti-EU groups can be identified as Eurosceptics. The European United Left/Nordic Green Left is opposed to the EU as it currently stands and to some of the values underpinning the integration process. Its members reject the economic values at the basis of European integration and strongly criticize the EU: "the confederal group of the European United Left is deeply committed to European construction but one of a different type than the one currently in place. (...) A different Europe which would wipe clean the democratic deficit as it is confirmed by the Maastricht Treaty and the monetarist and neoliberal policies that come with it. The EU is not a victim of the current economic, financial, environmental and global food crisis but one of its motors".[18] Similarly, the Europe of Freedom and Democracy (EFD) and its successor, the Europe of Freedom and Direct Democracy (EFDD) group, as well as the Europe of Nations and Freedom group (ENF) display a strong opposition to the European project. Their members tend to be opposed to the idea of supranational integration, essentially in the name of the defence of national sovereignty. The EFDD states in its charter that it opposes further European integration that would exacerbate the present democratic deficit and the centralist political structure of the EU. It "favours an open, transparent, democratic and accountable cooperation among sovereign European states and rejects the bureaucratization of

Table 3.2 Eurosceptic MEPs—7th legislature (2009–2014, opening session)

	EUL/NGL	Greens/EFA	S&D	ALDE	EPP	ECR	EFD	NA	TOTAL
Belgium						1		2	3
Bulgaria								2	2
Czech Rep.	4					9			13
Denmark	1						2		3
Germany	8								8
Estonia									0
Ireland	1								1
Greece	3						2		5
Spain	1	2							3
France	5						1	3	9
Italy							9		9
Cyprus	2								2
Latvia	1					1			2
Lithuania						1	2		3
Luxembourg									0
Hungary						1		3	4
Malta									0
The Netherlands	2					1	1	4	8
Austria								5	5
Poland						15			15
Portugal	5								5
Romania								3	3
Slovenia									0
Slovakia							1		1
Finland							1		1
Sweden	1	2							3
UK	1					26	13	3	43
Total	35	4	0	0	0	55	32	25	151
									20.5%

Source European Parliament, http://www.europarl.europa.eu/elections2014-results/en/election-results-2009.html [21]

Table 3.3 Eurosceptic MEPs—8th legislature (2014–2019, opening session)

	EUL/NGL	Greens/EFA	S&D	ALDE	EPP	ECR	EFDD	ENF	NA	TOTAL
Belgium						4		1		5
Bulgaria						2				2
Czech Rep.	3					2	1			6
Denmark	1					4				5
Germany	8					6	1	1	2	18
Estonia										0
Ireland	4					1				5
Greece	6					1			5	12
Spain	11									11
France	4						1	20	3	28
Croatia						1				1
Italy	3					2	17	4		26
Cyprus	2					1				3
Latvia						1				1
Lithuania						1	1			2
Luxembourg										0
Hungary									3	3
Malta										0
The Netherlands	3					2		4		9
Austria								4		4
Poland						19	1	2	1	23
Portugal	4									4
Romania						1		1		2
Slovenia										0
Slovakia						3				3
Finland	1					2				3
Sweden	1	4					2			7
UK	1					21	22	1	1	46
Total	52	4	0	0	0	74	46	38	15	229
										30.5%

Source European Parliament

Europe and the creation of a single centralized European superstate".[19] In a similar vein, members of the ENF group "reject any policy designed to create a supra-state or a supra-national model. The opposition to any transfer of national sovereignty to supranational bodies and/or European Institutions is one of the fundamental principle uniting Members of the ENF".[20]

In addition to these MEPs, members of the Swedish Green Party were also included (on the basis of interviews with these MEPs). A survey of the literature on Euroscepticism confirms this classification (esp. Barbieri 2015; De Sio et al. 2014; Hartleb 2011; Mudde 2014; Taggart and Szczerbiak 2008) (Tables 3.2, 3.3).

4.2   Patterns of Euroscepticism

The graph and tables in the previous section attest that the group of Eurosceptic MEPs is very heterogeneous, coming from a majority of Member states as well as covering the entire partisan spectrum. Recently, Usherwood (2014) rightly noted "in all the media hype, it has been forgotten that 'Euroscepticism' doesn't really exist, at least in the sense of a coherent ideology. (…) The differences between Eurosceptic parties in the European parliament are as big as the range of ideologies represented in the chamber as a whole". As shown by the analysis of their charters, some political groups strongly oppose integration and the EU while others are more moderate or solely focus on opposition to the EU. In order to differentiate them on the continuum explained previously, interviews were carried out with Eurosceptic MEPs. As explained, although the conceptualization of Euroscepticism corresponds to a single continuum, the work of Kopecky and Mudde should be borne in mind. More precisely, the distinction between opposition to European integration and the values underlying it and opposition to the EU and its institutions is very relevant, and MEPs were asked about their preferences on the two issues. On the basis of these interviews, three main positions could be found.

The first one is a principled opposition to institutionalized cooperation at the European level, be it economic or political, if it entails pooling or sharing sovereignty. It corresponds to hard Euroscepticism. These Eurosceptics are opposed to European integration and its basic ideals: "I am totally opposed to the whole concept. My own view is that I would be quite happy with a group of independent nation states trading and cooperating together" (interview with MEP15). They criticize the transfer of powers from the national to the supranational level, and most of them would advocate for an exit from the EU (what Mudde and Kopecky call isolationists). For them, the only desirable form of cooperation is purely voluntary and usually takes the form of a free-trade agreement although some are inspired by other forms of voluntary cooperation: "The European Union is an artificial political construction and it is failing. Here is something as a working model, the British Commonwealth, which is a loose association of people with a simple understanding who want to work together. (...) Why can't we have a Commonwealth of Europe?" (Interview with MEP57). Their opposition is not restricted to the integration process as they are very hostile towards the EU and its institutions which are considered to be corrupt, antidemocratic and beyond reform. Therefore, they do not develop arguments or ideas to improve the institutional architecture of the Union: "There is no reform needed, we need to renegotiate the membership of our country to the EU and fight for sovereign states" (interview with MEP97). They view the EP as worthless, as lacking influence and are usually in favour of its disappearance although some of them would keep a deliberative forum, as long as it does not have any constraining power: "If it didn't pretend to be a parliament, if we are talking about a body that occasionally meets to exchange views across Europe, possibly to reduce tensions, I have no objection to that as long as it is a forum, with no legislative powers" (Interview with MEP4).

A second position can be characterized as intergovernmentalism. These Eurosceptics are not opposed to their country participating in an institutionalized cooperation at the European level but this cooperation should be intergovernmental. Member states should be the centre of power: "we do not want the EU as it exists, The European project should be similar to what it was at the very beginning that is, a European cooperation between sovereign states, without a parliament and with a strong Council where states decide" (Interview with MEP85). They consider that the nation state is the irreplaceable framework for democracy and accept only a confederation or an intergovernmental Europe. They often consider that the integration process has gone too far and oppose any further transfer of power. Many of them believe that the integration process should be restricted to an internal market, without a level above the nation state: "my ideal Europe is actually to go back to the European Economic Communities. The only thing that brought prosperity is the internal market. Europe started as a market, it became an economic union and for us, it was enough" (Interview with MEP39). As far as the institutions are concerned, these Eurosceptics are in favour of reforms which would enhance the powers of Member states. They are opposed to the Community method as well as codecision and would give a permanent veto power to the Member states in the Council. Logically, they favour a weakening of the power of supranational institutions, especially the Commission and the EP. They would like powers to be transferred from the EP to the national parliaments, although they acknowledge the relevance of the EP as a forum for the defence of national interests: "Wouldn't it be actually better if MEPs all together keep the parliament but the parliament was actually composed of national parliamentarians, and some of the Committee of the Regions, that would mean that there would be absolutely no feeling that this is being done to us because you would have a delegation of members from the Scottish parliament, the UK parliament, the Assemblée nationale in France actually sitting in the EP with very direct link to domestic politics" (Interview with MEP13).

A third stance refers to reformism or soft Euroscepticism. These MEPs tend to consider European integration as a necessary evil or an unwanted constraint and they oppose further integration without major reforms in the process: "I think the idea of European integration is natural, logical, necessary but we need to think about the form and content of this integration" (Interview with MEP42). They accept the principle of institutionalized cooperation, a more or less integrated market as well as the transfer of sovereignty to the supranational level but they would like to limit this kind of transfer. They criticize the so-called federal idea of Europe (European superstate or United States of Europe) but consider that supranational cooperation is needed, especially to deal with transnational challenges such as the environment, organized crime: "We are not opposed to the membership to the Union as such, it is not an ideological question or us. It's rather that in our opinion, the EU should concentrate on those functions which bring added-value to everybody" (Interview with MEP75). For most of them, reflection is needed on the added value of the integration process and reform, and in a rather fundamental way, on the division of powers between the national and supranational levels. The EU should focus on common strategies and put more emphasis on subsidiarity. Regarding the EU, these MEPs concentrate their criticism on the lack of democracy, accountability and transparency of its institutions and decision-making process. They perceive the institutions as overly elitist and develop narratives to reform the way these institutions work: "For a start, I would make the Council of Ministers completely transparent, I mean they are the most secret organization in Europe, they meet in secret, they don't produce minutes of their meetings. I would insist on complete transparency and openness for the Council. I would also insist that we have democratic elections for the European Commission and that we certainly don't appoint Commissioners because they are not accountable to anyone at all now" (Interview with MEP60). At the same time, these Eurosceptics are usually positive towards the EP, seen as the only legitimate institution representing citizens and compensating the technocratic character of the Commission. As noted by this interviewee: "I fought against the Lisbon Treaty but not on these issues. I do hope the implementation of the treaty will enhance the role of the EP. If the EP has a stronger role, we are going in the right direction, towards more democracy in Europe" (Interview with MEP56). Nevertheless, they still consider that the EU needs major reforms, and enhancing the EP's role is not enough.

5   CONCLUSION

Oppositions to Europe have proven to be particularly complex, underpinned by both strategic and ideological factors, and prone to change according to the national context as well as the developments of the EU itself. In other words, Euroscepticism is a moving target, very much like the EU (Kny and Kratochvil 2015). This has sparked lively discussions as to its conceptualization but to date, there still is no commonly accepted definition.

This chapter has provided an overview of these discussions and has positioned this research within the literature on Euroscepticism. By doing so, it highlighted the gaps this book intends to address. First, while most analysis concentrates on the national level, this study focuses on the supranational level. Combining the literature on Euroscepticism with research on political opposition, it is possible to consider Euroscepticism as a form of anti-system opposition, directed against the status quo, namely the European project. Euroscepticism therefore qualifies the attitudes of opposition to European integration and/or the EU. Unlike the work of scholars from the "Sussex school" or "North Carolina school", the aim here is not to seek to uncover the causes of Euroscepticism. Rather, the objective is to understand how Eurosceptics perceive and carry out their representative mandate once elected to the EP and to explain the variation in this regard. On the basis of an analysis of MEPs' voting behaviour, EP groups' platforms and interviews, this chapter identified the Eurosceptics, and we can now turn to mapping their strategies.

NOTES

1. For alternative typologies, see Flood and Usherwood (2007), De Wilde (2010), Vasilopoulou (2009).
2. There are, of course, exceptions as several European countries, including Belgium, Spain, Italy and the UK, have been faced with challenges and demands from autonomist or ethno-regionalist parties, questioning the legitimacy of state authority and demanding a major revision of the institutional structure of the state. See also L. De Winter, Gomez-Reino, P. Lynch, *Autonomist Parties in Europe: Identity Politics and the revival of the territorial cleavage*, Barcelona, ICPS 2006.
3. H. Rosenthal and E. Voeten (2004) have indeed demonstrated that two dimensions structured the French National Assembly under the Fourth Republic: the left/right economic dimension and the pro/anti-regime dimension, provoking instability in the cabinets and the political regime.
4. It is particularly difficult to determine a priori precisely what European integration is. Indeed, on the one hand, the EU is rapidly evolving and stimulates constant debates over its nature and orientation. And, on the other hand, the actors may have varying interpretations of integration. Thus, we are not here to propose a definition of integration but to examine whether or not the opposition expressed is directed towards the integration process and its underlying values as perceived by the actors. For academic discussions on the meaning of integration, see: M. Eilstrup-Sangiovanni, *Debates on European Integration. A Reader*, Basingstoke, Palgrave McMillan, 2006. For a discussion of actors' visions on integration and the EU, see also: O. Costa, P. Magnette, «Idéologies et changements institutionnel dans l'Union européenne. Pourquoi les gouvernements ont-ils constamment renforcé le Parlement européen?», *Politique européenne*, no. 9, 2003, pp. 49–75.
5. Interviews with MEPs confirmed that these texts were considered as symbols of integration and the synthesis of previous treaties reforming the EU.
6. Resolution on the Ratification procedures of the treaty establishing a Constitution for Europe and a communication strategy concerning this same treaty, 2004/2553(RSP), adopted 14 October 2004.
7. Opinion of the parliament on the treaty to establish a Constitution for Europe, 2004/2129(INI), adopted 12 January 2005.
8. Resolution of the European parliament on the 60th anniversary of the end of World War II in Europe (8 May 1945), adopted 12 May 2005.
9. The period of reflection: the structure, subjects and context for an assessment of the debate on the European Union, 2005/2146(INI), adopted 19 January 2006.

10. European parliament resolution on the next steps for the period of reflection and analysis on the Future of Europe, adopted 14 June 2006.
11. Report on the road map for the Union's constitutional process (2007/2087(INI)), adopted 7 June 2007.
12. Leinen Report on the convening of the Intergovernmental Conference (IGC): the European parliament's opinion (Article 48 of the EU Treaty) (11222/2007 – C6-0206/2007 – 2007/0808(CNS)), adopted 11 July 2007.
13. Corbett/Mendez de Vigo Report «The Treaty amending the Treaty on European Union and the Treaty establishing the European Community», 2007/2286(INI), adopted 20 February 2008.
14. For individuals who were absent during one to four of these votes, the missing value was replaced by the average obtained from the other votes.
15. It is of course impossible to determine the reasons justifying the attitude of an elected official on a particular vote. Following the example of R. Scully, we have thus coded abstention as midway between a positive and a negative vote (see Scully 1998). Indeed, we argue that through an abstention, an elected official, to some extent, takes a position. Rather than being absent for the vote, the official votes in an active manner, and this vote does not accept the proposed text without going so far as to oppose it. This may reflect a lack of knowledge of the dossier (for a new member) but especially a distancing from the group's position without being disloyal. This is particularly the case for members of principal groups such as the EPP and the PES under the sixth legislature which have encouraged their members to vote in favour of the texts, considered to be fundamental. An abstention in this case may be seen as a refusal to accept a key text on integration and the future of the EU without going so far as a frontal opposition. This is why such an attitude was attributed a value of 0.5.
16. The discourse of elected officials during the debates related to these votes and the justification of their votes were analysed. This allowed me to capture their motivations as to their voting behaviour but also to ensure that I did not include any Europhile MEPs in the group.
17. It should be noted that the database covered all of the 2004–2009 legislature and due to the number of departures and arrivals during the legislature, there were 865 elected officials (and not 785).
18. Constitutional declaration of the EUL/NGL group, adopted on 14 July 1994, last consulted on 6 July 2016. Presentation of the EUL/NGL group [http://www.guengl.eu], last viewed on 6 July 2016.
19. EFDD charter, http://www.efddgroup.eu/about-us/our-charter, last viewed 6 July 2016.

20. Charter of the ENF group, http://www.enfgroup-ep.eu/charter/, last viewed 6 July 2016.
21. Lisbon Treaty was implemented, and Croatia became a member of the EU during the 7th legislature. As a result of the Lisbon Treaty, the number of MEPs increased by 18 MEPs, and Croatia elected 12 MEPs in 2013. The EP was temporarily constituted of 754 MEPs. Most of these new members were not Eurosceptic, except for an extra Austrian MEP from the BZÖ and an extra Dutch MEP from the PVV as well as two Eurosceptic Croatian MEPs (one seating in the ECR and the other in the EUL/NGL).

REFERENCES

Abbarno, A., & Zapryanova, G. (2013). Indirect effects of Eurosceptic messages on citizen attitudes toward domestic politics. *Journal of Common Market Studies, 51*(4), 581–597.

Barbieri, G. (2015). He's worse than me: The Eurosceptic parties at the turning point. *Partecipazione e conflitto, 8*(1), 97–117.

Bartolini, Stefano, et al. (2012). *Europeanisation and party politics: How the EU affects domestic actors, patterns and systems.* Colchester: ECPR Press.

Batory, A., & Sitter, N. (2008). Protectionism, populism, or participation? Agrarian parties and the European questions in Western and East Central Europe. In P. Taggart & A. Szczerbiak (Eds.), *Opposing Europe? The comparative party politics of Euroscepticism* (Vol. 2, pp. 52–74). Oxford: Oxford University Press.

Benedetto, G. (2008). Explaining the failure of Euroscepticism in the European parliament. In P. Taggart & A. Szczerbiak (Eds.), *Opposing Europe? The comparative party politics of Euroscepticism* (pp. 127–150). Oxford: Oxford University Press.

Berger, S. (1979). Politics and antipolitics in Western Europe in the seventies. *Daedalus,* 27–50.

Bouillaud, C. (2008). S'opposer à la constitution européenne dans l'enceinte du PE comme indicateur robuste d'euroscepticisme (2005–2007). In L. Neumayer, A. Roger, & F. Zalewski (Eds.), *L'Europe contestée. Espaces et enjeux des positionnements contre lintégration européenne. Michel Houdiard Éditeur* (pp. 159–184). Paris.

Brack, N., & Startin, N. (2015). Euroscepticism: From the margins to the mainstream. *International Political Science Review, 36*(3), 239–249.

Brack, N., & Costa, O. (2012). *Euroscepticism within EU institutions: Diverging views of Europe.* London: Routledge.

Brack, N., & Weinblum, S. (2011). Political Opposition: Towards a Renewed Research Agenda. *Interdisciplinary Political Studies, 1*(1), 69–85.

Conti, N. (2016). The Italian political elites and Europe: Big move, small change?, *International Political Science Review*, online first.

Costa, O. (2001). *Le Parlement européen, assemblée délibérante*, Brussels: Editions de l'Université de Bruxelles.

Costa, O., Roger, A., & Saurruger, S. (2008). Les remises en cause de l'intégration européenne. Introduction. *Revue Internationale de Politique Comparée*, *15*(4), 533–539.

Crespy, A., & Verschueren, N. (2009). From Euroscepticism to resistance to European Integration: An interdisciplinary perspective. *Perspective on European Politics and Society*, *10*(3), 377–393.

Dahl, R. A. (1971). *Polyarchies: Participation and opposition*. New Haven: Yale University Press.

Dahl, R. A. (1999). Can international organizations be democratic? A skeptic's view, *Democracy's edges*, 19–36.

Delmotte, F. (2007). Les résistances à l'Europe au prisme de la sociologie historique de Norbert Elias. In J. Lacroix & R. Coman (Eds.), *Les résistances à l'Europe. Cultures nationales, idéologies et stratégies d'acteurs* (pp. 17–29), Bruxelles: Editions de l'Université de Bruxelles.

De Sio, L., Emanuele, V., & Maggini, N. (2014). *The European Parliament Elections of 2014*, CISE.

De Vries, C., & Edwards, E. (2009). Taking Europe to its extremes. *Party Politics*, *15*(1), 5–28.

De Wilde, P. (2010). *Under what conditions does Euroscepticism flourish? An evaluation of different approaches and empirical findings*. Olso: Trial Lecture.

De Wilde, P., & Trenz, H. J. (2012). Denouncing European integration: Euroscepticism as polity contestation. *European Journal of Social Theory*, *15*(4), 537–554.

Down, I., & Wilson, C. (2008). From 'permissive consensus' to 'constraining dissensus': A polarizing union? *Acta Politica*, *43*(1), 26–49.

Dye, D. T. (2015). *Interpreting Euroskepticism(s): The Anti-establishment parties of the 2014 Euro-elections and their challenges to Integration*. Paper presented at the EUSA Biennial Conference, Boston, 5–7 March.

Emanuele, V., Maggini, N., & Marino, B. (2016). Gaining votes in Europe against Europe? How national contexts shaped the results of Eurosceptic Parties in the 2014 European parliament elections. *Journal of Contemporary European Research*, 12(3), 697–715.

Flood, C. (2009). Dimensions of Euroscepticism. *Journal of Common Market Studies*, *47*(4), 911–917.

Franklin, M., Marsh, M., & McLarren, L. (1994). Uncorking the bottle: Popular opposition to European unification in the wake of Maastricht. *Journal of Common Market Studies*, *32*(4), 455–473.

Giacone, A., & Olivi, B. (2007). *L'Europe Difficile*. Paris, Gallimard: Histoire Politique de la Construction Européenne.

Gifford, C. (2008). *The making of Eurosceptic Britain: Identity and economics in a post-imperial state*. Londres: Ashgate.

Harmsen, R. (2005). L'Europe et les partis politiques nationaux: les leçons d'un non-clivage. *Revue internationale de politique comparée, 12*(1), 77–94.

Harmsen, R. (2010). Concluding comment: On understanding the relationship between populism and Euroscepticism. *Perspectives on European Politics and Society, 11*(3), 333–341.

Harmsen, R., & Spiering, M. (2004). *Euroscepticism: Party politics, national identity and European integration*. Amsterdam: Rodopi.

Hartleb, F. (2011). After their establishment: Right-wing populist parties in Europe. *European View, 10*(2), 267–268.

Helms, L. (2008). Studying parliamentary opposition in old and new democracies: Issues and perspectives. *The Journal of Legislative Studies, 14*(1), 6–19.

Hix, S., Noury, A., & Roland, G. (2007). *Democratic politics in the European parliament*. Cambridge: Cambridge University Press.

Hobolt, S. (2015). The 2014 European elections: Divided in unity? *Journal of Common Market Studies, 53*(S1), 6–21.

Hooghe, L., & Marks, G. (1997). The making of a polity: The struggle over European integration. *European Integration Online Papers, 1*/004.

Hooghe, L., & Marks, G. (2007). Sources of Euroscepticism. *Acta Politica, 42*(2–3), 119–127.

Hooghe, L., & Marks, G. (2009). A Post-functionalist theory of European integration: From permissive consensus to constraining dissensus. *British Journal of Political Science, 39*(1), 1–23.

Ionescu, G., & De Madariaga, I. (1968). *Opposition: Past and Present of a Political Institution*, Londres: The New Thinker Library.

Jensen, C., & Spoon, J.-J. (2010). Thinking locally, acting supranationally: Niche party behavior in the European Parliament. *European Journal of Political Research, 4*(2), 174–201.

Katz, R. (2008). Euroscepticism in parliament: A comparative analysis of the European parliament and National parliaments In P. Taggart & A. Szczerbiak, *Opposing Europe? The Comparative Party Politics of Euroscepticism: Volume 2*, 151–180. Oxford: Oxford University Press.

Kircheimer, O. (1964). *Politik und Verfassung*. Frankfurt am Main: Suhrkamp.

Kný, D., & Kratochvíl, P. (2015). Caught in the deviation trap. On the fallacies of the study of party-based Euroscepticism. *Czech Journal of Political Science, 3*, 200–215.

Kopecky, P., & Mudde, C. (2002). The Two Sides of Euroscepticism. Party positions on European integration in East Central Europe. *European Union Politics, 3*(3), 297–326.

Krouwel, A., & Abts, K. (2007). The structure of political discontent: A typology of eurorejectionism. *Acta Politica, 42*(2/3), 252–270.

Leconte, C. (2010). *Understanding Euroscepticism*. Palgrave MacMillan: Basingstoke.

Lees, C. (2002). *'Dark Matter': Institutional constraints and the failure of party-based euroscepticism in Germany* (OERN Working Paper. 8).

Lindberg, L., & Scheingold, S. (1970). *Europe's would-be polity: Patterns of change in the european community*. Cambridge: Harvard University Press.

Magnette, P., & Papadopoulos, Y. (2008). *On the politicization of the European consociation: A middle-way between Hix and Bartolini* (p. C0801). Eurogov: European governance papers.

Marks, G., & Wilson, C. J. (2000). Past in the Present: A cleavage theory of party response to European integration. *British Journal of Political Science, 30*(3), 433–459.

Marks, G., Wilson, C. J., & Ray, L. (2002). National political parties and European integration. *American Journal of Political Science, 46*(3), 585–594.

McElroy, G., & Benoit, K. (2010). Party policy and group affiliation in the European parliament. *British Journal of Political Science, 40*(2), 377–398.

Mény, Y. (2009). *La construction d'un parlement: 50 ans d'histoire du Parlement européen. 1958–2008*, Luxembourg.

Mény, Y. (2012). Conclusion: A Voyage to the Unknown. *Journal of Common Market Studies, 50*(S1), 154–164.

Morgan, G. (2005). *The idea of a European superstate. Public justification and European integration*, Princeton, Princeton University Press.

Mudde, C. (2011). Sussex v. North Carolina. The comparative study of party-based Euroscepticism. *SEI Working paper*, 121:1–32.

Neuhold, C., & Settembri, P. (2009). Achieving consensus through committees: Does the European parliament manage? *Journal of Common Market Studies, 47*(1), 127–151.

Neumayer, L. (2008). Euroscepticism as a political label: The use of European Union issues in political competition in the new member states. *European Journal of Political Research, 47*(2), 135–160.

Neunreither, K. (1998). Governance without opposition: The case of the European Union. *Government and Opposition, 33*(4), 435–438.

Nivet, B. (2016). Union européenne: une dépolitisation propice au populisme. *La revue internationale et stratégique, 84*, 16–27.

Otjes, S., & van Der Veer, H. (2016). The Eurozone crisis and the European parliament's changing lines of conflict. *European Union Politics, 17*(2), 242–261.

Proksch, S.-O., & Lo, J. (2012). Reflections on the European integration dimension. *European Union Politics, 13*(2), 317–333.

Raunio, T. (2007). Softening but persistent: Euroscepticism in the Nordic countries. *Acta Politica, 42*(2/3), 191–210.

Roger, A. (2007). Les résistances partisanes à l'intégration européenne. Un objet de comparaison à consolider. In Lacroix, J., & Coman, R., *Les résistances à l'Europe. Cultures régionales, idéologies et stratégies d'acteurs*, (pp. 31–48). Brussels: Editions de l'Université de Bruxelles.

Ross, G. (2011). *The European Union and its crisis. Through the eyes of the Brussels' Elite*. Basingstoke: Palgrave McMillan.

Sartori, G. (1966). Opposition and control problems and prospects. *Government and Opposition, 1*(1), 149–154.

Schapiro, L. (1965). Foreword. *Government and Opposition, 1*(1), 1–6.

Scully, R. (1998). MEPs and the Building of a 'Parliamentary Europe'. *The Journal of Legislative Studies, 4*(3), 92–108.

Scully, R. M. (2005). *Becoming Europeans. Attitudes, behaviour, and socialization in the European parliament*. Oxford: Oxford University Press.

Serricchio, F., Tsakatika, M., & Quaglia, L. (2013). Euroscepticism and the global financial crisis. *Journal of Common Market Studies, 51*(1), 51–64.

Sitter, N. (2001). The politics of opposition and European integration in Scandinavia: Is Euroscepticism a government-opposition dynamic? *West European Politics, 24*(4), 22–39.

Steenbergen, M., Edwards, E., & De Vries, C. (2007). Who's cueing whom? Mass-elite linkages and the future of European integration. *European Union Politics, 8*(1), 13–35.

Szczerbiak, A., & Taggart, P. (2000). Opposing Europe: Party systems and opposition to the union, the Euro and Europeanisation. *OERN working paper*, 1.

Szczerbiak, A., & Taggart, P. (2002). The party politics of euroscepticism in EU member and candidate states, *SEI working paper*, 51.

Taggart, P. (1998). A touchstone of dissent: Euroscepticism in contemporary Western political systems. *European Journal of Political Research, 33*(3), 363–388.

Trenz, H-J., & De Wilde, P. (2009). Denouncing European integration, Euroscepticism as reactive identity formation. *Arena Working Paper*, 14.

Usherwood, S. (2005a). Opposition to the European Union in the UK: The dilemma of public opinion and party management. *Government and Opposition, 37*(2), 211–230.

Usherwood, S. (2005b). Realists, sceptics and opponents: Opposition to the EU's Constitutionnal Treaty. *Journal of Common European Research, 1*(2), 4–12.

Usherwood, S. (2007a). Sceptical or simply opposed? Anti-EU groups and the constitution In A. Cohen & A. Vauchez (eds.), *La Constitution européenne: élites, mobilisations et votes*, 167–180. Brussels: Editions de l'Université de Bruxelles.

Usherwood, S. (2007b). Proximate factors in the mobilization of Anti-EU groups in France and the UK: The European Union as first order politics. *Journal of European Integration, 29*(1), 3–21.

Usherwood, S., & Startin, N. (2013). Euroscepticism as a Persistent Phenomenon. *Journal of Common Market Studies, 51*(1), 1–16.

Usherwood, S. (2014), The Eurosceptic paradox, *EPERN*, available at https://epern.wordpress.com/2014/06/09/the-eurosceptic-paradox/.

Van Ingelgom, V. (2014). *Integrating indifference: A comparative, qualitative and quantitative approach to the legitimacy of European integration.* Colchester: ECPR Press.

Vasilopoulou, S. (2013). Continuity and change in the study of euroscepticism: Plus ça change? *Journal of Common Market Studies, 51*(1), 153–168.

Verney, S. (2011). Euroscepticism in Southern Europe: A diachronic perspective. *South European Society and Politics, 16*(1), 1–29.

Verney, S. (2015). Waking the 'sleeping giant'or expressing domestic dissent? Mainstreaming Euroscepticism in crisis-stricken Greece. *International Political Science Review, 36*(3), 279–295.

Voeten, E., & Rosenthal, H. (2004). Analyzing roll calls with perfect spatial voting: France 1946–1958. *American Journal of Political Science, 48*(3), 620–632.

CHAPTER 4

Strategies of Eurosceptic MEPs

Euroscepticism is far from being a recent phenomenon and since early on in the EP's history, there have been MEPs opposed to the European project. This pro-/anti-integration division is very salient today, especially with the increase in the number of Eurosceptic MEPs after the 2014 EU elections. However, despite their persistent presence, these actors remain largely unknown. While EP specialists tend to neglect Eurosceptic MEPs as a result of their minority position, the literature on Euroscepticism has focused primarily on the national level. So far, the literature on opposition to Europe within the supranational institutions remains limited (Brack and Costa 2012, 2018).

As an attempt to fill this gap, this chapter examines how these dissenting voices act once elected to the EP. It focuses exclusively on Eurosceptic MEPs in order to explore how they conceive of and carry out their mandate. To do so, the concept of role as defined by the motivational approach is used to articulate MEPs' perceptions and motivations as well as their attitudes and parliamentary practices. The chapter provides a typology of the roles assumed by Eurosceptic MEPs: the Absentee, the Public Orator, the Pragmatist and the Participant. These roles are ideal-types of strategies: the characteristic attitudes, behaviours and goals of each role were deliberately exaggerated in order to highlight their specificities and to demonstrate the differences among these four roles.

Relying on an interpretative and inductive approach, this typology is based on the analysis of data collected during interviews with MEPs

© The Author(s) 2018
N. Brack, *Opposing Europe in the European Parliament*,
Palgrave Studies in European Union Politics,
https://doi.org/10.1057/978-1-137-60201-5_4

(as well as assistants and EP public servants), on the analysis of their parliamentary activities and on the observations of group meetings. The typology presented here is the result of a permanent interaction between this data and the effort to conceptualize ideal-types. The role is a complex and dynamic configuration of characteristic objectives, attitudes and behaviours. The categorization of MEPs within the ideal-types was done in two stages. Priority was given to actors' discourse and vision of their mandate in order to understand how they perceive and carry it out as well as why they act one way rather than another (Hooghe 2001, p. 11; Navarro 2009, p. 123). Data relative to their behaviour within the chamber were then analysed to determine their priorities and the way in which they invest their (limited) time and (scare) resources. This two-step approach tests the extent of the correspondence between their perception of their mandate and their implementation thereof. In other words, it monitors the relevance of the identified role in accordance with the motivational approach. Rather than relying on a single indicator, these elements were combined to develop the typology and categorize every MEP interviewed into the ideal-type which most closely resembles him or her.[1]

This typology should be understood as an attempt at classification to understand the paradoxical situation faced by these anti-system actors whereby they must act within the very system they condemn. It is not meant as a value judgement of their attitudes and behaviour or a way to distinguish "good deputies" from "bad". Contrary to the idea generally conveyed by the media, the typology attests that these elected representatives propose an alternative but no less legitimate interpretation of their mandate, given the expectations and constraints they face.

1   THE ABSENTEE

Though often clearly identified by both MEPs and observers, this type of elected representative is rarely incorporated into any analysis (with the exceptions of Bale and Taggart 2006; Navarro 2009). This is explained partly by the fact that a lack of involvement in the EP is not restricted to Eurosceptics (Costa 2001, pp. 415–417; Kauppi 2005) as well as by the challenge of collecting data on this type of MEP, particularly through interviews. It is argued here that while a lack of involvement in their mandate is not limited solely to Eurosceptics, it has a special meaning in their case. More than being a residual category, the Absentee is a role ideal-type in the same way as Public Orator, Pragmatist and Participant. Absentees are characterized by two main indicators: a comparatively low involvement in the assembly and a concentration of their activities at the national level and in their constituencies. They receive little satisfaction from their European mandate and prefer to serve at the national or local level.

1.1 Reduced Involvement in the Chamber

Weak involvement of MEPs identified as Absentees can be interpreted as an exit strategy from the work of the parliament, motivated by a total refusal to engage in the workings of the institution or by indifference towards the European mandate: "No, I don't want to get involved in this! It's not a full-time job that I'm doing here. Most of the MEPs, they are involved, they have contacts with lobbyists, groups, they are doing amendments. But I don't" (Interview MEP 54).

Considering their limited capacity for action, this type of MEP believes that any activities undertaken within the institution would be futile. For Absentees, it matters little on which committee(s) they sit as they consider this to be secondary and do not actively participate in committee work. Indeed, most Absentee MEPs do not regularly attend meetings and would rather send their assistants to represent them (interview with MEPs, parliamentary assistants and EP officials). Absentees do not seek to oversee a report or hold responsibilities within the EP and its organs and are not involved in the work of their group or delegation: "We did not come here to be part of it" (Interview with MEP 5).

This same logic applies to other parliamentary activities. So even if Absentees follow the voting instructions of their national delegation or their group, they have a very realistic view of the impact of their vote: "I don't think it matters by the way because even if we sit there to blow bubbles it doesn't matter, they are going to push the laws through anyway. So the whole thing is pointless. It's just a question of principle I'm talking about now, practically it doesn't really matter. That's the balance we have to strike. [...] The problem we've got, you see, is the more we do here, even voting, the more we add legitimacy to this place, and it's got no legitimacy, so we've to be careful in how we get involved here, so I get involved as little as possible because I think it is a dreadful place" (Interview with MEP 7).

Similarly, and contrary to the Public Orator, interventions in plenary sessions assume no special significance for this category of MEP. Thus, even the Absentee with a relatively elevated number of interventions in the plenary will derive little satisfaction from it: "Yes I do [speeches], but it's in an empty chamber. It's a waste of time, it's not a debating chamber. You got 1 or 2 minutes. And it isn't that difficult to get minutes. But it's not a debate as a British would understand! You can't interrupt, people stand up, they don't speak but read, everybody sleeps, it's an empty chamber, it's not taken seriously" (Interview with MEP 10).

1.2   Emphasis on the National Level

While neglecting the parliament, Absentees are very active at the national and local levels. When interviewed, most MEPs of this type acknowledge that they spend most of their time at the national level and attend parliament only a few days per month. In effect, Absentees see their role as a promoter of Euroscepticism in national public opinion through interventions in the media (radio, TV and internet), dissemination of DVDs, meetings and school visits. Their (limited) presence in the EP gives them access to information about the EU which can then be transmitted to the local or national level (Interviews with MEP 46 and MEP 3): "My main responsibility is to find out the truth of what the EU is doing to democracy and expose it to the people in the UK" (Interview with MEP 96).

The Absentee's main source of satisfaction is derived not from a nonconformist attitude, an interest in efficiency or a desire to influence, but from an ongoing campaign against the EU in order to influence national public opinion: "Our concern is that our voters be informed of our actions through our media and through the media in general. We all have a mechanism to disseminate our work to ensure that the French see our policy markers on all these issues at the European level too, it is not in fact obvious but, nevertheless, each day we still have some input in the press" (Interview A # 9).

While certain Absentees are motivated by activism, we must also consider the more utilitarian and opportunistic Absentees. Indeed, Absentees may be motivated as well, at least in part, by MEP benefits such as compensation, salary, prestige and media access: "I am more interested in what the MEP status can provide me with, it provides me with a platform, I go on television and radio, because I am a MEP. (…) The letters MEP mean the doors are open for you in Britain to speak to associations, businesses, schools, universities, colleges" (Interview with MEP 7). Thus, they attend plenary sessions to avoid financial penalties designated to combat Absenteeism but generally are not involved in group, delegation or parliamentary committee meetings.

Finally, others should be labelled as "utilitarian Absentees": their participation in European elections is largely driven by national political considerations and by a desire to take advantage of the electoral system for the EP which is more favourable to small fringe parties, especially in countries with a first past the post system such as the UK and France. European elections tend to be second-order elections favouring the emergence of protest parties (Reif and Schmitt 1980). The European mandate is thus seen as an opportunity to get attention at the national level and as a platform to increase visibility and gain legitimacy, all the while being only minimally involved in the EP. This is then seen as a mandate "by default", providing an ersatz power (Kauppi 1996, p. 11) to such actors waiting for a "better" mandate.

> I am very skeptical and critical of this system but I wanted to come here and see for myself as I've been for two terms a Finnish parliamentarian and 6 years in the committee for the finish parliament which deals with European Union matters. And I wanted to meet the heart of darkness and now I've met it and I'm going back to the Finish politics. So my successor is going take my seat within a month. (Interview with MEP46)

1.3   Characteristic Behaviours of Absentee MEPs

In terms of behaviour, MEPs identified as Absentee form a relatively homogenous group (Table 4.1). Firstly, most of them had comparatively low attendance records, though they were more present in plenary sessions than any other type of meeting (groups, delegations and committees).[2] While, on average, the Eurosceptics interviewed in the framework of this research have had an attendance record above 85% of the votes, MEPs close to the Absentee type were on an average present for 70% of the roll call votes.

They further characterized themselves through a limited involvement in any kind of parliamentary activity. Thus, these MEPs have not been in charge of any reports nor have they produced any written opinions. Most have not proposed or signed any written declaration. As an example of their low involvement in their respective parliamentary committees and their lack of interest in the legislative process, these MEPs have introduced between 0 and 4 amendments to reports during a legislature.

Table 4.1 Activities of MEPs close to the ideal-type of absentee (July 2004–July 2016), $N = 9$

Name	Participation in RCV (%)	Reports	Written declarations	Speeches	Motions for resolutions	Opinions	Questions	Amendments
Mean	70.97	0	0.17	28.17	0.7	0	30.23	1.31
Median	66.7	0	0	16	0.5	0	9	1
St Deviation	18.56	0	0.35	23.21	0.74	0	41.63	1.26
Minimum	42.76	0	0	9	0	0	1	0
Maximum	91.6	0	1	70.5	2.3	0	113.5	3.5

Sources European Parliament and votewatch (author's own calculations)

Except for one MEP who was vice-chairman of a committee (but left the EP as soon as he could to return to the national level), none of these MEPs exercised any responsibility within the EP and its bodies.

Absentees are less homogeneous when it comes to the number of speeches in the plenary. On average, they made 28 speeches but this number varied from 9 to 70 speeches during the period under study. Some take more pleasure than others in expressing themselves during the plenary without giving it much importance. Finally, parliamentary questions are the only activity in which certain Absentees involve themselves; these do not require an actual physical presence in the EP. On average, these MEPs asked 30 questions during a parliamentary term. These questions were frequently used to defend their specific interests. Indeed, analysis of their written questions (though there were few) revealed regular allusions to their constituents, their district and to national issues. The objective may then be to defend individual cases or obtain information which can be used in their Eurosceptic campaign. In fact, this activity allows them to make pledges to their constituents and obtain an official statement from the Commission that they can then use at the national level: "Sometimes, if I'm dealing with a constituent who is just, feels betrayed and let down, and I'm feeling very sorry for him, I put a parliamentary question down, just to say, there is absolutely nothing I can do about, I would put a parliamentary question down because, at least, that's all I can do" (Interview with MEP 10).

To sum up, the Absentee role allows for an exit strategy from supranational institutions through a lack of involvement in parliamentary work and a claim of proximity (true or not) to their constituents and fellow citizens through strong activity at the national level.

2   THE PUBLIC ORATOR

Guided by a taste for anti-conformism and an attitude of frontal opposition, Public Orators prioritize two aspects of their mandate: public speaking and research and dissemination of negative information on European integration. They take great satisfaction from reactions to their behaviours and grand gestures. Like the Absentees, they are not interested in negotiating with colleagues or in developing a reform program for the EU. But unlike the Absentees, they choose to be present within the assembly and exercise their mandate at the supranational level to denounce the system by all the means at their disposal.

2.1   A Strategy of de-Legitimization of the Institution from Within: The Importance of Public Interventions

The main objective of Public Orators is to publicize and defend their positions by all means necessary, "the main thing I do is speak and argue against European integration" (interview with MEP 40). They exploit any information in support of their positions, especially regarding the deficiencies and failures of European integration, its institutions and elites. Public Orators see themselves first and foremost as representatives in permanent opposition: "My main role is to speak, talk and stand for the people" (interview with MEP 22). They believe that their role is to speak on behalf of Eurosceptic citizens, neglected by European institutions or, in other words, to "represent people who thought I should be their voice there" (interview with MEP 55). Public Orators seek first and foremost to delegitimize the institution by speaking in public.

Therefore, the vast majority of their activities consist of general accusations of failure and of the negative consequences of integration. Their interventions do not address the content of specific European policies but seek to break down the so-called consensus within the assembly. Therefore, unlike the Absentees, it is important for them to be present in the EP to express their opposition: "I was elected because I reflected a political philosophy, and I maintained that political philosophy so I attempted to put my particular point of view into every debate, every discussion that I can. That means turning up, the empty chair philosophy doesn't work over here unless you have unanimity and everybody has to be there and everybody has to agree. So turning up to the meetings, getting speaking time, I am not here to make this place work better, I am not here to help this thing exist, I am to criticize, criticize, criticize. In committee, they call me mister no, I say no to everything" (Interview with MEP 57).

Even though Public Orators are relatively present in parliament, they are not very interested in the "traditional" aspects of parliamentary activities. They take little part in other activities of the EP. They prefer to uphold their campaign of denunciation and maintain a balance between their presence within the system and their desire not to be integrated into the system they criticize. They believe they should "be present and play an active part. Some people go further and say one should play a constructive role. Well it's difficult to play a constructive part in an institution we don't agree with" (Interview with MEP 4).

Public Orators do not seek responsibility within the assembly, generally are not assigned reports and are rarely involved in parliamentary committee work. Moreover, they tend to rely solely on a contentious use of possibilities to propose resolutions and amendments such as censure motions and requests for a total rejection of the EU budget. Voting is subject to this same attitude of frontal opposition. While voting lists are prepared by parliamentary assistants and discussed during group or delegation meetings, Public Orators vote against the vast majority of texts, regardless of the policy area. They believe their role is to oppose nearly everything since they are opposed to parliament's legislative powers and, more generally, to EU competences: "We vote against anything that recognizes the EU as an entity. We tend to vote against most things" (Interview with MEP 8).

2.2 Use and Abuse of the Rules of Procedure

Public Orators are by no means cut off from the institution: a comprehensive understanding of the parliament and its bodies' formal and informal rules allows them to achieve their goal of obtaining speaking time. This ideal-type of role demonstrates the need to distinguish between the various aspects of socialization and more particularly between institutional learning and acculturation ("going native"). While Public Orators are essentially in a position of direct opposition and do not change their views towards European integration as a result of their mandate (contradicting the theory of acculturation), they are nevertheless socialized, in the sense of learning the rules of the institution.

Their behaviour in the chamber is clearly different from that of the other types. Indeed, they do not hesitate to resort to insults or personal attacks which allow them to garner the attention they desire. They take great satisfaction in the publicity resulting from their interventions and their "disobedience to EU protocol" (Interview MEP 98). Feeling discriminated against and/or marginalized, Public Orators can disrupt parliamentary work or create controversy, arguing that their mandate is to stimulate debate by breaking up what they perceive as the overly consensual nature of the EP. Some go so far in their nonconformist behaviour that they end up expelled from their EP group, although expulsion is in general very rare in the EP (Hix et al. 2007). The case of Helmer, a British conservative MEP (who switched party to become a member of UKIP in 2012), illustrates both the Public Orator's mastery of institutional rules as well as their non-compliance through a non-conformist attitude. Following a stunt in a plenary session, Helmer was excluded from the EPP-ED Group of the 6th legislature. In a debate held in May 2005 on a motion of censure against the European Commission,[3] Helmer relied on his knowledge of institutional rules to obtain a public intervention: "None of us, Eurosceptics, were allowed speaking time in the debate, but I found an obscure parliamentary rule, the 141, to ask a question and have a forty seconds speech. And in that speech, I strongly criticized the for trying to keep the debate out of the Parliament, to swipe it under the carpet. And I criticized the leader to put pressure on us. This was regarded as causing great offence. [...] They gave me 5 minutes to apologize and instead I spent the 5 minutes explaining why it was a good idea to fire me. As a result of which, I was expelled from the EPP, which I'm really pleased about".

Because of this type of attitude, Public Orators maintain poor relationships with MEPs from other political groups and, in particular, with large groups. Indeed, this ideal-type enjoys some recognition, in the sense of identifiability. Eurosceptics from other ideal-types, particularly the Pragmatists and the Participants, rely on Public Orators as a reference point from which they can distinguish themselves. Similarly, non-Eurosceptic MEPs and assistants clearly identify them: "You don't see them as engaged. The way they work is strange and they have this sort of moral conflict that they must have between saying we must be out of Europe and at the same time, they are earning a very good living from it. They'll just vote against everything, we see this from time to time again, they don't engage at committee level and then they become really vociferous at plenary level. Why didn't you table amendments at committee level?"

But Public Orators are indifferent to this since their purpose is not to negotiate a compromise with their colleagues. In contrast to the effective MEP described by Corbett (2002, p. 4) as "someone who is able to explain, persuade and negotiate with colleagues from 15 different countries", these MEPs evaluate their effectiveness in light of the responses to their actions and behaviour.

2.3   Dissemination of Negative Information About the EU at All Levels of Power

The second fundamental aspect of this ideal-type is the significance accorded to researching and disseminating negative information on the EU and European integration, at any territorial level, including the supranational one. Indeed, like the Absentee, Public Orators consider it as their duty to inform the public of EU decisions and their negative consequences. But unlike the Absentee, they also seek to remind their colleagues that EP decisions are not supported by a segment of the population: "what we do in the parliament, on any issue which is essentially pro-integration/anti-integration, we are going to lose the vote by definition. One of the things we do is simply get up as often as possible and remind them that people out there take a different view, and I get a perverse satisfaction out of that, because they hate it, they hate to be reminded that ordinary people out there on the streets take a different view on this matter" (Interview with MEP 40).

They frequently update their websites, are very aware of new forms of communication (blog, twitter and Facebook), maintain close relationships with the press and are available for anyone wishing to contact them: "I talk a lot in committee and in plenary, interventions are the parliamentary tool I use the most, my role is to lead the opposition. But I dedicate about 40% of my time to the press, debates, communication with voters and the party" (Interview with MEP 39). Their presence in the EP is conditioned not only by the satisfaction derived from their public speaking but also by the need to collect and disseminate negative information of any kind on European institutions: "the only way to fight is to be elected. Once in the machine, you get information that you can use to further advance your fight against it on the ground" (Interview with MEP 78). This same search for information can be found in the type of written questions posed to the Commission. Generally, they do not pertain to the content of European or national policies or projects, but tend to remain general in nature, even contentious or ironic. For example, they will question the contribution of European integration to peacekeeping on the continent or the costs related to European Commissioners and their bodyguards, allowing them to collect financial information which they can then mobilize in their speeches critical of the EU.

2.4   *Characteristic Behaviours of Public Orators*

Analysis of Public Orators' activities and their responsibilities within the parliament demonstrates that they form a relatively cohesive group, distinguished from others by their lack of involvement in the legislative process, their lack of responsibilities within the EP and the priority given to individual action, especially speeches. If we refer to (Table 4.2), one can see that the main behavioural characteristic of this ideal-type is the priority given to speeches in plenary session. On average, they gave 344 speeches per parliamentary term, whereas on average the Eurosceptics interviewed in the framework of this research gave 219 speeches per legislature. The Public Orators' focus on speeches goes hand in hand with a limited investment in other types of activities and, in particular, in the "positive tools" at their disposals such as reports, opinions and amendments. Only 2 MEPs identified as Public Orators out of 23 were rapporteur, one of which abandoned his task before the report was voted in plenary. Similarly, only one MEP of this type has overseen the writing of an opinion for his committee. And most of these MEPs proposed a limited number of amendments: while on average, Eurosceptics interviewed for this research proposed 43 amendments throughout a parliamentary term, MEPs close to the Public Orator type only proposed on average 17 amendments per legislature.

This group is heterogeneous regarding the number and nature of their parliamentary questions. Indeed, while some asked very few questions, especially during the 6th legislature, others were particularly active, asking up to 388 questions. Content analysis of their written questions to the Commission over the course of three years does not reveal a homogeneous focus of representation. While some tend to concentrate on the national, regional and local levels, others ask questions related to the European level. Meanwhile, those who are the most active in parliamentary questions tend to focus on the relations between the EU and third countries, Turkey in particular (due to their negative stance towards the country's accession to the EU). Finally, none of the Public Orator MEPs have exercised responsibility in the EP, except for one who is co-president of an EP political group. This demonstrates both their desire not to take part in the institutional system and their strained relations with their colleagues, as responsibilities in the EP depends on the endorsement of other MEPs through a vote (in committee or delegation).

In brief, this role provides, to those who endorse it, the opportunity to develop an essentially negative strategy vis-à-vis the European polity: it means being present in the heart of the system to denounce it with no desire to reform it, while adopting a posture external to this system through non-compliance with its rules and norms.

Table 4.2 Activities of MEPs close to the ideal-type of public orator (July 2004–July 2016), $N = 24$

	Participation in RCV (%)	Reports	Written declarations	Speeches	Motions for resolutions	Opinions	Questions	Amendments
Mean	85.50	0.06	1.9	344.39	8.73	0.06	91.79	16.7
Median	88.39	0	0	245	2	0	69.65	7
St Deviation	12.97	0.23	4.21	291.2	15.12	0.3	98.28	24.05
Minimum	53.22	0	0	48	0	0	2	0
Maximum	98.24	1	18.5	934.5	58	1.5	388.5	100

Sources European Parliament and votewatch (author's own calculations)

3   THE PRAGMATIST

As its name suggests, this ideal-type is characterized by pragmatism or, more precisely, by a dual strategy whereby, on the one hand, they seek to achieve concrete results while, on the other hand, not compromising their Eurosceptic beliefs. Guided by a desire to be efficient, Pragmatists are characterized by a greater investment in the EP's daily work, a tendency to follow the assembly's rules and a willingness to change, in a targeted and limited way, the system of which they are critical.

Like the Public Orators and Absentees, the Pragmatists are aware they belong to a minority with little chance of changing the direction of European integration or of upholding their views in the assembly. While they may share some characteristics with the Public Orators, Pragmatists offer a completely different implementation of their European mandate. It matches the MEPs described by Costa (2002a, p. 110) as "motivated by the interests of efficiency which encourages them to not remain in a sterile opposition". As one interviewee claims, "it is not only opposition, it is constructive opposition which makes reports and proposals" (interview with MEP 31).

Although they refuse any compromise on their Eurosceptic beliefs, their dissatisfaction with the EU does not result in an outsider position, unlike the two previous roles. Rather, Pragmatists try to find a balance between the promotion of their convictions and the pursuit of tangible results without intending to disrupt the functioning of parliament or undermining the European political system. They also emphasize their mission of representation, in the sense of "acting on behalf of" and believe they have a quasi-imperative mandate linking them to their constituents, fellow citizens or political party. Thus, they have developed a dual strategy, consistent with their perception of a European representative mandate: as Eurosceptics, they see themselves as opposition actors, but also, as MEPs, they wish to emphasize the constructive nature of their opposition and their willingness to get involved to make a difference through their actions. As noted by this representative "As MEP my role is to control legislation and see what I can achieve case by case but as a Eurosceptic, my role is to oppose… (…) and even as MEP, I could make a difference in important areas". (Interview with MEP 16)

Two categories of Pragmatists can be found, each focusing on a different aspect.[4]

3.1   First Subgroup: Emphasis on Control

The first group emphasizes its mission of control over legislation. They see themselves as the watchdogs of European institutions. They conceive of and carry out their mandate in order to amend and control, in very specific areas, the initiatives of their peers and other European institutions. "I think we should participate in legislative work and the control of parliament and I think it's important that we use the resources at our disposal as MEPs to perform these tasks" (Interview with MEP 12).

They also rely on the EP to regulate their national government. Parliamentary questions are considered a very important tool as they allow them to carry out their mission of control, including over the use of budgetary resources, government compliance with European commitments, or even respect for the principles of subsidiarity and transparency: "We ask the Commission and the Council to stress that the government does take actions or not" (Interview with MEP 6). The answers to these questions are then used not so much for the purpose of activism but for politicizing the national debate on the EU or for controlling their national government.

However, their involvement in parliamentary work is limited to policies in which they believe the EU has a role to play and they tend to be specialized in these specific areas: "in areas where we think the EU has a role to play, such as the single market, environmental issues, climate issues, things for which it makes sense to deal with at the European level, in these areas, we try to provide an alternative majority. But we are not willing to compromise on our way of thinking that the EU already decides too much over the national states and on more and more issues we need to work to give competences back to the national states" (Interview with MEP 87).

While the control function tends to prevail for this type of Pragmatist, it is nevertheless important to them to stay in contact with their constituents and representational activities occupy a significant part of their agenda. Thus, it is essential for this subgroup of Pragmatists to report on their actions at the national level, including through explanations of vote.

3.2   Second Subgroup: A Strategy of Defence of Territorial Interests

While all Pragmatists value the national level as they consider it the legitimate arena for political action, the second category is fundamentally guided by the defence of national or regional interests within the assembly: "to me, the most important responsibility is to work for the interest of the people of your country, whatever is their interest. I am in the committee of regional development and the fisheries committee so I see what I can do to help fishermen or regional development in my country" (Interview with MEP 93). This subgroup relies on the European mandate to solve regional and national problems, and their presence in the assembly is driven by this consideration. Their action is primarily instrumental, and the parliament is used as a forum for the defence of specific interests which they cannot effectively defend at the national level. And as explained by this MEP: "I'm at the service of the Cypriot citizens and I expect my political activities to help the major problems of my country, to promote peace in my country and I think through the enlargement of the EU" (Interview with MEP 53).

Thus, members of this subgroup mobilize all the parliamentary tools at their disposal to attract the attention of their peers and of European institutions to the specific problems faced by their region or country. They remain very active at the national level and hope to obtain additional resources for their territory, as a kind of pork barrel politics: "One must never forget, I am the expression of the people, thus, [my role is] to change as much as possible in the direction of improving democracy and the effectiveness of the European institution through policy, and secondly to activate myself to do everything possible to give answers to the territory, to respond to their needs, to, why not, bring money, assistance, be it from a social, economic or institutional point of view…" (Interview with MEP 43).

3.3   Investment in a Broad Range of Parliamentary Activities

The perception of their mandate developed by the Pragmatists, whether of the first or second category, implies greater investment in the work of the parliament and its bodies as well as the mobilization of a much broader range of activities than that of the Public Orators and Absentees. They consider committee work to be an essential tool to achieve their objectives, given the significance of this body of legislative activity and control of the EP (observations of group meetings and interviews with Pragmatist MEPs). As noted by a Pragmatist MEP, "I would say the most important is the work in the committees, putting the amendments, controlling powers, controlling the budget, the legislation process"

(Interview with MEP 16). Pragmatists derive great satisfaction from their commitment to their committees, which allows them to defend the interests that are most important to them and control the content of European policy: "The most important thing is to be present, to be diligent. We were elected to be there. For example, I sit in the Industry, Energy and Research Committee and it deals with very important issues for the future of Europe. One must be present in order to inform oneself in order to vote and to inform the citizens, in order to be able to participate on important issues such as REACH, Galileo, etc." (Interview with MEP 44).

They also invest considerable time and resources to focus the attention of their colleagues on specific issues, through motions for resolutions and written statements. They seek reports and opinions in the policy areas which interest them and accept the principle of negotiation with their colleagues: "Our aim is to change the EU and the Eurozone from inside the institutions. As a political party we are in opposition, in a group labelled as Eurosceptic. European integration is not going well so we are proposing another view. And the first goal is that we would like to open a debate inside the EU about the single currency" (Interview with MEP 84). To do so, they establish contacts with officials from other institutions to increase the effectiveness of their actions all the while criticizing the functioning of the institution. They also file numerous amendments, seen as the most useful tool at their disposal in the EP, given the difficulty for small groups and Eurosceptics to obtain reports. "In the last mandate I was very active in putting down parliamentary questions, because we were seekers after truth and very curious about all sorts of things, that was useful in terms of getting information. But in terms of actually doing something with it, putting down amendments is obviously the key way and which way influences how the legislation is going to go, I focus on the written work and the committee work" (Interview with MEP 13).

Voting is not the subject of an objection on principle. Pragmatists tend to modify their voting behaviour depending on the public policies being considered. Thus, they may vote favourably on all matters related to the internal market or environmental policies or to regional development because this matches the idea that there is added value in the EU that these are policies in which they have been particularly involved or because they serve their territory.

3.4   *A Difficult Balance to Maintain: Respect for the Rules and Refusal to Compromise*

This type of MEP also tends to respect the EP's written and unwritten rules. The language and rhetoric of their interventions in plenary are less confrontational than those of Public Orators and these interventions, even if they are numerous, are not considered by them as the most effective tool in exercising their mandate. One of the Pragmatists' concerns is to distinguish themselves from the Public Orators whose behaviour they condemn as excessive.

As a result of their respect for codes of conduct within the institution, Pragmatists maintain better relationships with their colleagues from other groups and are often recognized for their investment, their constructive attitude and/or their expertise on certain issues. They can take the lead on technical reports, particularly non-legislative opinions and initiative reports and have responsibilities within the delegations and parliamentary committees. When asked about her mandate and the opportunity to hold responsibilities in the assembly, this MEP said she was opposed to her country's accession to the EU, but nevertheless: "you need to be present in the parliament, you must be engaged, you must have the arguments, you must be active in the group, the committees, in plenary. So if you are active and you really show other members that you are engaged, that you are willing to work, work hard" (Interview with MEP 59).

However, while being integrated within the institution appears meaningful within the context of a limited number of policies, Pragmatists do not consider compromising their beliefs towards integration and the European institutions, even if this prevents them from influencing certain policies or holding responsibilities within the EP. Thus, one MEP noted that: "We have to find a balance but it is difficult because I am critical and opposed to the official policies and it is difficult you understand. If I was in favour of this, our work would be much easier" (Interview with MEP6). On these aspects, Pragmatists maintain an attitude of opposition and all their activities are essentially based on and judged according to their Euroscepticism. They can then vote against everything they consider to be inappropriate to deal with at the supranational level, file numerous amendments to repatriate powers to the national level or refuse to join a group because it would require them to compromise on some of their opinions. In addition, they remain very aware of the relative impact of their investment not only on the parliament's legislative work but also on the direction of the European project and keep a certain distance with respect to their mandate: "I am elected to come here and do what I can for the people I'm elected by, so I take my role seriously, but I don't kid myself that that's going to change the UK relationship with the EU" (Interview with MEP 18).

3.5   Characteristic Behaviours of the Pragmatists

If we refer to (Table 4.3), we can see that the Pragmatists' behaviour within the parliament is more heterogeneous than the two previous types. Indeed, their involvement in a broader range of activities leads to greater variation in the individual interpretation of the role.

First, more Pragmatists have exercised a position of responsibility within the EP than Absentees and Public Orators. Under the 6th legislature, a majority of them held positions of responsibility but, with the exception of two MEPs, they were chairs or vice-chairs of parliamentary delegations or committees with weak legislative impact. During the 7th term, only a minority of Pragmatist MEPs succeeded in obtaining positions of responsibility. However, they did receive more sought-after positions including the (vice) presidency of the Fisheries, the Environment, Public Health and Food Safety, the Foreign Affairs and the Employment and Social Affairs Committees (non-attached members being excluded from the distribution of posts). Under the 8th legislature, only a minority have held positions of responsibility, mostly within their political group or as vice-chair of delegations.

Overviewing the activities of Pragmatists also demonstrates their involvement in the various facets of parliamentary work. Like the Public Orators, the Pragmatists use individual-type actions such as questions and speeches. On average, these MEPs have asked many more questions than their colleagues from the other types, as they see it as their mission to control the work of the institutions and to bring national issues to the attention of their colleagues. On average, they ask 141 questions during a legislature, whereas the average of the number of questions of Eurosceptics interviewed during this study is 100 questions per parliamentary term. They also give many speeches, although less than the Public Orators. However, they also use the other tools at their disposal. Thus, their investment in their respective Commission appears to pay off with the allocation of reports and opinions. Two-third of these

Table 4.3 Activities of MEPs close to the ideal-type of pragmatist (July 2004–July 2016), $N = 46$

	Participation in RCV (%)	Reports	Written declarations	Speeches	Motions for resolutions	Opinions	Questions	Amendments
Mean	88.19	1.63	3.63	264.97	39.22	1.6	141.76	60.51
Median	88.69	1	2.5	157	22.5	1	76.25	59
St Deviation	7.27	2.43	3.27	315.55	52.14	2	160.68	41.14
Minimum	63.67	0	0	17	0	0	5	0
Maximum	98.99	14	16	1307	237.5	9	657.5	161

Sources European Parliament and votewatch (author's own calculations)

MEPs have been in charge of reports and opinions for their committees. Similarly, Pragmatists filed a large number of amendments, with an average of 60 amendments per MEP per legislature (compared with an average for interviewed Eurosceptics of 43 amendments). While this suggests their willingness to make changes to European legislation, the number of amendments can vary greatly between them, depending on their level of involvement in their respective committees and the group in which they sit. Finally, they are the MEPs who propose the highest number of motions for resolution, reflecting their will to promote reforms of the EU and its policies inside the institutions.

In sum, the role of the Pragmatist gives those who endorse it limited and targeted influence and control over European legislation through an attitude of constructive opposition and meaningful involvement in parliamentary work. Guided by a desire for efficiency, they develop a dual perception of their representative mandate and try to find a balance between pragmatism and idealism all the while being aware of the difficulty of maintaining this balance.

4   THE PARTICIPANT

This ideal-type refers to a process of socialization in a broad sense, in the form of institutional learning, "by which individuals transform themselves from organizational outsiders to participating insiders" (Scully 2005, p. 79). The Participant is characterized by his/her willingness to appear as an MEP like any other and adapt his/her behaviour to the rules of the game so as to achieve his/her main objective: influence over the European legislative process.

4.1   Looking "like Any Other" MEP

The Participants see themselves first and foremost as legislators, whose mandate is to influence European policies. They want to "formulate European initiatives, discuss them with other MEPs and find a middle ground that can be shared" (interview with MEP 48). When asked about her role, this elected representative defined herself not as an opposition player, but by her institutional affiliations and responsibilities within the EP: "the duties of a MEP are to inform, engage, share and represent the citizens of Europe. We have a pretty important and delicate role. I try to never miss all the works regarding the committees, from the committee meetings to the shadow meetings, the coordinators meetings as I am coordinator of the Libe committee and I follow many reports. I am currently rapporteur on two reports and I am shadow rapporteur on many other dossiers of the Libe committee, in particular those on migration and the defence of fundamental rights as well as on the legal affairs committee (…)" (Interview with MEP 91).

To satisfy their desire for influence, they invest the majority of their time in the chamber and its bodies. As noted by a representative of this type, the European mandate involves immersion in European issues, "we must become involved in the institution and society, once engaged in Europe, we cannot have other responsibilities, it requires serious investment in institutional work" (interview with MEP 56). Unlike the Public Orators and the Pragmatists, Participants not only know and respect the formal and informal rules governing the operation of the EP but adjust their behaviour to them. They subscribe to the rules of political deliberation. Within the context of the EP, this means developing negotiating skills, seeking the broadest possible coalitions and accepting compromise, with the parliament being regarded as "the place where resolutions are prepared in the spirit of consensus and compromise. Compromise is a European value I think" (Interview with MEP 42). They can, occasionally, disregard their Eurosceptic beliefs in order to conform to the rules and thus receive consideration.

> Here we don't work on an isolated basis, never. You have your political point of view and your ideological background and this is of course mirrored in the proposals you present but then we work on the basis of cooperation with the other groups. At the end, what counts is really what we can do, and not what any member in particular can do. (Interview with MEP 38)

Participants therefore consider it essential to be accommodating and willing to compromise during negotiations. They believe that negotiation is the best way to obtain a final result that corresponds, at least in part, to their beliefs. They are also aware that the legislative process takes place at an inter-institutional level and that the EP must have a unified position with regard to the Council in order to be heard (interview with parliamentary assistants). Thus, an MEP of this type states that a successful MEP "should be able to pass a legislative package of measures, to reach consensus between parties in order to prepare the vote. So he should be a good negotiator- he should be able to work across parties since the EP is different from national parliaments and requires a consensus" (interview with MEP 52).

Parliamentary committees are seen as the best political space for them to reach their goal. These committees are the principal venue for the socialization of MEPs where take place most of the deliberations, the legislative and technical work and especially negotiations (Costa and Brack 2011, pp. 107–108; Neuhold 2001).

> We want to be critic but we also want to be part of the solution. (…) and I think the main duty or responsibility a MEP has is on the legislative/directive/regulation front within the parliament, which means you need to be fully involved and engaged with your committee work. MEPs who don't attend committees cannot be active MEPs. I am not talking here of people who are president of the parliament or some other roles. But if you don't actively engage in the committee work, you cannot expect to be participating in the working of this parliament. So the first duty is contributing in that way, on legislation. (Interview with MEP28)

In maintaining good relationships with colleagues, they can obtain legislative reports that they can then draft in such a way that they will be accepted by their fellow MEPs. For example, a member of the ALDE group described a report written for the Committee on Budgetary Control by a well-known Eurosceptic as follows: "One would not be able to distinguish his report from a report which had been written by someone else. He plays the game". Participants appear indeed to play along and consider it important to show others that they are valuable and responsible partners in committees, despite their Eurosceptic views.

4.2   Eurosceptics Guided by a Search for Influence

However, all of their activities are conditioned by their quest for influence. The choice of committees on which they serve tends to be determined by the competences of the latter.

> In Italy, I was on the institutional affairs committee, but here the institutional affairs committee has no real power. In Italy, I voted on constitutional laws, I made my contribution to change the constitution, on parliamentary immunity, on the transfer of power from the states to the regions. Here, the Constitutional Committee can only make proposals but

cannot make decisions. The Lisbon Treaty is not at the parliamentary level, we have only taken a position, we can take positions and give opinions but we cannot amend the treaty. But I can make amendments to family law, company law, etc. So this is why I prefer the Legal Affairs Committee. (Interview with MEP 51)

Similarly, while, in principle, Participants mobilize all parliamentary tools at their disposal, Participants have a predilection for reports, opinions, amendments and questions, considered to be the most effective and interventions in plenary generally confined to areas related to their parliamentary committees. As this MEP explains it, "interesting things do not happen there, they happen upstream but when it comes to the plenary, it's testimony, the hemicycle is a place of testimony" (interview MEP 9). They thus focus on the means by which they can have an impact before the plenary meeting, during informal meetings or coordinators meetings.

> Amendments and reports. Also, I organize and negotiate the voting with the other members of my committee, so that we can get a sufficient number of votes for a proposal. If I should put them according their degree of importance I would say/ first doing reports- this is the most important activity, then second- reaching and negotiating the majority in the committee and third- speaking in the Chamber. I think that speeches are more for publicity- to get visibility; the most important work is in the committees and the reports. (Interview with MEP 52)

This can lead to frustration on the part of this type of MEP, especially when sitting in small EP groups. Indeed, in the EP, success depends on finding a large majority, i.e. on convincing members of larger groups. Some MEPs may find it more difficult to achieve their goals due to the rules governing the functioning of the EP, including the distribution of reports and opinions according to the D'Hondt method (interview MEP 62).

Participants derive great satisfaction in contributing to negotiations and influencing the legislative process. Therefore, it is not about denouncing the EU in plenary, controlling the initiatives of their peers or providing solutions for their territory, but about participating in the EU decision-making process, even if this requires compromises on their Euroscepticism.

> Yeah, I mean, if, you can get a report carried by the majority, that reflects not only what the industry itself wants but also it enables you to have a

serious input of that, where you are perhaps shaping the policy, by you know certain aspects guiding the industry, but also bending the commission to your beliefs, I think that is quite important, it does give you a feeling of achievement. (Interview with MEP 60)

They also seek to perform duties and responsibilities within the chamber (to chair committees and delegations) and are involved in the development of rich networks of contacts in the EP but also the Commission, the Council and the Permanent Representations. They are generally involved in multiple intergroups, forums and discussion groups and dedicate a lot of time and resources to more informal activities such as meetings with lobbyists, working lunches and dinners which will be useful to them later. They greatly appreciate "to have access to influential people and being able in their own small way to influence events. It gives them a great deal of pride to think that they were able to move the situation to a better way because they were there, because they were able to speak to a Commissioner for example" (Interview A # 10).

4.3   Complex Relationships with Their Constituents?

While Participants believe that their tasks are primarily at the supranational level and require commitment and a significant presence in the EP, this does not mean they are cut off from the national and local political arenas. Indeed, they try to maintain a connection with their constituents and fellow citizens through their websites, newsletters, local assistants and constituency visits during weekends and the so-called green weeks. But unlike the Pragmatists, the Participants do not intend to solve local problems or to politicize the national debate but rather to "educate" their fellow citizens on European issues and to promote their work, or even the work of the EU in some respects. This can also cause a lag between the MEP and his/her voters, whether on their vision of the EU (although the representatives define themselves as Eurosceptics) or their expectations about the role of the representative Participants may then have the feeling of being torn between the expectations of voters and the way in which they perceive their role.

What is true is here we see what the EU is concretely and how it can be positive, we understand better through our work here.(...) but voters live this less concretely, those who truly travel in Europe are quite minority but here is a tower of Babylon. I think the concrete and direct experience, including participation in things, if it is not obtuse, and that is not full of a priori, it is indeed, we feel better, we better see the bottle half full [rather than half empty]. (Interview with MEP 9)

It's not easy to find enough possibilities [to go home] and if you're at home, every time the people are interested but they complain because they don't hear about you when you're not there. They don't know what we are doing, I invite people to come here or in Strasbourg to discuss with them, to show how we are working, what is possible and what is not possible and they are interested but 3 months later, they still complain because they don't hear about you in the news in the region [...] My role is to be here and see what I can do. But a lot of the left members think it is easier on the national level to defend our views but I think in the area of globalization, it's not possible, you've to act at all levels and I try to get more influence in my own political group and party for this thinking. (Interview with MEP 62)

Additionally, the national or local level may also serve as a fallback position for disappointed Participants, who, having failed at reaching their goal at the supranational level, may then tend to invest in the party or local tasks. Indeed, if the Participants are unable, for various reasons, to be influential in the EP, they may withdraw and regret choosing the European mandate.

Well I was interested in European politics before, I was a member of the parliament and of the European integration committee. Here my main responsibility is to take part in the parliamentary work, in the plenary sessions and the committees, delegations, and so on. To be part of the functioning of the Parliament. (...) But well I can tell you, as a politician, the most satisfying part of my job is to be local councillor of my town, I've been local councillor for 20 years and this is the most satisfying part of politics because you can directly see the outcomes of your decisions. In the EP, it's much more difficult to see the real outcome. (Interview with MEP 19)

4.4   The Characteristic Behaviours of the Participant MEPs

The involvement of the Participants in all EP activities, both formal and informal, causes a certain heterogeneity of the practices of MEPs in this ideal-type. Their quest for responsibilities within the assembly is not always successful although some have held important positions within the EP such as the (vice) chair of sought-after committees (Internal Market, International Trade, Constitutional Affairs, Industry, Research and Energy) or even the position of Quaestor over the course of the 3 legislatures under study. The others then fall back on functions within their group or delegation. During the 8th legislative term, a minority obtained positions of responsibility in the EP but again, some scored sought-after positions such as the (vice) presidency of the special committee on taxation, of the International trade committee or of the employment and social affairs committee.

Regarding their parliamentary activities, MEPs close to the Participant type are characterized by three main elements. First, in comparison with MEPs of the other ideal-types, they use relatively few individual-type actions such as questions and speeches. Indeed, on average, these MEPs have asked only 47 questions per term (while Eurosceptics interviewed for this study asked on average 100 questions per legislature) and they gave only 63 speeches on average during a legislature (the average for Eurosceptics being 219 per term). Secondly, as they try to look like any other MEP, they do not resort to a particular type of activities and they stand out from the other ideal-types through moderation in all of their activities. Finally, as these MEPs concentrate on influencing the legislative process and are involved in all types of parliamentary activities, they have, for the most part, been in charge of reports and opinions. On average these MEPs have taken the lead on more than 2 reports during a parliamentary term, which is twice as many as the average Eurosceptic MEP (Table 4.4).

In summary, like the Pragmatists, the Participant matches the posture of an insider seeking change from within the system of which he is critical. However, guided by a desire for influence, they focus on the legislative aspects of the European mandate. Rather than trying to maintain a balance between the search for concrete results and their Eurosceptic beliefs, Participants do not see themselves as opposition players and adapt their practices to the rules of the institution.

5   Conclusion

Eurosceptic MEPs are at the centre of a paradox: they are particularly successful during EU elections, campaigning on the basis of a Eurosceptic platform but once elected to the EP, they have to operate in an institution, and more generally a political system, they

Table 4.4 Activities of MEPs close to the ideal-type of participant (July 2004–July 2016), $N = 22$

	Participation in RCV (%)	Reports	Written declarations	Speeches	Motions for resolutions	Opinions	Questions	Amendments
Mean	86.56	2.78	1.67	65.32	26.62	1.52	49.28	51.19
Median	88.66	2.25	1.4	48.4	16.15	1.25	28.75	42.15
St Deviation	8.1	2.49	1.68	48.83	29.06	1.43	47.69	42.22
Minimum	69.91	0	0	17	1	0	4.5	3
Maximum	96.92	8.5	6	206.5	99	4.5	168	192

Sources European Parliament and votewatch (author's own calculations)

strongly criticize or even oppose. Despite the extensive literature on Euroscepticism and abundant research on the EP, little is known about the individual activities of MEPs and on how they perform their representative function. The aim here was therefore to propose an in-depth and comparative analysis of the strategies developed by Eurosceptic MEPs as anti-system actors.

This chapter has examined how these actors cope with the tension between the Eurosceptic platform on the basis of which they were elected and the tasks and expectations arising from their representative mandate. Relying on the concept of role and an inductive methodology, it analysed how Eurosceptics conceive of and carry out their parliamentary mandate. The idea was to understand the roles played by Eurosceptic MEPs.

A typology of four ideal-types of roles has been developed: the Absentee, the Public Orator, the Pragmatist and the Participant. Analysis has shown that, like any elected representative, Eurosceptics interpret their mandate so as to match both their visions of the role of the MEP and the presumed expectations of their electorate. Given the constraints they face and the lack of consensus on the best way to exercise the European mandate, they offer alternative ways of conceiving of and inhabiting the parliamentary function, which could differ from those of their colleagues. Moreover, unlike some studies on roles (see Price 1985; Van Vonno 2012), no role-switching was observed. Although the study period is relatively short, the actors remained faithful to their role in parliament over the course of three legislatures, confirming the hypothesis of Searing (1994) according to which individuals primarily interpret one role.

The analysis also demonstrates that, beyond their Eurosceptic position, there is a diversity in the ways Eurosceptics conceive of and carry out their European mandate. They do not all adopt an attitude of protest but exhibit diversified attitudes and behaviours, some being relatively well integrated into the parliamentary game. As noted by Birenbaum (1992) in his study of the French National Front, we should refrain from a simplistic interpretation of the practices of anti-system actors.

Eurosceptic MEPs can remain in an outsider position by endorsing the Absentee or Public Orator roles. The Absentee reflects a position of retreat from the institution but not to the point of total withdrawal. Indeed, unlike some national parties such as Sinn Fein whose elected representatives refused to sit in the British Parliament on principle (see Usherwood 2008), Absentees actually fill their seats but are not much involved in parliamentary work. This type of MEP is not interested in the European mandate and is only active at the national or regional level as they see their role as promoting Euroscepticism at home. Absentees derive great satisfaction from carrying out a permanent campaign against the EU in their country and use the European mandate as a way of obtaining information, resources, visibility and legitimacy. Meanwhile, Public Orators are more present in the EP but are not involved in the traditional aspects of parliamentary work. This type of MEP sees his/her role as being an opposition speaker whose mission is to delegitimize the institution and the EU through speeches in plenary. Such MEPs take great pride from the reactions aroused by their anti-conformist behaviour and do not seek to participate in the legislative or oversight function of the parliament. In doing so, they claim, their opposition to the EU from within the institution by refusing to accept the risks of participating in the deliberations.

But Eurosceptic MEPs may also adopt an insider position and assume the roles of the Pragmatist or Participant. The Pragmatist is driven by a desire to be efficient and seeks a balance between achieving concrete results and promoting his/her Eurosceptic views. Such MEPs develop a dual conception of their role: as MEP on the one hand, he/she wants to be constructive and contribute to the oversight function of the parliament or represent the national interest in the EU but as Eurosceptic on the other hand, he/she does not want to compromise his/her point of view on Europe. As they maintain a posture of opposition, this prevents them from having any real impact on sensitive policies. Finally, the Participant wants to appear as any other MEP and certainly not as being in opposition. Motivated by a desire to influence the legislative process, these MEPs are very much involved in all aspects of parliamentary work. They seek responsibilities within the chamber and adapt their behaviour to the EP's rules and the expectations of their colleagues.

Now that it has been established that, beyond their shared opposition to the EU, Eurosceptic MEPs develop heterogeneous strategies within the institution, the next step is to explain the diversity of their roles. The next two chapters address one of the main challenges of role theory, i.e. explaining the elected representative's choice of a role. They are dedicated to examining the impact of two key elements: the institutional context and individual preferences.

NOTES

1. For each established roles, each MEP has his/her own individual interpretation. But the aim here is to reconstruct principal roles with sufficient
   generality to provide a typology of roles summarizing their patterns and
   characteristics (see Searing 1994, p. 369).
2. The attendance rate does not adequately reflect their investment since on
   the one hand, it only allows to control the presence of the elected representatives in the building and not their participation in debates and, on
   the other hand, MEPs must sign a register during the plenary sessions to
   receive their allowances, motivating them to be present.
3. The censure motion was aimed primarily at the European Commission
   President, Barosso as the MEPs suspected conflicts of interest. Indeed,
   Barroso had spent his vacation on the yacht of a Greek shipowner after
   his nomination as the head of the Commission. Soon thereafter, the
   Commission approved Community funding for this shipowner. This generated a series of parliamentary questions as well as a request for debate.
   A group of MEPs who were unsatisfied and complained about the
   Commission's lack of transparency on this question, introduced a censure
   motion, obliging the president of the Commission to respond to parliamentary questions during a debate in the plenary session.
4. In practice, these categories are not water tight: in the interpretation of the
   role of the pragmatist, MEPs have two types of consideration at the heart
   of their actions.

REFERENCES

Bale, T., & Taggart, P. (2006). *First-timers yes, virgins no: The roles and background of new MEPs*. SEI working papers, 89.

Birenbaum, G. (1992). Le front national à l'Assemblée (1986–1988)—Respect
et subversion de la règle du jeu parlementaire. *Politix, 5*(20), 99–118.

Brack, N., & Costa, O. (2018). Euroscepticism in the EU institutions: A persistent and embedded phenomenon. In B. Leruth, N. Startin, & S. Usherwood
(Eds.), *The routledge handbook of euroscepticism*, London: Routledge,
forthcoming.

Brack, N., & Costa, O. (2012). *Euroscepticism within EU institutions: Diverging
views of Europe*. London: Routledge.

Corbett, R. (2002). A very special parliament: The European parliament in the
twenty-first century. *The Journal of Legislative Studies, 8*(2), 1–8.

Costa, O. (2001). *Le Parlement européen, assemblée délibérante*. Brussels:
Editions de l'Université de Bruxelles.

Costa, O. (2002a). Les députés européens entre allégeances multiples et logique d'institution. *Journal of European Integration, 24*(2), 91–112.

Costa, O. (2002b). Le travail parlementaire européen et la défense des intérêts locaux. Les députés européens dans la gouvernance multi-niveaux. In O. Nay & A. Smith (Eds.), *Le gouvernement du compromis. Courtiers et généralistes dans l'action politique* (pp. 195–225). Paris: Economica.

Costa, O., & Brack, N. (2011). *Le fonctionnement de l'Union européenne.* Brussels: Editions de l'Université de Bruxelles.

Hix, S., Noury, A., & Roland, G. (2007). *Democratic Politics in the European Parliament.* Cambridge: Cambridge University Press.

Hooghe, L. (2001). *The European commission and the integration of Europe. Images of governance.* Cambridge: Cambridge University Press.

Kauppi, N. (1996). European union institutions and French political careers. *Scandinavian Political Studies, 19*(1), 1–24.

Kauppi, N. (2005). *Political power in the European parliament.* Manchester: Manchester University Press.

Navarro, J. (2009). *Les députés européens et leur rôle. Sociologie interprétative des pratiques parlementaires.* Brussels: Editions de l'Université de Bruxelles.

Neuhold, C. (2001). The 'Legislative Backbone' keeping the Institution upright? The Role of European Parliament Committees in the EU Policy-Making Process. *European Integration online Papers, 5*(10).

Price, K. C. (1985). Instability in representational role orientation in a state legislature: A research note. *Western Political Quarterly, 38*(1), 162–171.

Reif, K., & Schmitt, H. (1980). Nine second order national elections: A conceptual framework for the analysis of European election results. *European Journal of Political Research, 8*(1), 3–44.

Scully, R. M. (2005). *Becoming Europeans. Attitudes, behaviour, and socialization in the European parliament.* Oxford: Oxford University Press.

Searing, D. (1994). *Westminster's world. Understanding political roles.* Cambridge: Harvard University Press.

Usherwood, S. (2008). The dilemmas of a single_issue party–The UK Independence Party. *Representation, 44*(3), 255–264.

Van Vonno, C. M. (2012). Role-switching in the Dutch parliament: Reinvigorating role theory? *The Journal of Legislative Studies, 18*(2), 119–136.

CHAPTER 5

The EP, an "Unrewarding" Location for Eurosceptics?

Roles are embedded within a particular institution. As Searing noted (1994, p. x), "political roles are the place where individual choices meet institutional constraints". According to the motivational approach, institutional context is a key to understand the roles developed by parliamentarians. Institution can be defined as rules and procedures, both formal and informal, which structure social interactions and give political actors incentives (Davison et al. 2005; Helmke and Levitsky 2004; North 1990). These rules define the scope of permissible action and influence actors' ability to achieve their objectives by encouraging or discouraging certain kinds of behaviour. In other words, rules have a double-edged quality: they are at both constraining and empowering for elected representatives (Sheingate 2010, p. 168; see also Giddens 1984). But institutions empower and constrain actors differently, depending on multiple factors such as their skills or professional experience but mostly on the parliamentarian's position within the institution (Costa 2001; March and Olsen 2005; Searing, 1994). Along with other works in legislative studies, it is argued here that the rules of the game have an impact on the way (Eurosceptic) elected representatives conceive and carry out their mandate.

This chapter aims therefore at systematically identifying the constraints and resources deriving from the institutional context which influence the room for manoeuvre of Eurosceptic MEPs and their perceptions of institutional reality. Doing so makes it possible to determine to what extent the formal and informal rules of the EP affect the

© The Author(s) 2018
N. Brack, *Opposing Europe in the European Parliament*,
Palgrave Studies in European Union Politics,
https://doi.org/10.1057/978-1-137-60201-5_5

roles they play. The evolution of the chamber's formal rules is studied first. The analysis shows that political groups have become key actors in the functioning of the EP at the expense of individual parliamentarians' rights. Individual legislators' room for manoeuvre has decreased, and their behaviour has become much more constrained over time. The second part of this chapter is devoted to the examination of the informal rules of the European parliament and their influence on the roles of Eurosceptic MEPs. Three main elements are studied here: the way the EP works; membership in a political group and the effect of the cordon sanitaire around some Eurosceptics. The analysis highlights the impact of these formal and informal rules on the roles played by Eurosceptic MEPs. Although the formal rules apply to all MEPs, which should have the same parliamentary rights and privileges, there is a differentiation among MEPs as a result of parliamentary organization (Strøm 2012, p. 97). The rules of procedure have fundamentally changed over time and now tend to marginalize individual parliamentarians as well as small groups. The informal rules reinforce this trend and incentivize Eurosceptics to integrate the institution, in the roles of Pragmatist or Participant while discouraging MEPs from staying at the margins (as Absentees and Public Orators).

1   THE INFLUENCE OF FORMAL RULES ON EUROSCEPTIC STRATEGIES

The formal rules regulating the EP are contained in the chamber's Rules of Procedure (RoP). These rules frame the daily activities within the EP. They define the MEPs' room for manoeuvre, their relations to their political group as well as the relations between political groups (Kreppel 2002, p. 9). Unlike many national parliaments whose organization depends on constitutional rules, organic laws or a priori control of their procedural rules by external bodies, the EP has full autonomy in defining its organization. MEPs are therefore free to determine their deliberation methods. They can change their RoP as they want (Costa 2010). Nonetheless, this text has been at the heart of power struggles as the distribution of power among actors in the chamber is at stake (Brack et al. 2015; Kreppel 2002). It has been frequently reformed: in the 30 years after the first direct elections of MEPs, there were 17 editions of the RoP (1979–2009). The text was again deeply reformed after the adoption of the Lisbon Treaty and has been reformed once again in

December 2016. These changes were necessary for the EP not only to face its growing empowerment after each treaty reform but also to cope with the increasing number of MEPs after each enlargement and deal with new situations, such as behaviours deemed inappropriate by MEPs. For instance, the rules regarding the transparency register and the standards of conduct of Members were changed after a scandal involving three MEPs accepting money in exchange for amendments to proposed legislation.[1] The reforms of the rules have rationalized parliamentary work, i.e. procedures have been increasingly codified, individual MEP's room for manœuvre has been restricted and the division of labour within the chamber has been enhanced (Costa 2001, p. 305). This has allowed the EP to become more efficient, maximize its impact on the legislative process and claim new powers (Corbett et al. 2007; Hix 2002b; Kreppel 2002, 2003). Through its various reforms, the RoP has become increasingly precise and complex: whereas in 1979, the text was 42 pages long, with 54 rules and 2 annexes, in January 2017, it contains over 230 rules and 7 annexes, for a total of 158 pages.

The changes went beyond what was technically required and deeply changed the internal organization of the EP as well as the intra-institutional relationships between actors within the EP (Kreppel 2003, p. 898). This section will not evaluate all the modifications of the rules and their impact on the EP (see Brack et al. 2015; Kreppel 2002; Williams 1995). It will concentrate rather on the consequences of the rationalization of parliamentary work on the activities of Eurosceptic MEPs. The rules relative to the rights of individual MEPs will be examined before evaluating the empowerment of political groups. Then, the particular situation of non-attached MEPs will be analysed to highlight their marginalization from parliamentary activities. Finally, the growing constraints on parliamentarians' behaviour will be examined.

1.1 An Increasingly Reduced Scope for Individual Action

As noted by Corbett et al. (2007, p. 56), the individual *backbencher* can play a considerable role in the EP. With very little rules regarding the tasks and duties of an MEP and in the absence of a clear majority/opposition cleavage to frame parliamentary behaviour, an MEP is relatively free to define his/her priorities and to get involved (or not) in the various aspect of the European mandate. To do so, he/she can rely on the rights granted by the RoP.

First, an MEP can ask written questions to European institution. And as the previous chapter has shown, parliamentary questions are considered to be a useful tool by some Eurosceptics, especially the Absentee and Pragmatist. Through parliamentary questions, they have access to information or can control the actions of the Commission, the Council, the European Central Bank or even their national government. However, since the 2008 reform, this activity is framed by the principles laid down in Annex II. Whereas before, parliamentarians were totally free to ask their questions on the topics of their choosing and in the way they wanted; now, their questions should be concise (no more than 200 words), contain an understandable interrogation, not contain offensive language and not relate to strictly personal matters. Moreover, since January 2017, the number of questions has been limited to 20 written questions over a rolling period of 3 months.

Second, an MEP can participate during question time, although here again, the number of questions and follow-up questions have been reduced over time. Question time remains a platform relatively free of constraints for individual MEPs. But a single member cannot ask a question for oral answer with debate, the threshold being a committee, a political group or one-twentieth of parliament's component Members (rule 138).

Third, any MEP can intervene during plenary sessions through various procedures. He or she can take the floor at the end of the debate through the catch-the-eye procedure if he/she could not get speaking time during the debate itself. MEPs can also make personal statements to rebut any remarks that have been made about them in person in the course of the debate or about opinions that have been attributed to them, or to correct observations that they themselves have made (rule 164). Individual MEPs can also make a one-minute speech to draw parliament's attention to a matter of political importance or raise the blue card to ask a question to the person speaking in plenary.

Finally, any MEP also has the right to propose amendments in the committee he/she is a member of, which is an important resource for Eurosceptics endorsing the roles of Pragmatist or Participant. Any MEP can also table a motion for a resolution on a matter falling within the spheres of activity of the EU, with a maximum now set at one per month (art. 133). Although it rarely leads to the adoption of that kind of motion through the EP, this type of individual initiative gives MEPs some visibility, notably towards their voters. Until the 8th legislature, any MEP could also table a written declaration but this now requires 10 MEPs from at least 3 political groups (art. 136), and the possibility disappeared in January 2017.

These possibilities are significant resources for Eurosceptic MEPs and give them some room for manoeuvre, especially in plenary session. However, at the beginning of the 1990s, they could use two other options, whose impact on parliamentary activities was more important. They could table amendments in plenary sessions (art. 69, 1991), whereas now, this prerogative lies solely with the responsible committee, a political group or at least 40 MEPs (art. 169).[2] They could also ask for a referral back to committee, entailing the suspension of the discussion of the report (art. 103, 1991). This could be used as a filibustering technique but is now reserved for political groups or at least 5% of parliament's component Members (art. 188).

Overall, the rules offer some room for manoeuvre for dissenting voices within a political group or a coalition of individual MEPs to trigger various procedures, notably to obstruct parliamentary work (Corbett et al. 2007, p. 56). However, the impact of those possibilities is limited, and their scope has been progressively reduced. If, in most chambers, members wanting to filibuster can extend the debates, table a large number of amendments or use procedural and interruptive motions, these tools are not efficient in the EP. Indeed, the multiplication of speeches is no longer possible, and the massive tabling of amendments does not significantly delay the adoption of a report (Costa 2001, p. 429). Only procedural motions remain: verification of the quorum, points of order, moving for the inadmissibility of a matter, closure of these debates or adjournment of a vote. But many of these rights are only open to a political group or to at least 40 Members, and procedural motions need to be approved by the majority of the chamber. And, because of abuse by some parliamentarians, especially Eurosceptics, filibustering opportunities have been reduced, and rules have been reformed to avoid future misuse. The rules were changed during the 6th legislature after numerous abuses by several MEPs, and now, the EP's president has the power to "put an end to the excessive use of motions such as points of order, procedural motions, explanations of vote and requests for separate, split or roll-call votes where the President is convinced that these are manifestly intended to cause and will result in, a prolonged and serious obstruction of the procedures of the House or the rights of other Members" (art. 164a).

1.2   The Growing Importance of Political Groups

Along with diminished rights for individual MEPs, the rationalization of parliamentary work went hand in hand with the empowerment of political groups. Through various reforms, EP political groups have become key players in the chamber. Before the direct election of the EP, several rules granted rights to political groups but also to a small number of MEPs, which meant MEPs could remain non-attached without facing too many constraints. Over time, however, the number of parliamentarians required to exercise the same rights as a political group has progressively increased. For instance, candidates to the EP presidency can be nominated by a political group, whatever its size or one-twentieth of parliament's component Members (rule 15), whereas it was possible for 4.59% of the chamber to nominate a candidate in 1994 and for 2.44% in 1981 (art. 12, 1981). Similarly, a committee, a political group or at least 5% of parliament's component Members may put a question with oral answer (rule 128), whereas it was possible for 1.95% of MEPs to do so in 1991 (rule 58). At the beginning of the 1970s, political groups were mentioned in only 6 rules; in 1981, 22 rules referred to them, and groups have progressively received exclusive prerogatives rules (Kreppel 2002, p. 115). For instance, only a group may designate a coordinator or shadow rapporteur (rule 205 and 205a). Overall, "groups control the deliberation because of the extended rights the Rules of Procedure grant them, because of the control they have over the hierarchical bodies of the assembly and because of the role they play in the functioning of parliamentary committees" (Costa 2001, p. 306).

The reforms have not only empowered the political groups at the expense of individual parliamentarians, they have also consolidated the power of the two largest groups (Christian-democrats and socialists). After the Maastricht Treaty, the rules were once again modified, and the functioning of the Conference of the Presidents changed. The 1993 modification altered the electoral system by introducing the weighted vote: if a consensus cannot be reached, the matter is put to a vote subject to a weighting based on the number of MEPs in each political group. In a way, it institutionalized the co-management of the EP's organization by the two main groups. Bringing together between half and two-thirds of the MEPs, they share the presidency and most of the vice-presidencies of the EP since the mid-1980s as well as many chairmanships of committees and delegations because of the D'Hondt rule. Furthermore, since the 1993 reform, they can impose their point of view in the Conference of the Presidents because of the weighting of the votes. Smaller groups, where most of the Eurosceptics are found, are generally subjected to the rule of the two largest groups when these reach an agreement beforehand (Brack et al. 2015). As this MEP notes, "the big negative tendency is to pretend the increased number of MEPs requires to drastically limit the expression of political pluralism beyond the two main political families, for instance through amendments and committee debates. It's a permanent struggle. Most of the time, it's lost because the two largest groups rule and the others are just tolerated".

Political groups control every aspect of parliamentary life and are key players in the institution. They manage the legislative and non-legislative activities in the EP and control the access to resources such as the agenda-setting or the allocation of reports and responsibilities. On the contrary, the freedom of action of individual MEPs has been tightened. Like any other parliamentarians, Eurosceptics have some room for manoeuvre, but the powers of isolated MEPs are limited in scope and now require some coordination, within a group or with like-minded colleagues. But collective action at the supranational level has been problematic for many Eurosceptic MEPs, especially from right-wing nationalist parties (Halikiopoulou and Vasilopoulou 2014). As explained by Hanley (2007), because these MEPs are hostile to the EU, it is quite logical that they oppose any institutionalized cooperation at the European level. Eurosceptic political groups are often technical alliances rather than ideological groupings, and cooperation among radical right MEPs is usually fragile and short-lived (Brack and Startin 2017; Fieschi 2000; Startin 2010). Fringe EP groups grant more freedom to their national delegations as the national level remains the main framework for Eurosceptics: "if you are a member of a political group, you have some privileges but our first priority is to be independent in our activity and to focus on the national level and our party" (interview with MEP 73). Most Eurosceptic MEPs tend to conceive of and carry out the parliamentary mandate as an individual task, and few consider the collective dimension of parliamentary work, depriving themselves from the rights granted by the rules to groupings meeting the threshold of one-twentieth of parliament's component Members.

1.3   The Situation of Non-attached MEPs: An Increasing Marginalization

The reforms of the rules have not only empowered political groups at the expense of individual MEPs, but they also have penalized non-attached MEPs, most of whom are Eurosceptic.

Indeed, because of their fringe position within their national political arena and their ideological orientations, these MEPs are unable or unwilling to join a group or to form one or even to act in a coordinated manner. As this EP civil servant (CPE #3) explains, "this is always the problems for the non-attached members. They come from different horizons and we cannot put them together to vote. They belong to the same parliament, they have been elected as the others but as far as the organization is concerned, they cannot be a political group because there is a threshold. As a result, they are involuntarily non-attached and we cannot force them to be organized". If at some point, there has been a coordination, especially among radical right members, in order to allocate speaking time in plenary, they are usually not numerous enough to use the tools at the disposal of a political group or of the threshold established in the RoP. Because of their inability to cooperate, non-attached MEPs have been deeply impacted by the gradual reduction of individual member's rights granted by the RoP: "I have seen that colleagues who are non-attached are in fact very limited in their actions and have a lot of obstacles by the actual rules of procedure" (Interview with MEP 90).

These obstacles are one of the main drivers behind the attempts by radical right MEPs to form a group, as exemplified by the pressure by Marine Le Pen to create the new radical right group ENF during the 8th legislature. Non-attached MEPs are given less logistical and financial resources than groups and are excluded from most of the organizational aspects of the institution (Clinchamps 2006, p. 282). They are unable to influence the decision-making process within the institution as they do not have voting rights and no longer have the right to choose their own representative to the Conference of Presidents. Indeed, the two largest groups sought (and achieved) to reduce the representation (without voting right) of the non-attached in the Conference of the Presidents from two to one representatives. After the implementation of the Lisbon Treaty, the RoP was changed, and the nomination procedure for the representative of the non-attached members to the Conference of the Presidents modified. Whereas, historically, non-attached MEPs could choose their representative, it is now the EP President who designates the representative. Officially, the aim was to put an end to the continuous struggles of the non-attached to choose their representative. But the reform also gives the opportunity to the President to choose a conciliatory member (interview CPE #2).

Additionally, non-attached members cannot nominate shadow rapporteurs or coordinators. They are therefore excluded from the coordinators' meetings which are crucial for committee work. Indeed, coordinators play a key role in the management of committee work and reports, and it is during these strategic meetings that report allocations, agenda-setting and the political priorities of the committee are debated and decided (interview CPE #8). These meetings were informal until the 7th legislature but have since then been mentioned in the rules. Rule 205 stipulates that the status of coordinator is for members of political groups only. Non-attached are therefore excluded: "we cannot attend the coordinators and chairmen's meetings and as a result, we are cut off from the actual functioning of the Parliament because everything is decided there" (Interview MEP 85). Some questioned the discriminatory nature of this rule and informal practices developed: whereas several committee chairs authorized the attendance of non-attached members or of civil servants as observers during coordinators' meetings, others were opposed to it (interview CPE #6). This led to the adoption of an interpretation of rule 205 in 2012, which now mentions that "Non-attached Members do not constitute a political group within the meaning of Rule 32 and they cannot therefore designate coordinators, who are the only Members entitled to attend coordinator meetings. (…) In all cases, non-attached Members must be guaranteed access to information, in accordance with the principle of non-discrimination, through the supply of information and the presence of a member of the non-attached Members' secretariat at coordinator meetings".

In a nutshell, non-attached members are, comparatively to other MEPs, marginalized by the rules of procedure of the EP. They do not have influence in the Conference of Presidents or on the decisions made between political groups, and they are excluded from the coordinators' meetings. Furthermore, because of the formal rules, they have very limited access to responsibilities within the chamber and a very limited impact on the legislation-making process. For some non-attached members, this situation is a burden on their activities, and on the way, they conceive of their mandate: "I think it's important to use all the tools at our disposal to carry out our mandate as European parliamentarians and that's why I consider it very serious that non-attached members do not have the same means and opportunities as the colleagues belonging to a political group. I think non-attached members should also be able to propose amendments in plenary, be candidate to various positions, should have the same resources, secretariats, etc." (Interview MEP 12). They tend to concentrate on plenary meetings rather than on committee work as they are rather unlikely to become rapporteur, and the likelihood of becoming one will depend on relatively random factors such as the personality of the individual MEP, the size of the committee and its political culture (interview CPE #6). This exclusion from areas of parliamentary work tends to trigger a feeling of political impotence among non-attached members: "being non-attached is not easy, notably because not everybody gets along. And we do not have a great room for manoeuver, we cannot work on the legislation because we are very seldom in charge of reports, we cannot submit amendments in plenary, all this is quite discriminatory" (interview A #9). The discrimination against non-attached members entailed by the rationalization of deliberation is a recurring issue within the EP. It refers to a larger debate regarding the balance between the efficiency of parliamentary work and democracy within the chamber, notably through political pluralism and parliamentary minority rights (Brack et al. 2015). Non-attached members claim they should have the same rights as the members of political groups, in the name of democracy. MEPs from the main groups argue that the efficiency of parliamentary work is the best guarantee for the legitimacy of the institution and the implementation of parliamentary democracy at the EU level.[3] Any upgrade in the rights of non-attached members tends to be followed by other rules constraining their room for manoeuvre (see Settembri 2004). Some non-attached therefore feel strongly discriminated against: "the rules are always interpreted to our disadvantage. Even when the Court ruled in our favour, then the EP changed the rules so that we don't have access to this or that anymore. You have to understand who the non-attached are: the non-popular ones, those who do not have many political friends in the parliament and nobody is interested in our rights" (Interview with MEP 58).

1.4   *A Progressive Reduction of Speaking Time*

Because of the rules, many Eurosceptic MEPs, among which those who are non-attached members, tend to turn to individual types of actions such as parliamentary questions and speeches in plenary session; the various reforms of the rules also limited the time allocated to debates. Indeed, in order to deal with the empowerment of the EP as well as with the increased number of MEPs, parliamentarians seem to have favoured efficiency and a focus on the legislative process (Rasmussen and Toshkov 2011). Legislative debates now occupy the bulk of the agenda. This went hand in hand with an increased codification of the parliamentary proceedings and a limitation of speaking time. The various options for MEPs to speak in plenary session have been progressively reduced, penalizing the elected representatives who favour this type of actions such as public orator and, to a lesser extent, Pragmatist Eurosceptics.

The reforms have quite limited speaking time for questions. The post-Maastricht reform of the rules removed the possibility of oral questions without debate. Half a day during plenary sessions used to be allocated to such questions, granting 10 min of speaking time to the author(s) of the question, with a short reply from a representative of the relevant EU institution (rule 59, 1991). It also reformed the procedure of oral questions with debate, by increasing the number of MEPs required to ask such a question (from 7 to 40) and reducing the number of minutes for the question (from 10 to 5). At the same time, the procedure of Question time, introduced after the accession of the UK, was modified to reduce the time allocated to debate. The post-Maastricht reform removed the possibility of a one hour debate after Question time and reduced the number of complementary questions to the Commission and Council. The current RoP caps the number of complementary questions.

The rules give MEPs other opportunities for supplementary speaking time, although these have also been reduced. As explained previously, because of abuses from a minority of MEPs, the speaking time allocated to procedural motions (referral back to committee, closure of a debate, adjournment of a debate and vote, and suspension or closure of the sitting), points of order and personal statement has been changed from three to one minute per member. Moreover, to use a point of order, the MEP should be able to mention the exact rule he or she refers to, leading some MEPs to become masters of the rules of procedure.

Voting explanations are another opportunity for MEPs to speak during a plenary session. But here again, the speaking time has diminished, and more importantly, the 1994 reform of the rules allowed the President to postpone the explanations after the vote, reducing the attractiveness of this speaking time. MEPs wanting to explain their vote can no longer hope to extend the debate through an explanation of vote and are often speaking in a chamber whose ranks are emptying (Corbett et al. 2007, p. 57). However, as shown in Chap. 4, it remains a popular tool for a category of Eurosceptics who seek to reach their voters through their statements.

The constant reduction of speaking time has triggered hot debates in the EP. On the one hand, members of the larger groups and the hierarchical bodies within the assembly consider that these reforms are necessary to increase the institution's efficiency: "Parliament will have more legislative powers and we must get ready to place legislating at the heart of our work" (Leinen, S&D). One the other hand, members of smaller groups denounce this vision, considering that these reforms "to turn our Parliament into a bureaucratic machine where the role of individual MEPs and minority groups and even the committees must be subject to the growing, partly arbitrary, decision-making power of the Conference of Presidents and the administration" (Frassoni, Greens/EFA).[4] Several Eurosceptic MEPs argued, during the revision relating to the standards of conduct of MEPs that this reform "flouts parliamentary democracy" (Lang, Non-attached), considering that "interruptions in debates and a visible display of different opinions are part and parcel of normal parliamentary practice." (Meijer, EUL/NGL) and that the reform is "an attempt, in the name of the smooth functioning of Parliament, to use policing and sanctions in order to restrict and control the expression of reaction, protest or disagreement and terrorise those Members who wish to express their opposition" (Pafilis, EUL/NGL).[5]

New procedures were introduced in order to compensate for the reduced speaking time while limiting filibustering tactics. Since the 2009 reform, any member can hold up a blue card to indicate they would like to ask a question to another MEP giving a speech. If both the speaker and the President agree, then the Member will have half a minute to ask the question (rule 162). Finally, after each debate, up to five speakers are selected on the "catch-the-eye" principle, whereby the President selects members indicating their wish to speak. If this is the case, then the member will have up to a minute to give a short speech. But overall, the trend is toward a greater emphasis on legislative activities rather than plenary debates.

1.5   *A Stricter Regulation of Members' Behaviour*

The behaviour of MEPs has become increasingly regulated, especially since the 2000s. The aim was not only to manage disruptions to the proceedings but also to control more tightly the activities of individual parliamentarians.

In addition to the 2008 and 2014 reforms regulating the form and content of parliamentary questions, the rules regarding the behaviour of MEPs in plenary session have also been changed in reaction to disruptions. A first reform occurred after two incidents in the late 1980s[6], which increased the powers of the EP's president and included sanctions for troublemakers. But it was not enough to discourage further disruptions. In 2005, British and Polish Eurosceptic MEPs refused to lower their banners opposing the vote on the European constitution despite the orders of the President. Their "not in my name" campaign disrupted the launch of the official information campaign on the Constitution, leading to agitation and scuffles, inside and outside the hemicycle.[7]

This type of incidents showed the limits of the rules: existing sanctions, notably expelling the troublemaker(s) from the plenary session and his/her deprivation of voting rights, were rarely applied as they infringe on the MEP's representative mandate.[8] As noted by this EP official, "there were doubts about what was legally possible and it was never used because the sanctions would go far and posed too many practical problems. The issue was therefore to find a way to discourage people from disrupting the proceedings. We have to guarantee the liveliness of the debates, to ensure the freedom of speech in the parliament but when the freedom of speech of some limits the freedom of speech of others…".

As a result, an in-depth reform was carried out in 2006 to regulate MEPs' behaviour. Principles of conduct and new sanctions were introduced in the rules of Procedure.[9] For the first time, the EP's rules included values, norms and principles that its members have to respect, such as the dignity of the parliament and the smooth conduct of parliamentary business. Since 2017, the rules also state that "Members shall not resort to defamatory, racist or xenophobic language or behaviour in parliamentary debates, nor in that context shall they unfurl banners" (rule 11). The rules also specify that "a distinction should be drawn between visual actions, which may be tolerated provided they are not offensive and/or defamatory, remain within reasonable bounds and do not lead to conflict, and those which actively disrupt any parliamentary activity whatsoever" (rule 166). They also extend the responsibility of MEPs to his/her entire staff, who must now respect the rules of conduct applicable to elected officials and, secondly, to all the EP buildings as assistants had participated in some disrupting events in the past.[10] Despite a careful phrasing, these rules govern MEPs' behaviour more strictly. New penalties were also introduced in 2006 and strengthened in 2017. They may now consist of one or more of the following measures: a reprimand, forfeiture of entitlement to the daily subsistence allowance for a period of between two and thirty days; temporary suspension from participation in all or some of the activities of parliament (for a period of between two and thirty days, without prejudice to the right to vote in plenary); and prohibition of the Member from representing the parliament on an inter-parliamentary delegation, inter-parliamentary conference or any inter-institutional forum, for up to one year and, in the case of a breach in the obligations of confidentiality, a limitation in the rights to access confidential or classified information for up to one year. These sanctions may be doubled in case of repeated offence.

The enforcement of these new sanctions is still quite controversial. It is sometimes difficult to identify all the troublemakers in case of a collective incident such as during the signature of the European Charter of Fundamental Rights in 2007, and some MEPs, such as the former Green President Cohn-Bendit, have been opposed to the exclusion of MEPs in the name of democracy. Overall, penalties are rarely applied.[11]

If these reforms have restricted the room for manoeuvre for Eurosceptics, they have also unexpectedly provided some of them with new opportunities, especially for public orators. The reforms have given them new arguments to denounce the European regime. As they see themselves as opposition speakers, they seek to break the so-called consensual nature of the chamber and express their views by all means. The new sanctions have therefore a limited effect on their "outrageous" behaviour and their untimely speeches. This is indeed one of the justifications for the increase in penalties as the hierarchy of the EP (mostly the Bureau) feels powerless to avoid such (repeated) behaviour. If they consist of a reprimand or fines, these sanctions give public orators the publicity they seek, and they can present themselves as victims of the system, as attested by the reactions in the media regarding the sanctions against Farage.[12] And if the sanctions consist of an exclusion from the EP's activities, it could be problematic to dismiss duly elected representatives and harm the institution's legitimacy.

In a nutshell, the formal rules have evolved in a dramatic way over the last 20 years. Although all MEPs are subject to the rules of procedure, they are crucial to understanding the room for manoeuvre of Eurosceptic members. The rationalization of the chamber's functioning led to the empowerment of political groups at the expenses of individual

MEPs. The latter have seen their rights, and the scope of their freedom shrink over time. As noted by Bardi and Ignazi (2004, p. 51), "for the individual MEP, whether marginal or marginalized within a group or non-attached, there are only crumbs: the meticulous and complete architecture of the EP leaves little room for manoeuver for free electrons, contrary to what happens in many national parliaments". Eurosceptics have few choices. They either integrate the EP's structures in order to be involved in parliamentary work and influence the decision-making process (through the roles of Pragmatist or Participant) or remain at the margins and resort to individual-type of actions such as speeches and questions (through the roles of Public Orator or Absentee). But the gradual reduction of debate and speaking time as well as the stricter regulation of parliamentary behaviour tend to deter from an excessive exit from traditional parliamentary activities on the one hand and to give new means for MEPs willing to denounce the system from the inside through nonconformist attitude (notably the public orators) on the other hand. But as the next section will show, it is mostly the informal rules which are constraining for Eurosceptic MEPs. Informal rules reinforce the impact of formal rules, leaving Eurosceptics with very limited options, between an insider and an outsider strategy within the institution.

2   INFORMAL RULES: A FURTHER RESTRICTION ON EUROSCEPTICS' ROOM FOR MANOEUVRE

Political actors respond to a combination of formal and informal incentives, and both should be taken into account to understand the institutional context in which elected representatives act (Helmke and Levinski 2004; Waylen 2010). The same applies to MEPs, whose behaviour is also conditioned by a series of non-written institutional rules, norms and traditions (Abélès 2001, p. 37). These informal rules can constitute both a resource and a constraint for Eurosceptic MEPs. This section first examines the way the EP works and how this affects the room for manoeuvre of Eurosceptic MEPs. It will then concentrate on the informal rules governing report allocations, and finally, it considers the consequences of political affiliation for Eurosceptics' strategies. Throughout the analysis, it will be shown how these informal rules act mostly as a constraining element for Eurosceptic MEPs, limiting the range of available strategies.

2.1   A Compromise-based Chamber

A first series of constraints for Eurosceptics stems from the position of the EP within the institutional system of the EU as well as the way the chamber works. For a long time, the EP was reduced to a talking shop: its members could devote a lot of time to debates in plenary, adopt ambitious resolutions and afford a more conflictual style with the other institutions (Costa 2001; Yordanova 2011). But the empowerment of the EP required a rationalization of its functioning: it led to a more efficient decision-making process and allowed the institution to have a united, and more moderate, position vis-à-vis the other institutions (Kreppel 2002, p. 101). But it also changed the way it operates, with a stronger emphasis on expertise, the need for pragmatic and variable coalitions and a decision-making process essentially based on compromise. In other words, we moved from a debate democracy to a negotiation democracy, as the MEPs became mostly experts whose aim is to reach an acceptable compromise: "the European Parliament is without doubt the best example of a watering down of debates and the empowerment of a negotiation democracy" (Abélès 2001, p. 134). The bulk of the agenda is now devoted to legislating, leaving little time for debates on the future of the EU which the EP has no formal power anyway. With the rare exceptions of debates on resolutions regarding treaties reforms, there are very few opportunities for discussions on the scope of European integration or the transfer of powers from the national to the supranational level. Yet, it is precisely on these issues related to national sovereignty and the pro-/ anti-EU dimension that many Eurosceptics have been elected. The lack of debates on those issues within the chamber makes it difficult for them to represent and stand for their voters and political platform.

More importantly, the way the EP works is characterized by a tendency to reach a compromise, requiring large coalitions across the left-right cleavage (Costa 2001, p. 328). The consensual nature of the chamber—some scholars even talking of an "institutionalized consensus" (Benedetto 2008) is derived from the internal decision-making mode, especially the proportional representation according to the D'Hondt method (Westlake 1994). Although coalitions may vary according to the issue under consideration, the EP tends to be dominated by a grand coalition composed of the Christian-democrats (EPP) and the Socialists (S&D), sometimes with the Liberals (or the "2 + 1 coalition") (Settembri 2006). This can be explained by several elements:

the ideological proximity between the two main political groups on fundamental issues (a social market economy and further integration in Europe), the technical nature of the texts under discussion which may reduce political competition; the moderating role of expertise; the pressure to overcome the high majority requirements imposed by the treaties; and the common desire of the two main groups for the EP to have a unified and strong position vis-à-vis the other institutions (Corbett et al. 2007; Corbett 1998; Costa 2001; Hix et al. 2007; Judge and Earnshaw 2008; Kreppel 2002). The tendency to resort to large coalitions is a way of simplifying the complexity of parliamentary work through division of labour among groups (Settembri 2006). It has three major implications for Eurosceptic MEPs.

First, the main groups work together on sensitive policies and issues. They do not want or need the support of small and marginal groups and can therefore avoid any compromise with Eurosceptics. As noted recently by the leader of the parliament's centre-right EPP group, Manfred Weber, "it is crucial this stability is safeguarded. We want to make sure that the role of radical and extremist MEPs is limited and that they cannot influence major EU decisions" (EU observer, 24 November 2016). Contrary to the situation of some anti-system actors in national parliaments, Eurosceptics are not numerous enough and are too fragmented within the chamber to have any blackmailing power (Benedetto 2008). Moreover, the decision-making rules give large groups forming a coalition a de facto veto power on the content of each report, forcing the minority to either seek the support of at least one of the two main groups for their text or amendment to be adopted (Hausemer 2006, p. 513) or to give up.

Second, the consensual nature of the decision-making process in the EP, combined with the technicality of the texts and the valorisation of expertise, leads to a lack of conflict within the European political system. As Neuhold and Settembri (2009, p. 135) found out in their study, EP committees play a key role in producing compromise: "while fulfilling the task of preparing the vote of the plenary, they are almost inevitably successful in building and offering a consensual deal". Votes in all committees and under all procedures are virtually unanimous, and political conflict is particularly weak. Any potential conflict tends to be dealt with ex ante, through an agreement between the most important parties. This tendency deters the emergence of a conflictual style within the EP and reduces the potential for constructive opposition. It keeps the EP from being the institutional forum for the expression of political opposition (Kohler 2014; Mair 2007; Neunreither 1998).

Third, the mode of deliberation with the EU, combined with the lack of electoral connexion at the European level tends to give incentives to MEPs to join the camp of compromise, or at least to be involved in legislative activities rather than remain in permanent opposition. At the national level, opposition parties can be rewarded by voters for systematic opposition. In the EP, on the contrary, Eurosceptic MEPs cannot hope to replace the governing coalition formed by the main groups whereas an involvement, even limited, could be synonymous of influence (Settembri 2006).

2.2   A Further Constraint for Eurosceptic MEPs: The Allocation of Reports

The situation of Eurosceptic MEPs is further constrained by the system for the allocation of resources in the EP, which is the D'Hondt method (i.e. proportional system, allocating resources depending on the size of each EP group). This method ensures the control of large groups over all facets of parliamentary activities. Not only do they cooperate closely during the legislative process, but they also control the Conference of the Presidents, share among themselves most of the chairmanships and vice-chairmanships, and they are overrepresented in the allocation of legislative reports.

MEPs derive substantial benefits from sitting in the two large political groups in terms of the informal arrangements inside the chamber, especially regarding reports. Being in charge of a report is considered to be one of the most important tasks for an MEP (Judge and Earnshaw 2008, p. 176). Yet, the allocation of reports is not defined in the rules of procedure and remains informal. It happens according to a complex bidding system, favouring a proportional allocation among party groups according to the size of their delegation. But the exact rules can vary from committee to committee, leading some to compare it to horse-trading or an elaborate poker game (Høyland 2006, p. 32; Hausemer 2006, p. 510). Basically, each political group has a quota of points, according to its size, and has to bid on each report, the value of each report being decided by the coordinators' meeting (codecision and budgetary reports are usually costlier) (Kaeding 2005; Yordanova 2011). To avoid a group saving its points to win an important or salient report, every group has to participate in the bid on each report (Yoshinaka et al. 2010). If, in theory, the allocation is proportional to the size of the group and should be fair for all national delegations within groups, studies have demonstrated that in practice, some actors are better placed than others to be rapporteurs (Yordanova 2011). More precisely, they showed that the system is not strictly proportional, and a series of factors influence the allocation of reports (Benedetto 2005; Høyland 2006; Kaeding 2005; Mamadouh and Raunio 2003; Yordanova 2009). The likelihood of being in charge of a report depends on the political affiliation of an MEP, his/her nationality, ideology, attitude towards European integration and the position of his/her national party at the national level. As a result, socialists and Christian-democrats tend to be overrepresented during report allocations and members of the three main groups (socialists, Christian-democrats and liberals) obtain most of the codecision and budgetary reports (Benedetto 2005; Kaeding 2005). Moreover, MEPs whose national party is in government are more likely to become rapporteurs, whereas MEPs from new Member states tend to be disadvantaged during their first term (Høyland 2006; Hurka and Kaeding 2012). Conversely, MEPs with extreme views, i.e. whose political positions are far from the median representative in the chamber, can only hope for minor reports, in low-saliency policy domains (Hausemer 2006).

Eurosceptic have very limited opportunities to be in charge of a report at all (Yoshinaka et al. 2010; Settembri 2004). Indeed, the leaders of the main political groups make sure that Eurosceptic MEPs are not in a position to promote their Eurosceptic views through important reports or exert influence on sensitive issues (interview CPE #8). It is not surprising to observe that Eurosceptic MEPs feel strongly discriminated against: "what I do feel though is that the ECR group within the parliament is not treated fairly, people appear to think less of us because we are in the ECR than they would have done had we been in the EPP. I don't really know why because it's a bit short-sighted but that's the way it is" (Interview with MEP 18). Radical right MEPs in particular have to face a "cordon sanitaire". With the majority of the chamber being hostile to their presence, these MEPs tend to be excluded from parliamentary activities, especially from responsibilities (Kestel 2008; Startin 2010). For instance, when radical right parties managed to form a (technical) group between 1984 and 1994, none of its members were elected as chairman of a committee, and the group was excluded from inter-group cooperation (Fieschi 2012). And the Identity, Tradition, Sovereignty radical right group (ITS, constituted and dissolved in 2007) was the only group not to be granted any report, chairmanship or vice-chairmanship of committee (Almeida 2010, p. 248). The issue of the cordon sanitaire resurfaced in October 2015 when a radical right MEP's amendment in the environment committee in order to ban a dangerous pesticide triggered a debate among the two main political groups on how to deal with such situations. In both groups (S&D and EPP), the French national delegations pushed for a strong cordon sanitaire so that no amendment from the radical right could be supported by the members of the S&D and EPP, whatever the content of the amendment.[13] This "political quarantine" is not limited to the radical right, as under the 8th legislature, the EFDD group has also faced the same obstacle: some of its members were candidates for vice-chairmanships which they were supposed to obtain according to the D'Hondt rule in use in the EP. But the proportional allocation of responsibilities according to the D'Hondt rule was bypassed by the main groups to avoid giving institutional positions to the EFDD: "we have had first-hand experience of that cordon sanitaire by the time we entered into the EP. We were denied all of the institutional positions in the parliamentary committees as well as the vice-presidency of the Parliament's Bureau. Here they have adopted the D'Hondt method, which is a gentlemen's agreement, that is to say, it is not an established rule but rather an agreement that was always followed and always respected by all parliamentary groups. This year, it was decided not to respect it and we were denied the charged which have been attributed to other parliamentary groups. This is not fine because democracy must respect majorities, minorities, oppositions and above all give everybody the possibility to establish a reputation. This is the democracy, otherwise it is a dictatorship of the majority" (Interview with MEP 91).[14]

In the light of this, Eurosceptics face a set of constraints. They generally belong to small groups; their political party, with some exceptions, is in the opposition at the national level, and their views are usually far from the median MEP, including on European integration. They are thus unlikely to be in charge of a (salient) report. Non-attached MEPs and small groups are, unsurprisingly, underrepresented in the report allocation and are responsible for less salient reports, worth few, or even no points in the bidding process (Almeida 2010, p. 248). One must add to this marginalization a tendency of

Eurosceptics to exclude themselves from the process. Indeed, they are in charge of few reports not only because of their radical positions but also because some of them do not want to be. Undeniably, as reports do not deal with central issues of their political programme, they trigger less interest on the part of Eurosceptics. Moreover, in order for a report to be adopted, the rapporteur needs to moderate his or her own opinion to achieve a centrist compromise and win the support of a majority of colleagues. This perspective is not attractive for elected representatives who have campaigned on an anti-establishment platform (Almeida 2010, p. 249). This dual process of marginalization due to the informal rules and of auto-exclusion explains the underrepresentation of Eurosceptics in the allocation of reports: "on the one hand, we are allocated very few reports, either because MEPs are not interested, because they don't want to be involved directly in the EP, or because the parliamentary committee does not want to give us sensitive reports. So we have the ones that are not really interesting. And when we may have an interesting report, the risk is to make a report that is politically unacceptable for the majority of the parliament. So for instance, Mr. X had a report for the constitutional affairs committee and of course, it was considered as unacceptable, unadoptable. The report remained at the committee stage and was never sent to the plenary. It shows the problem for our type of political group: either the MEP accepts a report, asks the staff of the committee to do it and ends up with a report he or she does not want to approve or the MEP writes it himself or herself and loses the majority to support it" (Interview CPE #2).

2.3 Parliamentary Group Affiliation

A last set of informal rules derive from the political affiliation of an MEP. As explained earlier, belonging to a (large or small) political group in the EP affects the MEP's access to resources within the chamber. But it can also influence his/her room for manoeuvre because of the rules and internal structure of the group.

The choice of a group has a significant impact for Eurosceptic MEPs (Benedetto 2008, p. 130). Joining a large group or a group such as the Greens/EFA and UEN (6th legislature) means agreeing on the fundamental principles of the group, i.e. reaching a compromise with non-Eurosceptic colleagues, including on European integration. It also means respecting the desire of the political group to be cohesive and not defecting too often from the EP group's line. In exchange for that, the member gets opportunities to influence the decision-making process and access to important internal resources.[15]

In this regard, a distinction should be made between small and large groups on the one hand and small and fringe groups on the other. The two largest groups provide their members with more resources and opportunities within the EP. But this goes hand in hand with stronger constraints in terms of respecting the group, its hierarchy and its cohesiveness.[16] Indeed, large groups have more incentive to be cohesive in order to continue dominating the legislative process at the European level (Hix et al. 2007). But some Eurosceptics, including the British Conservatives, sat within the EPP but in a separate branch, called the European Democrats, in order to have access to the resources provided by a large group but with more freedom, notably on votes on issues that were salient for their electorate. They could influence the positions taken by one of the main groups from within and have access to responsibilities within the EP (reports, chairmanships) while having some room for manoeuvre.

On the contrary, members of small marginal groups such as Ind/Dem (6th term), EFD (7th term), EFDD (8th term) and EUL/NGL or ENF have much more freedom from their group. But the latter offers them little influence due to their small size and their status at the fringes of the political arena. The Communist group (EUL/NGL) has opted for a confederal structure, leaving their members to vote as they see fit. As one of its former presidents explains, this structure "was required due to differences in historical cultures in a specific context (…) we don't usually vote in group meetings and there is little voting discipline. The most important thing is to know where the misunderstandings can come from and if we differ in our views, we assume this difference" (interview with MEP 56). If the monthly group meetings aim at reconciling the points of views, debates can be heated as the group is still characterized by several divisions, ranging from European integration to agriculture and fisheries policies. They share the same voting lists but sometimes for totally different reasons, and MEPs do not feel constrained by group discipline (interview A #3). Similarly, the charter of the Ind/Dem group (2004–2009), EFD group (2009–2014) and EFDD group (2014–2019) ensures the freedom to its members to vote as they see fit in the name of respect for national differences. These groups were created on the "agree to disagree" principle on many policies and therefore remain more technical groupings (rather than political ones): "it is a marriage of convenience. I am often on the same side as UKIP and opposed to the 5 star movement. We all share ideas such as the dislike of the Euro, of the EU bureaucracy but we can have different opinions about a lot of policies but it's not a problem" (Interview with MEP 76). Their members share a same opposition to the EU but have diversified preferences regarding numerous public policies. For instance, it can happen that during group meetings, some national delegations argue in favour of a common European immigration policy while other delegations are favourable to exiting the EU and do not want any common policy at all. This leads to contradictory voting behaviour in plenary, with some MEPs voting against proposals from their own EP group. Cohesion is therefore particularly low. However, it is worth noting that this type of group, especially the Ind/Dem group during the 6th legislature, tends to encourage an oppositional style from their members. Because leader(s) of the group as well as some national delegations see and present themselves as the only opposition in the chamber, they do not tolerate behaviour that could be perceived as too positive towards the EP.[17] Similarly, the newly constituted ENF group leaves great room for manoeuvre to its members and national delegations. Its charter explicitly states that "the parties and individual MEPs of the ENF Group recognize each other's right to defend their specific unique economic, social, cultural and territorial models". They can therefore vote and act as they see fit.

Members of the other small groups are in an intermediary situation. Small non-radical groups seek to achieve good internal cohesion in order to have some weight in the decision-making process whenever possible. However, national delegations among those groups remain the key elements, and MEPs have some freedom from their EP group on the topics relevant to their national party. For instance, each year, regionalist MEPs from the Greens/EFA group negotiate a work programme with the Greens (Brack and Kelbel 2016). Eurosceptic MEPs within the group do not feel obligated by the group's voting instructions, especially on topics related to the integration process (interviews with MEPs 49 and 29). Under the 6th legislature, the EUN group presented itself as a right-wing conservative and nationalist group. It was highly cohesive on economic questions but was very divided on institutional and constitutional issues (Brack 2008) as the national delegation remained the main principal of MEPs from that group. The ECR group for its part attempts to be cohesive not only on issues related to the left-right cleavage in order to appear as a partner for the EPP but also on topics regarding European integration to show its opposition to a federal Europe. But the daily activities are organized by the national delegations, which issue voting instructions. Group meetings tend to be rather short and aim at accommodating the interests and preferences of the various delegations without constraining them too much (meeting with D. Eppink, 17 September 2012 and interviews A #6 and #8).

Finally, non-attached members are per definition totally free. They have little institutional resources at their disposal but do not have to compromise with colleagues from other political parties. As summarized by a non-attached MEP: "we are not in a fraction, so we are freer to vote and speak in an independent way, according to the party programme and we do not have to make compromise" (Interview with MEP 68). They are only accountable to their national party and to voters.

In short, informal rules in the EP reinforce the effect of the formal rules: they also a source of resources but mostly of constraints for Eurosceptic MEPs. They restrict their room for manoeuvre. As noted by Settembri (2006, p. 24), "at the micro level, MEPs seem to be driven by a somewhat similar "be in" imperative, given that the EP institutional context makes much more remunerative in political terms a proactive participation than an enduring and consistent opposition. This is so because the system provides deputies with great incentives to come to an agreement and equally great disincentives to be against, especially on a permanent basis". The institutional context gives therefore incentives to Eurosceptics to either be involved in the parliamentary work, through the roles of pragmatist or participant, or to stay at the margins, with the roles of Public Orator and Absentee.

3   Conclusion

Roles are the interplay between institution and individual preferences (Searing 1994). Legislative rules and structures steer individual member's choices in certain directions, by encouraging and discouraging certain kinds of behaviour. The aim of this chapter was to examine the effect of the institutional context on the strategies available to Eurosceptic MEPs. More particularly, it analysed whether the roles played by Eurosceptics are influenced by the formal and informal rules of the EP.

A first part was dedicated to the formal rules. Indeed, parliamentary organization and procedures define a large part of the repertoire of parliamentarians' strategies (Strøm 2012, p. 97). This chapter showed that to deal with the empowerment of the institution and the increasing number of MEPs as well as the technicity of legislative proposals, the parliament has attempted to preserve its efficiency and ensure its legitimacy in the face of other institutions through frequent reforms of its Rules of Procedure. These reforms have progressively changed the rules of the game. They altered the balance of power between actors and led to a specialization and division of labour. They empowered political groups at the expense of individual MEPs, reduced the time allocated to debates and regulated more strictly the behaviour of elected representatives. A second part explored the constraints coming from the more informal rules, i.e. from how the chamber works and from the consensus-oriented decision-making process. The analysis revealed how the functioning of the EP as well as membership in a political group has consequences for the room for manoeuvre of Eurosceptics. Formal but mostly informal rules give incentives to Eurosceptic MEPs to "be in", to get involved in parliamentary work and to seek to influence the decision-making process. In other words, they incite them to play the role of Participant or Pragmatist. On the contrary, the rules tend to discourage Eurosceptics to stay in permanent opposition, synonymous of marginalization.

The institutional context impacts the range of roles available to Eurosceptic MEPs by affecting their room for manoeuvre. Rules help form a parliamentarian's sense of satisfaction or frustration inside the institution. Representatives may therefore not desire institutional influence, especially if they know that the formal and informal rules make it unlikely that they will be able to satisfy that goal in the future (see Davison et al. 2005). Eurosceptics have the choice between an insider and an outsider position. As they belong to a minority whose point of view has little chance of prevailing, they can be involved in the EP and join one of the non-fringe groups. Thereby, they accept some restraints but hope to benefit from the advantages and resources that belonging to such a group bring. As the next chapter will show, members of "larger" groups as well as of the Greens/EFA, UEN and ECR tend to play the roles of Pragmatist and Participant. Or Eurosceptics can remain in permanent opposition to reject the institution and any compromise. With limited resources, they tend to be structurally marginalized and to turn away from traditional parliamentary work to focus on individual-type actions. They then pursue a strategy of hindrance (Public Orator) or of empty chair (Absentee).

If the analysis sheds light on the variation between an insider (Pragmatist and Participant) and outsider (Public Orator and Absentee) strategies, the institutional context alone does not fully explain the roles of Eurosceptics. Due to the formal and informal rules, MEPs are more or less free to pick and choose a role but then they tailor it to suit their individual preferences. The next chapter will therefore be devoted to the other variables put forward by the literature and further test the hypothesis that roles are the result of the interaction between the institutional context and individual preferences.

NOTES

1. MEPs were contacted by fake lobbyists (actually Sunday Times journalists pretending to be lobbyists), and three MEPs accepted to submit amendments in exchange for money. These kinds of practices were not covered by the RoP. The rules were changed, and now, the Annex I on the Code of Conduct for Members of the European Parliament with respect to financial interests and conflicts of interest stipulates that MEPs should respect several principles such as disinterest, integrity, openness, diligence, honesty, accountability and respect for the parliament's reputation. They should refrain from obtaining or seeking to obtain any direct or indirect financial benefit or other reward.

2. This reform was highly contested at the time by many MEPs, especially by those who were non-attached. They considered this reform as a seizure of their rights as in most Member states, an individual MEP can table amendments in plenary sessions (Settembri 2004, p. 155).

3. See, for instance, the speeches of non-attached members during the debate on the report on the reform of the rules of procedure after the Lisbon Treaty, 23 November 2009, report D. Martin A7-0043/2009.

4. See speeches of Jo Leinen (S&D) and Monica Frassoni (Greens/EF) during the debate on the general revision of the Rules of Procedure, (report A6-0273/2009 Corbett), 5 May 2009.

5. Voting explanations on the Onesta report (A6-0413/2005), on the amendments to be made to the European Parliament's Rules of Procedure relating to standards for the conduct of Members of the European Parliament, 18–19 January 2006.

6. In 1988, Reverend Paisley disrupted the speech of Jean-Paul II and was expelled from the chamber. A year later, members of the radical right

protested against their exclusion from the allocation of responsibilities within the EP and provoked a brawl in the chamber.

7. N. Smith, «Vote no protest sparks EU scuffles», *The Telegraph*, 13 January 2005.

8. The sanctions were applied once in December 1997, against a Portuguese MEP who hit one of his Danish colleagues after a heated debate regarding subsidies for tobacco production. See Corbett et al. (2007), p. 181.

9. Onesta report A6-0413/2005 on the amendments to be made to the European Parliament's Rules of Procedure relating to standards for the conduct of Members of the European Parliament (2005/2075 (REG)).

10. The Corbett report of 2016 on the general revision of the rules proposes to extend this measure to any person for whom the member has arranged access to parliament's premises or equipment.

11. Giertych was sanctioned with a reprimand for the use of the parliamentary logo and diffusion of a racist pamphlet entitled "civilisation at war in Europe", which was against the fundamental values of the EU. N. Farage was more severely sanctioned for his insulting comments on the then President of the European Council Van Rompuy in a plenary session. As he refused to apologize, the President of the EP decided to deprive the British politician of 10 days of allowance (i.e. 2980€). In 2015, a Polish MEP (Korwin-Mikke) and Italian MEP (Buananno) were fined for a Nazi salute and references in the chamber and were suspended for ten days.

12. See in particular "Killing Dissent in Europe: Mr. Nigel Farage won't be the last victim", The Commentator, 24 September 2012.

13. See for instance Euractiv, "National Front stung in attempt to ban bee pesticide", 16 October 2015, http://www.euractiv.com/section/sustainable-dev/news/national-front-stung-in-attempt-to-ban-bee-pesticide/.

14. During the midterm changeover in January 2017, one MEP from EFDD became vice-chair of the JURI committee.

15. Most groups try to maintain high internal cohesion in order to have a united position during votes in order to influence the decisions. As highlighted by scholars, a significant part of the influence of EP groups depends on their cohesiveness, i.e. on the will of their members to abide by the group's rules and constraints (Bowler and Farrell 1995: 211).

16. Under the 6th legislature for instance, two dissenting voices who criticized the hierarchy of the EPP-ED during a plenary session were expelled from the group and ended up sitting with the non-attached.

17. During the 6th legislature, a MEP from Ind/Dem was very much involved in his committee: he was vice-chairman, in charge of several reports and proposed numerous amendments. His commitment triggered

tensions within the group and was strongly criticized by some, who questioned his Euroscepticism during group meetings. He was asked to propose amendments in his own name or with the support of his committee rather than in the name of the group. After the 2009 election, his successor changed group. (Interview CPE #2, observation group meetings and interviews with parliamentary assistants).

REFERENCES

Almeida, D. (2010). Europeanized eurosceptics? Radical right parties and European integration. *Perspectives on European politics and society, 11*(3), 237–253.

Bardi, L., & Ignazi, P. (2004). *Il Parlamento europeo.* Bologne, Il: Mulino.

Benedetto, G. (2005). Rapporteurs as legislative entrepreneurs: The dynamics of the codecision procedure in Europe's parliament. *Journal of European Public Policy, 12*(1), 67–88.

Benedetto, G. (2008). Explaining the failure of euroscepticism in the European parliament. In P. Taggart & A. Szczerbiak (Eds.), *Opposing Europe? The comparative party politics of euroscepticism* (pp. 127–150). Oxford: Oxford University Press.

Bowler, S., & Farrell, D. M. (1995). The organizing of the European parliament: Committees, specialization and coordination. *British Journal of Political Science, 25*(2), 219–243.

Brack, N. (2008). "Are Marginal EP party Groups Cohesive? A Comparison of UEN, EUL/NGL and IND/DEM", Summer School of the standing group de l'ECPR Political parties and European politics, European University Institute.

Brack, N., & Startin, N. (2017). To cooperate or not to cooperate? The European radical right and pan-European cooperation. In J. Fitzgibbon, B. Leruth, & N. Startin (Eds.), *Euroscepticism as a transnational and pan-European phenomenon.* London: Routledge.

Brack, N., Costa, O., & Dri, C. (2015). Le Parlement européen à la recherche de l'efficacité législative: une analyse des évolutions de son organisation. *Bruges political research papers, 39.*

Brack, N., & Kelbel, C. (2016). The Greens in the European Parliament. In Van Haute, E. (ed), *Green Parties in Europe* (pp. 217–237). London: Routledge.

Clinchamps, N. (2006). *Parlement européen et droit parlementaire. Essai sur la naissance du droit parlementaire de l'Union européenne.* Paris: LGDJ.

Corbett, R. (1998). *The European parliament's role in closer EU integration.* Houndmills: MacMillan Press.

Corbett, R., Jacobs, F., & Shackleton, M. (2007). *The European parliament.* London: John Harper.

Costa, O. (2001). *Le Parlement européen, assemblée délibérante.* Brussels: Editions de l'Université de Bruxelles.

Costa, O. (2010, May 28). Peut-on délibérer à l'échelle supranationale? La délibération au Parlement européen entre pratique démocratique et méthode de décision. *communication présentée à la journée d'études du groupe intercentres Gouvernance et délibération, Sciences Po Bordeaux.*

Davison, D., Krassa, M., & Reagan, D. (2005). The behavioural consequences of institutional rules: Republicans in the US house. *Journal of Legislative Studies, 11*(1), 38–56.

Fieschi, C. (2000). European institutions: The far right and illiberal politics in a liberal context. *Parliamentary Affairs, 53*(3), 517–531.

Giddens, A. (1984). *La constitution de la société. Elements de la théorie de la structuration.* Paris: PUF.

Halikiopoulou, D., & Vasilopoulou, S. (2014). Support for the far right in the 2014 European parliament elections: A comparative perspective. *The Political Quarterly, 85*(3), 285–288.

Hanley, D. (2007). *Beyond the nation state. Parties in the era of European integration.* Palgrave MacMillan: Basingstoke.

Hausemer, P. (2006). Participation and political competition in committee report allocation under what conditions Do MEPs represent their constituents? *European Union Politics, 7*(4), 505–530.

Helmke, G., & Levitsky, S. (2004). Informal institutions and comparative politics: A research agenda. *Perspective on Politics, 2*(4), 725–740.

Hix, S. (2002a). Parliamentary behavior with two principals: Preferences, parties and voting in the European parliament. *American Journal of Political Science, 46*(3), 688–698.

Hix, S. (2002b). Constitutional agenda setting through discretion in rule interpretation: Why the European parliament won at Amsterdam. *British Journal of Political Science, 32*(2), 259–280.

Hix, S., Noury, A., & Roland, G. (2007). *Democratic politics in the European parliament.* Cambridge: Cambridge University Press.

Hoyland, B. (2006). Allocation of codecision reports in the fifth European parliament. *European Union Politics, 7*(1), 30–50.

Hurka, S., & Kaeding, M. (2012). Report allocation in the European parliament after eastern enlargement. *Journal of European Public Policy, 19*(4), 512–529.

Judge, D., & Earnshaw, D. (2008). *The European parliament.* Basingstoke: Palgrave Macmillan.

Kaeding, M. (2005). The world of committee reports: Rapporteurship assignment in the European parliament. *Journal of Legislative Studies, 11*(1), 82–104.

Kestel, L. (2008). Le Front national au Parlement européen: Professionnalisation politique et ressources partisans. In L. Neumayer, A. Roger, & F. Zalewski (Eds.), *L'Europe contestée. Espaces et enjeux des positionnements contre l'intégration européenne* (pp. 210–231). Paris: Michel Houdiard Éditeur.

Kohler, M. (2014). European governance and the European parliament: From talking shop to legislative powerhouse. *Journal of Common Market Studies, 52*(3), 600–615.

Kreppel, A. (2002). *The European parliament and supranational party system: A study in institutional development.* New York: Cambridge University Press.

Kreppel, A. (2003). Necessary but not sufficient: Understanding the impact of treaty reform on the internal development of the EP. *Journal of European Public Policy, 10*(6), 884–911.

Mair, P. (2007). Political opposition and the European union. *Government and Opposition, 42*(1), 1–17.

Mamadouh, V., & Raunio, T. (2003). The Committee System: Powers, Appointments and Report Allocation. *Journal of Common Market Studies, 41*(2), 333–351.

March, J. G., & Olsen, J. P. (2005). Elaborating the new institutionalism. *Arena working paper,* 11.

Neuhold, C., & Settembri, P. (2009). Achieving consensus through committees: Does the European parliament manage? *Journal of Common Market Studies, 47*(1), 127–151.

Neunreither, K. (1998). Governance without opposition: The case of the European union. *Government and Opposition, 33*(4), 435–438.

Rasmussen, A., & Toshkov, D. (2011). The Inter-institutional division of power and time allocation in the European parliament. *West European Politics, 34*(1), 71–96.

Searing, D. (1994). *Westminster's world. Understanding political roles.* Cambridge: Harvard University Press.

Settembri, P. (2004). When is a group not a political group? The dissolution of the TDI group in the EP. *The Journal of Legislative Studies, 10*(1), 150–174.

Settembri, P. (2006). *Is the European Parliament competitive or consensual… 'and why bother'?* In Conference "The European Parliament and the European Political Space", London.

Sheingate, A. (2010). Rethinking rules: Creativity and constraint in the US house of representatives. In K. Thelen & J. Mahoney (Eds.), *Explaining institutional change: Ambiguity, agency, and power* (pp. 168–203). New York: Cambridge University Press.

Startin, N. (2010). Where to for the radical right in the European parliament? The rise and fall of transnational political cooperation. *Perspectives on European Politics and Society, 11*(4), 429–449.

Strøm, K. (2012). Roles as strategies: Towards a logic of legislative behavior. In M. Blomgren & O. Rozenberg (Eds.), *Parliamentary roles in modern legislatures* (pp. 85–100). London: Routlege/ECPR studies in European Political Science.

Waylen, G. (2010). Researching ritual and the symbolic in parliaments: An institutionalist perspective. *The Journal of Legislative Studies, 16*(3), 352–365.

Westlake, M. (1994). *A modern guide to the European parliament,* Pinter Publisher.

Williams, M. (1995). The European parliament: Political groups, minority rights and the 'rationalizations' of parliamentary organization. A research note. In

H. Döring, *Parliaments and the majority rules in Western Europe* (pp. 931–404). New York: St Martin's Press.

Yordanova, N. (2009). The Rationale behind Committee Assignment in the European Parliament: Distributive, Informational and Partisan Perspectives. *European Union Politics, 10*(2), 253–280.

Yordanova, N. (2011). The European parliament: In need of a theory. *European Union Politics, 12*(4), 597–617.

Yoshinaka, A., McElroy, G., & Bowler, S. (2010). The appointment of rapporteurs in the European parliament. *Legislative Studies Quarterly, 35*(4), 457–486.

CHAPTER 6

Explaining the Roles of Eurosceptic MEPs

One of the main challenges of role theory is explaining the choice of a role. Members of parliament tend to have diverging views on representation, their mandate and on how they should behave. In the case of the EP, the rationalization of the chamber's work and the specialization of its members have not yet led to homogeneous strategies for MEPs, quite the contrary. Studies have revealed that there is still a lot of variation in the way MEPs conceive of and carry out their representative mandate (Navarro 2009; Scully and Farrell 2007). This heterogeneity of views and behaviours can also be found among Eurosceptics as they can choose among four roles: the Absentee, the Public Orator, the Pragmatist or the Participant.

To explain this variance among roles, three main elements are generally put forward in the literature: institutional variables, mainly the electoral system and the institutional context, cultural factors and individual-level variables. The structuring hypothesis of this book states that roles depend on the interaction between the institutional context and the MEPs' preferences regarding European integration and the EU. The previous chapter was dedicated to the institutional context. The analysis of the EP's formal and informal rules reveals that the institutional context is a key element to understand the roles played by Eurosceptic MEPs. Indeed, the rules of the game have an impact on the room for manoeuvre of Eurosceptic members and determine the range of strategies available to them. But the institutional context alone does not explain the variety of roles played by Eurosceptic MEPs. And it's

© The Author(s) 2018   147
N. Brack, *Opposing Europe in the European Parliament*,
Palgrave Studies in European Union Politics,
https://doi.org/10.1057/978-1-137-60201-5_6

time to turn to the second part of the hypothesis to test whether MEPs' preferences regarding the EU and European integration influence the role they chose to play. Whereas attitudes and preferences are usually used in the literature as "an explanatory complement" to other factors; it is argued here that MEPs' preferences are key to explaining their roles. In order to test this hypothesis, it will examine whether the roles played by Eurosceptics are influenced by the degree and nature of their Euroscepticism. But alternative hypothesis put forward by the literature will also be tested such as the impact of the electoral system as well as of nationality, political affiliation and political background of MEPs.

To do so, this chapter relies on two types of data. First, the interviews conducted with Eurosceptic MEPs provided information on their personal position vis-à-vis the EU and the integration process. They were asked how they would situate themselves regarding European integration, what they think of the EU and its institutions, which reforms were necessary and which power, if any, should be transferred to the EU or back to the national level. Second, for each of these MEPs, data were collected on their background (seniority in the parliament, previous political experiences), country, including its electoral system, and EP group. In order to examine the relation between the typology of roles and the other variables, a combination of methods is used. Indeed, qualitative analysis and bivariate analysis make it possible to assess the existence and strength of a relationship between the variables under consideration. Then, a multivariate analysis provides some answers as to the relation between all the variables in one model. The first two sections analyse individual-level factors: the first one will be devoted to the main argument, i.e. the impact of MEPs' preferences regarding Europe on their roles, while the second one will concentrate on the relationship between the background of MEPs and the roles they play. The third section will examine more macro-level elements, i.e. the relation between parliamentary roles, nationality, political affiliation and the electoral system. A final section aims at determining the key variables explaining the choice of a role by Eurosceptics. The analysis reveals the relevance of the degree and the nature of MEPs' opposition to the European political system to understand their strategies within the parliament. Beyond their shared Eurosceptic label, MEPs have diverging attitudes towards the EU and the integration process, ranging from a hard Eurosceptic position to a soft Eurosceptic stance. Taking an actor-centred approach, this chapter shows how important it is to take into account individual preferences regarding the political regime in order to understand the strategies of anti-system actors.

1   Parliamentary Roles and Attitudes Towards Europe

Attitudes towards European integration and the EU can be considered to influence the way MEPs conceive of and carry out their mandate. The study by Wessels (2005) for instance shows that MEPs have diverging preferences on the European political system as well as on the role of the EP and that these preferences influence their strategies. Similarly, Scully and Farrell (1995, 2007) noted that MEPs' attitudes towards the EP are essential to understanding how they see their representative mandate.

However, most of those works tend to see these preferences as secondary to other elements such as the electoral system or the social backgrounds of legislators. Here, these attitudes are at the core of the explanatory model. It is indeed argued that the roles played by Eurosceptics depend primarily on their attitudes towards European integration and the EU institutions.

Of course, the focus here is on Eurosceptic MEPs as anti-system actors. The analysis therefore concentrates on negative attitudes towards Europe. Nevertheless, research on Euroscepticism demonstrates that Eurosceptic actors have heterogeneous views on Europe, just as pro-EU actors do. They have diverging preferences as to what kind of cooperation is necessary and desirable at the European level and on the powers of each EU institutions.

The analysis of the interviews reveals three categories of attitudes towards Europe. Two correspond to the categories proposed by Szczerbiak and Taggart (2002, 2008) who distinguished soft and hard Euroscepticism. These two categories are seen here as a continuum with a middle category which corresponds to intergovernmentalism.

The first position corresponds to hard Euroscepticism, i.e. a principled opposition towards any institutionalized political or economic cooperation at the supranational level if it implies a loss of sovereignty. These MEPs are opposed to European integration and to its underlying principles. They stress the need to stop European integration and replace it with a form of free-trade agreement. They are often in favour of their country exiting the EU and reject any constraints on national sovereignty: "I think that in the future Germany should go out of the European Union because the European parliament is a copy of the parliament of the United States and we don't want that for Europe" (interview MEP 83). As a result, any transfer of power from the national to the supranational level is rejected by hard Eurosceptics. They usually argue for bilateral free-trade agreements between countries although some are more inspired by other forms of cooperation such as the Commonwealth (interview MEP 57). Unsurprisingly, hard Eurosceptic MEPs are very critical of the EU and its institutions, which are seen as corrupt, non-democratic and impossible to reform. Such MEPs do not propose arguments or plans to reform the institutional architecture of the EU: "The EU is beyond reform and it deserves to be put out of its misery. (…) It's taking too much power to the center and it does not respect the democratic wishes of the states" (Interview MEP 40). Their position on the EP is hostile as well. They consider it to be a useless institution, lacking any real power and are usually in favour of dismantling it although some of them would keep it as a forum for debates, as long as the EP did not have any constraining power. For instance, this MEP explains: "now would I be in favor of a forum like the EP? No if the EP didn't pretend to be a parliament, it would be ok, if we are talking about a body that occasionally meets for exchange of views across Europe, possibly to reduce tensions" (interview MEP 4).

A second position refers to intergovernmentalism. These Eurosceptics are not opposed to belonging to the EU or to an institutionalized cooperation at the European level, as long as it is an intergovernmental cooperation in which the Member states are central: "we do not want Europe as it is, with a president, a service for foreign affairs and a diplomatic service. We do not want to exit the EU like UKIP does. But Member states should remain sovereign, there shouldn't be any political integration or federal Europe" (interview MEP3). These MEPs consider nation states to be the only suitable and legitimate level for democratic governance and therefore, only an intergovernmental Europe or a confederation, leaving national sovereignty intact, is desirable for them: "I would go back to the start of the European project, which was a cooperation among sovereign states such as the Ariane project. I think we should go back to that and then decide what we want to do regarding our borders, our currencies, etc." (interview MEP 85). They usually consider that European integration has gone too far and opposed the pursuit of integration as it stands, let alone any further transfer of power to the EU: "I think it's gone far enough. I am not keen on further political

integration" (interview MEP 18). They are very critical of the orientations of the integration process and would generally go back to a previous stage of that process: "My opinion is that the process goes the
wrong way, it is a mistake, a mistake from the basis and I think that this
frame was wrong from the treaties of Maastricht and further" (interview MEP 6). If most stress their opposition to political integration and
would limit European cooperation to an economic union with a single
market, others emphasize their reluctance to the economic orientation
of the integration process. Especially since the global financial crisis,
some Eurosceptic parties argue for a profound reform of the economic
policies of the EU or even for their country to exit the Eurozone: "as
a movement, we have a fairly clear idea regarding the euro: we have
always said that we are not against Europe, we do not want to destroy
Europe but the Euro does not work and we want to get out of this
money" (interview MEP 89). Contrary to hard Eurosceptics, these
MEPs have ideas to reform the EU's institutional architecture in the
direction of a central place for Member states. They are usually against
the Community method and favour an intergovernmental method, with
unanimity as the voting system in the Council of the EU in order to
provide each country with a veto power: "the first thing I would do
is transfer more responsibilities to the Member states, in conformity
with the subsidiarity principle. The national level is the best to evaluate the situation and take appropriate measures" (Interview MEP 92).
They would like to reduce the powers of supranational institutions
especially the Commission and the EP in order to give more power
to the Council and to the European Council: "institutionally I would
close down the EP and have a 2 chambers system with the Council and
the national parliaments. Then I would take the right of initiative from
the Commission and give it to the Council and I would redefine the
objectives of the Court so that it can no longer make political decisions, but only a less ambitious way to interpret the law. The Economic
and social committee and the committee of the regions can disappear
because it's basically just a waste of money. On the division of powers,
I would put much more focus on elements of the treaties linked to economic growth, rather than social benefits or third countries aid, inferior
issues" (interview MEP 70). As a result, they favour a transfer of legislative power from the EP to national parliaments, although they are not
opposed to the EP as such which could be used as a forum to defend
national interests, as long as it does not have strong legislative powers.

The third and last position corresponds to soft Euroscepticism. It is a moderate opposition to the integration process, in particular as a political project. These Eurosceptics see European integration as an undesired constraint or even a necessary evil: "We want less EU. But there are topics that can only be solved at the European level, but it's not the majority, so we should reduce everything. Asylum policy makes sense at the European level. For foreign policy we also should try to find a common line. But it must not be an excuse for all the rest" (interview MEP 82). They accept the principle of an institutionalized cooperation, with a more or less integrated common market and some transfers of sovereignty but they want to limit these. They oppose any idea of a European superstate, of a United States of Europe, but consider that supranational cooperation is necessary in order to deal with cross-border issues or to defend their national interests on the global level: "We are in favour of the single market but against any federation. Certain decisions should be taken at the EU level for efficiency purposes: the environment, transnational crime, the economy" (interview MEP 23). According to them, we should re-evaluate the added-value of European integration to reform the balance of power between the EU and nation states and emphasis should be put on subsidiarity as well as the respect of diversity: "We want less EU, in the sense that only decisions that are really necessary should be taken by the EU. Now for a majority of the decisions, there is no need to take them here. But there are topics that can only be solved at the European level, but it's not the majority so we should reduce everything that is done here to a minimum. Asylum policy makes sense at the European level, foreign policy we should try to find a common line, it has to do with geographical arrangements as we understand ourselves as one bloc, environment might be something, but it must not be an excuse for everything but these are topics where we should work together more" (interview MEP 82). This group also includes "resigned" Eurosceptics, who would prefer a purely intergovernmental Europe or who even campaigned against their country joining the EU but who today argue that it is utopic to wish to rewrite history. They prefer dealing with the reality such as it is and adopting a more moderate position by concentrating their criticism on the EU. They consider that "EU integration is the future of the continent, it has to be done in a globalized world. It does not mean that I like it but it's like this" (interview MEP 63). As far as the EU is concerned, moderate Eurosceptics are essentially reformists: "I have been a long standing critic of what's going on in the EU. But I was never one of those people who said we have to leave. I never wanted to destroy the European Union. I saw that there are some merits to it and there are some advantages for us to belong to it, up to a point but we need major reform" (interview MEP 72). They denounce the lack of transparency and accountability of the EU as well as the elitist nature of its institutions. They stress the democratic deficit of the EU and develop ideas on ways to reform how the institutions work, to increase the transparency of the Council or the legitimacy of the Commission. These Eurosceptics are usually in favour of the empowerment of the EP: the chamber is seen as the only legitimate and democratic institution to represent citizens and counterbalance the technocratic nature of the Commission "Every strengthening of integration must also have a strengthening of democracy and of the role of the European parliament, which is the only institution elected by the people. Especially the role of the Council today is very bad and it is a clear obstacle to the integration. The role of parliament should be strengthened, and also the citizens' initiative should be reformed. It should absolutely become legally bounding in the sense that the commission should give an answer and should propose legislative acts answering to the citizens' initiatives" (interview MEP 90). However, they remain critical of the way the EP works and consider that in-depth reforms are needed to alleviate the democratic deficit: "I am not of the opinion that automatically granting new powers to the EP will make the whole decision-making process more transparent and easier" (interview MEP 61).

According to the hypothesis, it is expected that these diverging attitudes towards European integration and the EU influence MEPs' roles. More precisely, a stronger opposition to Europe will discourage Eurosceptic MEPs from being involved in parliamentary work and that they play rather the role of the Absentee or of the Public Orator. On the contrary, moderate Eurosceptics would want to engage themselves in the work of the EU and try to reform it from the inside, through the roles of Pragmatist or Participant.

If we look at the Table 6.1, we see that the data seem to validate the hypothesis. Hard Eurosceptics are only found among Absentees and Public Orators while soft Eurosceptics are mostly found among Pragmatists and Participants. Intergovernmentalists for their part are split: the majority of them play the role of Pragmatist but a significant minority is found among Public Orators and 13.8% of them are Participants. The vast majority of Absentees and Public Orators are hard

Table 6.1   Euroscepticism and parliamentary roles

			Euroscepticism			Total
			Hard Eurosceptic	Intergovernmentalist	Soft Eurosceptic	
Role	Absentee	Count	6	2	1	9
		%	28.6	6.9	2.0	8.9
	Public orator	Count	15	7	2	24
		%	71.4	24.1	3.9	23.8
	Pragmatist	Count	0	16	30	46
		%	0.0	55.2	58.8	45.5
	Participant	Count	0	4	18	22
		%	0.0	13.8	35.3	21.8
Total		Count	21	29	51	101
		%	100.0	100.0	100.0	100.0

$p < 0.001$; Cramer's $V = 0.556$, $\lambda = 0.314$

Eurosceptics while 65% of Pragmatists and 82% of Participants are soft Eurosceptics. The analysis also shows that these two variables are substantially related: the measure of association indicates that there is a significant relation between the level of Euroscepticism and the roles played by MEPs.

At this point, the hypothesis seems corroborated by the data: the roles played by Eurosceptic MEPs are indeed influenced by their attitudes towards Europe. A stronger opposition to Europe tends to lead MEPs to choose an outsider role, such as the Absentee and the Public Orators whereas soft Eurosceptics seem more likely to play the roles of Pragmatists or Participants. However, the literature on role theory puts forward an alternative hypothesis and other variables need to be tested in order to assess the relevance of the attitudes towards Europe for understanding the roles of Eurosceptic MEPs.

2   SOCIAL BACKGROUND AND PARLIAMENTARY ROLES

The social background of parliamentarians is often mentioned as an individual-level variable to explain the variation in the way they conceive of and carry out their mandate. Scholars have indeed argued that legislators come from various backgrounds and that roles cannot be explained by general elements such as nationality or the electoral system. They tend to emphasize the effect of previous political experiences, which could impact the way members of parliament react to their environment (Bale and Taggart 2006; Beauvallet and Michon 2010; Navarro 2007). Others consider that seniority is the key variable to understand the way elected representatives act. Mughan and his colleagues (1997) for instance show in their study on the House of Commons that the time spent in the institution influences the degree of radicalism of parliamentarians. The most radical members would gradually become socialized and less extreme in their behaviours and attitudes. According to this strand of research, there would thus be a relation between seniority and roles, either because of institutional socialization or because of the career interests of legislators (Beyers 2010; Lewis 2005).

Table 6.2 examines the relations between the roles played by Eurosceptics and their previous political experiences. These include any mandate at the local, regional, national or international level, from local councillor to civil servant in an international or European organization, before entering the EP. It could have been expected that people with previous experience would be more likely to play the game in the institution in order to be influential (Participant) or to defend local or regional interest in the chamber (for instance through the role of pragmatist). To a certain extent, the analysis reveals that Eurosceptics playing the roles

Table 6.2 Political experience and parliamentary roles

			Previous political experience		Total
			None	Yes	
Role	Absentee	Count	6	3	9
		%	66.7	33.3	100.0
	Public orator	Count	15	9	24
		%	62.5	37.5	100.0
	Pragmatist	Count	21	25	46
		%	45.7	54.3	100.0
	Participant	Count	7	15	22
		%	31.8	68.2	100.0
Total		Count	49	52	101
		%	48.5	51.5	100.0

$p > 0.1$, Cramer's $V = 0.237$, $\lambda = 0.087$

of Participant or Pragmatist tend to have had some political experience before entering the EP. Indeed, most of the Participants and the Pragmatists have had political experience at another level before being elected as MEP. Or, in other words, 75% of those with political experience before sitting in the EP play the roles of Pragmatist or Participant. At the same time, there is a significant minority of Absentees and Public Orators with political experience and of Pragmatists and Participants without any. Overall though, the relation does not seem significant ($p > 0.1$).

However, it must be noted that the size of the sample and the particular nature of the population under consideration do not allow to draw a general conclusion regarding the relationship between political experience and roles. There has been no in-depth analysis of the trajectories of Eurosceptics here as it is not the purpose of this study, contrarily to some studies in political sociology (Michon and Beauvallet 2010; Georgakakis 2012). But the results shown in Table 6.2 seem to go along with the conclusion of Wessels' study (2005) which demonstrated that the previous political experiences of legislators have a limited effect on their roles.

We now turn to seniority. The general idea within the literature is that the time spent in the institution will have an impact on the role played by a parliamentarian. In other words, does seniority in the EP lead to a moderation in the behaviour of Eurosceptic MEPs? Do more senior MEPs tend to play the roles of Pragmatist or Participant rather than remaining outsiders (Absentee and Public Orator)?

The analysis reveals that Eurosceptic MEPs in their first mandate (junior) tend to choose the roles of Pragmatist and, to a lesser extent, of Public Orator. But senior Eurosceptics (in their second mandate or later) tend also to be found among Pragmatists as well as among Participants (Table 6.3). The majority of Absentees (56%), Public Orators (71%) and Pragmatists (63%) are in their first mandate whereas 73% of Participants are at least in their second mandate. So contrary to the findings of Navarro (2009), there seems to be a moderate relation between seniority and roles ($p < 0.05$, Cramer's $V = 0.322$). Eurosceptics returning to the EP seem to a certain extent more likely to play the role of Pragmatist or Participant or Eurosceptics playing those roles are more likely to stand for election again and be re-elected.[1]

Table 6.3 Seniority and parliamentary roles

			Seniority		Total
			Junior	2nd mandate or more	
Role	Absentee	Count	5	4	9
		%	8.8	9.1	8.9
	Public orator	Count	17	7	24
		%	29.8	15.9	23.8
	Pragmatist	Count	29	17	46
		%	50.9	38.6	45.5
	Participant	Count	6	16	22
		%	10.5	36.4	21.8
Total		Count	57	44	101
		%	100.0	100.0	100.0

$p < 0.05$, Cramer's $V = 0.322$, $\lambda = 0.101$

3   POLITICAL AFFILIATION, ELECTORAL SYSTEM AND PARLIAMENTARY ROLES

A last set of factors put forward by the literature to explain the variation in the strategies developed by legislators is more general and refers to more macro-level elements such as the electoral system, political affiliation as well as political culture.

A recent study by Wessels and Giebler (2011) shows that parliamentarians have diverging views of their mandate and that this variation can be explained no so much by the electoral system but by their individual characteristics as well as their political affiliation. Hagger and Wing (1979) stressed the influence of nationality on the way MEPs perceive their mandate. And Katz (1999) argued that parliamentary roles can be explained by cultural factors, i.e. by national differences regarding the expectations and demands towards parliamentarians. He considers for instance that British legislators devote attention to their constituency not because of the electoral system since they are elected on closed lists but because of the British political culture.

The majority of studies though emphasize the key role of the electoral system: variations in electoral rules lead to different behaviours and views of representation among members of parliament (Bowler and Farrell 1993). Farrell and Scully (2007) analysed the role orientations of MEPs in order to show that nationality does not account for the variation in the way MEPs conceive of and carry out their mandate. More particularly, they revealed that MEPs coming from a country with open lists and a more personalized electoral system devote more time and attention to their constituency as well as to territorial representation. Indeed, open lists and the possibility to express a preference vote tend to put the focus on the individual candidate rather than the political party. Voters may reward or punish an MEP on the basis of his/her performance. Therefore, individual MEPs have an incentive to be responsive to voters and seek a personal vote (Hix and Hagermann 2009; Wessels 2005). But Farrell and Scully also show that if the electoral system influences the roles of MEPs, its impact remains moderate and does not fully account for the differences in their attitudes and behaviour. This has to do, among other things, with the relative uniformity of the electoral rules for EU elections: although each Member state can set its own procedure for the election of its MEPs in terms of ballot structure, district magnitude, etc., they have to respect a number of broad principles (proportional representation being the most important one in this case) which limit the possible variations of electoral systems. As a result, studies have shown that electoral system-related factors matter but are not all-important for shaping the attitudes and behaviours of MEPs, leading some to conclude that it is "not easy to explain individual subjective attitudes to the role of representative with broad and objective criteria" (Scully and Farrell 2007, p. 112).

The aim here is certainly not to settle the controversy on the respective impact of cultural factors vs electoral system-related variables but rather to examine their effect on the roles played by Eurosceptic MEPs. To do so, a bivariate analysis examines the relation between the typology of roles on the one hand and political affiliation, nationality and two electoral system-related factors on the other hand.

3.1   Political Affiliation and Parliamentary Roles

Table 6.4 shows the bivariate analysis between the roles of Eurosceptic MEPs and the EP group they belong to. Two main conclusions can be drawn from it. First, Eurosceptics from fringe right-wing political groups as well as non-attached members tend to remain outsiders. They mostly play the roles of Absentee or Public Orator. Indeed, 53.8% of non-attached members, 60% of the radical right ENF group and 34% of the members of Ind/Dem—EFD(D) choose the role of Public Orator. In addition to that, 15.4% of non-attached members and

Table 6.4   EP political group and parliamentary roles

			Ep group					
			Greens +GUE/ NGL	ECR + ED	Ind/ Dem + EFD(D)	ENF	NA	Total
Role	Absentee	Effectif	0	1	6	0	2	9
		% dans EP group	0,0%	4,3%	17,1%	0,0%	15,4%	8,9%
	Public orator	Effectif	0	2	12	3	7	24
		% dans EP group	0,0%	8,7%	34,3%	60,0%	53,8%	23,8%
	Pragmatist	Effectif	16	10	14	2	4	46
		% dans EP group	64,0%	43,5%	40,0%	40,0%	30,8%	45,5%
	Participant	Effectif	9	10	3	0	0	22
		% dans EP group	36,0%	43,5%	8,6%	0,0%	0,0%	21,8%
Total		Effectif	25	23	35	5	13	101
		% dans EP group	100,0%	100,0%	100,0%	100,0%	100,0%	100,0%

$p < .001$, Cramer's $V = .367$, $\lambda = .107$

17.1% of members of Ind/Dem and EFD(D) group choose the role of Absentee. However, it should also be noted that a significant minority of the members of ENF and Ind/Dem and EFD(D) groups play the role of Pragmatist. So the members of these groups tend to remain at the margin of parliamentary work, in part because of institutional constraints (see Chap 5) but are split, with some attempting to get involved, in a limited way, in the EP's work through the role of Pragmatist. Second, Eurosceptics from left-wing groups and from the ECR group mostly play the roles of Pragmatist or Participant. A majority of Eurosceptics from the left (Greens and EUL/NGL) play the role of Pragmatist while 36% of them choose the role of Participant. Overall, 35% of Pragmatists and 41% of the MEPs playing the role of Participant are found among left-wing Eurosceptics. Members of the ECR group play either the role of

Pragmatist or Participant. They are thus much more involved in parliamentary work and choose an insider strategy. While 45% of Participants are found among the members of the ECR group, half of the Public Orators and 67% of the Absentees are found among the Ind/Dem or EFD(D) groups. The members of these two right-wing Eurosceptic groups have very different strategies inside the chamber, compared to their colleagues from other political groups.

It seems here that political affiliation has an impact on the roles played by Eurosceptics. But this relation also refers to the institutional context. As shown in the previous chapter, the formal and informal rules of the EP limit some actors' room for manoeuvre. Fringe actors, i.e. radical right MEPs, non-attached members and to some extent members of the Ind/Dem and EFD(D) groups face significant constraints, notably because of the cordon sanitaire. These restrictions, combined with self-exclusion mechanisms, lead these MEPs to prefer individual-type actions, such as speeches rather than involvement in policy-making. Moreover, belonging to a political group also brings some constraints in terms of rules, norms and standards of behaviour. Although small groups, where most Eurosceptic MEPs sit, leave their members room for manoeuvre, one could hypothesize that there is a "valorization" effect of particular behaviours and attitudes among some groups. Indeed, if a role is dominant among a group, it could reflect the fact that particular behaviours tend to be appreciated and others discouraged. It appears from the interviews as well as from my observation of group meetings that the EUL/NGL group tends to promote a collective view of parliamentary work and some degree of involvement of its members in the work of the parliament. On the contrary, leaders of the Ind/Dem and EFD groups tended to encourage protest actions and were reluctant towards an active and positive involvement in parliamentary work. This was particularly the case in the 6th legislature within the Ind/Dem group.[2] It is therefore not surprising that a significant share of their members is found among Absentees and Public Orators.

Furthermore, it should be noted that it is not the individual MEPs but national political parties which decide on the choice of an EP group, on the basis of various criteria such as political congruence, pragmatism and the political context (Bressannelli 2012; Whitaker and Lynch 2014). The choice of a role might depend on the national party, more particularly on the type of party it is, what its goals are and how radical it is. On the one hand, MEPs from large or mainstream parties aim at governing at the national level and at influencing policies. On the other hand, we need to distinguish between small parties, which are moderate and want to be seen as potential coalition partners, and fringe radical parties. As noted by Deschouwer (2008), when a small party enters a governing coalition or supports the government, this creates tensions within the party. This is especially true for Eurosceptic parties as it entails forsaking their anti-establishment stance and moderating their principled opposition. Fringe parties, which do not seek to govern, can just concentrate on their opposition and their responsiveness to their voters, without moderating their stances.

The sample here is too limited to draw any conclusions on the relation between national parties and the roles of Eurosceptics. But we can see from Fig. 6.1 that some parties are more present in some roles. For instance, members of the British Conservatives, of the Polish PiS and of the Czech ODS tend to be mostly found among Pragmatists and Participants. They are members of mainstream parties at the national

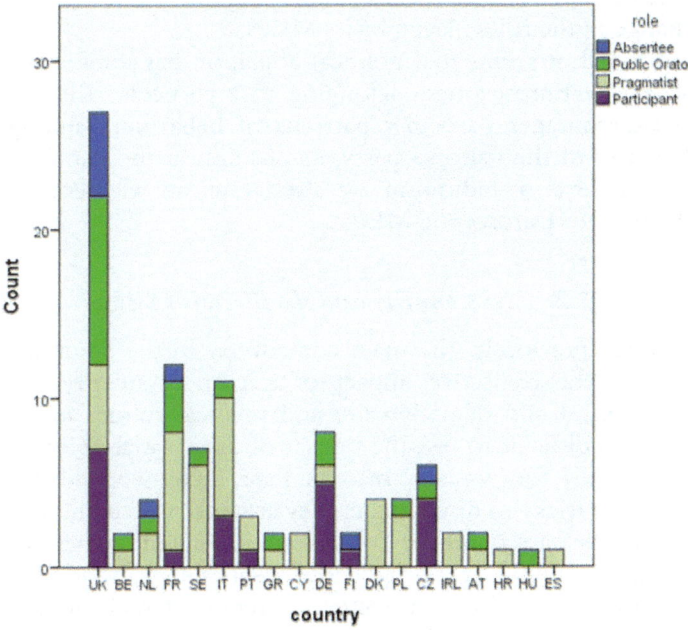

Fig. 6.1 Country and roles

level, which are or used to be in government; it is therefore not surprising that they want to be involved in the decision-making process in the EP and play insider roles. On the other side, members from UKIP, the Greek Golden Dawn and the Hungarian Jobbik exclusively play the role of Absentee and Public Orators. They oppose the EU as well as their national government, as part of their anti-establishment attitude and do not want to be part of it, through any positive involvement in the chamber. But Eurosceptic parties' strategies in the EP may change depending on their aims at the national level. For instance, the Italian Lega Nord tried to change its strategy inside the EP between the 6th and 7th legislatures. As the party wanted to be seen as a potential partner at the national level, it selected other candidates than its incumbents for the 2009 EU elections. It then encouraged its MEPs to be more constructive in their opposition and to improve their reputation within the EP, in other words to shift from a Public Orator role to a Pragmatist or Participant role (interview MEP 43). Similarly, although it is too soon to tell, the changes within the French Front national (Crépon et al. 2015; Startin 2014) and its increased share of seats in the EP could lead to some change in the roles played by its MEPs.

In a nutshell, it seems that political affiliation has some effect on the roles played by Eurosceptics. Belonging to a particular EP group reinforces or discourages particular patterns of behaviours among MEPs. The objectives of the national party, its position in the national political arena and its level of radicalism are also significant elements to understand the roles of Eurosceptic MEPs.

3.2   Nationality and the Electoral System

As mentioned previously, the main controversy in the literature on role theory is on the respective impact of electoral system-related factors on the one hand and of nationality and political culture on the other. However, it is difficult to test the impact of these variables empirically in the case of the EP for two main reasons. First, these two kinds of variables are particularly tricky to disentangle: they are interrelated and do not vary over time in the case of all the countries represented in the EP. Second, all Member states now have proportional representation for EU elections which reduces the variations in electoral system-related elements.

Therefore, two factors related to the electoral system are tested here: the ballot structure for EU elections and the type of electoral system for national elections. Using the work of Farrell and Scully (2010), two types of ballot structure are distinguished. On the one side, open list systems and systems allowing preferential voting are candidate-based: the focus is on the individual candidates. These are considered to be open list systems. On the other side, we have closed list systems: they are party-centred, since the party controls the list. It could be expected that MEPs elected on open list systems would be more likely to seek a personal vote, through an emphasis on the defence of local, regional or national interests (which are more prominent among the roles of Absentee and Pragmatist). Regarding the national electoral system, one must distinguish between countries with a proportional system and those with a majoritarian system. It could be expected that the electoral system influences the roles of Eurosceptic MEPs, especially for members of small parties. Indeed, countries with a proportional system offer more career opportunities to these actors, who could be elected at the national level. On the contrary, members of small parties from countries with a majoritarian system have fewer opportunities at the national level. The European mandate is then often the only available option for them to achieve parliamentary representation, as a mandate by default for the leaders of small Eurosceptic parties.

The analysis confirms the difficulty in analysing the relation between nationality and parliamentary roles. Indeed, Fig. 6.1 shows that some delegations are more likely to be found among particular roles: the British constitute a substantial share of the MEPs playing the role of Absentee and Public Orator, while the Germans are comparatively more present among the Participants and the Italians and French among the Pragmatists for instance. But the small size of each national delegation in the sample makes it impossible to draw any conclusions or examine any relationship ($p > 0.1$).

Regarding the electoral system, we can see from Table 6.5 that there does not seem to be a relation between the ballot structure at the EU level and the roles of Eurosceptic MEPs. Most Absentees are elected on closed lists, contrary to expectations. Although they put a strong emphasis on the local, regional and national level, it does not seem that this tendency comes from the ballot structure at the EU level. Most Public Orators and Participants are also elected on closed lists. It is only among Pragmatists that a majority is elected on open list systems. But the relation is not significant and it should be noted that this variable is correlated with the national electoral system (0.716^{**}). The electoral system

Table 6.5 Ballot structure in EU elections and parliamentary roles

			Electoral list EU elections		Total
			Closed	Open	
Role	Absentee	Count	6	3	9
		%	66.7	33.3	100.0
	Public orator	Count	17	7	24
		%	70.8	29.2	100.0
	Pragmatist	Count	20	26	46
		%	43.5	56.5	100.0
	Participant	Count	12	10	22
		%	54.5	45.5	100.0
Total		Count	55	46	101
		%	54.5	45.5	100.0

$p > 0.1$; Cramer's $V = 0.231$, $\lambda = 0.059$

and nationality are so intertwined that it is very difficult to analyse their respective impact on MEPs' parliamentary behaviour.

Finally, if we turn to the national electoral system, there seems to be a relation here (Table 6.6). Indeed, a majority of MEPs from countries with a majoritarian system at the national level can be found among Absentees and Public Orators (outsiders). On the contrary, a majority of Participants and Pragmatists come from countries with a proportional electoral system for national elections. So, the majority of MEPs from countries with a proportional electoral system for domestic elections are found among the MEPs playing the roles of Pragmatists and Participants whereas Eurosceptics from countries with a majoritarian electoral system tend to turn to the Public Orator role. But it should be noted that this is highly related to the country: it is mostly MEPs from fringe parties from France and the UK who are choosing the roles of Absentee and Public Orator. These parties have had little to opportunity to gain parliamentary representation at the national level and have had their main success in the EU elections. But once in the EP, they tend to choose an outsider strategy and remain at the fringe of parliamentary work, probably because of their strong opposition towards the EU and their anti-establishment stance, rather than because of the electoral system.

Overall, two conclusions can be drawn from these bivariate analyses. First, as hypothesized, the individual preferences of MEPs regarding European integration and the EU matter in order to understand how

Table 6.6 National electoral system and parliamentary roles

			National electoral system		Total
			Proportional	Majoritarian	
Role	Absentee	Count	3	6	9
		%	33.3	66.7	100.0
	Public osrator	Count	10	14	24
		%	41.7	58.3	100.0
	Pragmatist	Count	33	13	46
		%	71.7	28.3	100.0
	Participant	Count	14	8	22
		%	63.6	36.4	100.0
Total		Count	60	41	101
		%	59.4	40.6	100.0

$p < 0.05$, Cramer's $V = 0.294$, $\lambda = 0.083$

Eurosceptic actors conceive of and carry out their representative mandate. There is a substantial and significant relationship between the roles of Eurosceptics and their attitudes towards Europe. The more opposed an actor is to the EU and to the integration process, the more he or she will endorse an outsider position, playing the role of Absentee or Public Orator. On the contrary, soft Eurosceptics tend to play the roles of Participant or Pragmatist and want to be involved in parliamentary work. Often considered as a secondary factor (or even overlooked) by the literature, individual preferences seem in fact essential when examining the parliamentary roles of anti-system actors. Second, other factors also matter. Although the aim here is to test the relation between the degree and nature of MEPs' Euroscepticism and the roles they play, the analysis also reveals that seniority, political affiliation and the domestic electoral system seem to have some impact on the variance among the roles of Eurosceptic MEPs. More senior Eurosceptics are mostly found among insiders, i.e. Pragmatists and Participants. Those from right-wing fringe parties coming from countries with a majoritarian system tend to turn to the roles of Absentee and Public Orator. Eurosceptic MEPs from left-wing parties as well as from mainstream parties and those from countries with a proportional electoral system are more likely to play the roles of Pragmatist and Participant. However, it is very difficult to determine empirically the respective impact of nationality and of electoral system-related factors, especially given the relatively small sample of this study. These elements are intertwined, and it is probable that both play some role in the way Eurosceptic MEPs conceive of and carry out their mandate.

4   How to Explain the Roles of Eurosceptic MEPs?

So far, the analysis reveals that four variables seem to interact with the typology of roles: the attitudes towards European integration and the EU; seniority, political affiliation and the national electoral system. As a last test of the hypothesis, an ordered logistic regression was performed on the data. It allows to examine the relation between the ordinal dependent variable (the typology of roles) and the independent variables which were significant in the bivariate analysis in one single model rather than separately. It also provided information as to whether the main independent variable, i.e. preferences regarding European integration and the EU, is indeed the key to understanding the roles of Eurosceptics. The choice of an ordered regression is justified by the nature of the dependent variable. It has four categories, which can be seen as a continuum ranging from the most outsider stance, i.e. the least involved in parliamentary work (Absentee) to the institutional insider, i.e. the most involved in the EP (Participant). The reference category here is the Participant role, which is at one end of the continuum. The idea is therefore to measure the likelihood for an MEP to play the role of Participant, rather than the three other roles.

As far as the independent variables are concerned, only the factors who reached statistical significance at the stage of the bivariate analysis were selected, i.e. the level and nature of Euroscepticism, seniority, EP groups and the electoral system.[3] Regarding the electoral system-related variables, the ballot structure used during EU elections and the electoral system used for domestic elections are correlated (0.716**). Because of this, only one of them can be tested in the model. The electoral system used for domestic elections was included rather than the ballot structure for EU elections because the bivariate analysis showed a relation between the roles played by Eurosceptic MEPs and this variable, while no relation could be detected between the roles and the EU election ballot structure.[4]

Because of the small size of the sample, one must be cautious when interpreting the results. The aim here is to further test the impact of Eurosceptic MEPs' preferences regarding Europe on the way they conceive of and carry out their mandate and to compare it with the other

Table 6.7 Ordered logit model for the typology of role, by significant independent variables

	Estimate	S.E.	95% Confidence interval	
			Lower bound	Upper bound
Hard Euroscepticism	−4.364***	0.888	−6.101	−2.627
intergovernmentalism	−1.456*	0.551	−2.540	−0.372
Soft Euroscepticism	0[a]			
Non-attached	−2.239**	0.829	−3.953	−0.704
ENF	−2.349*	1.222	−4.744	−0.046
I/D + EFD(D)	−1.572*	0.698	−2.940	−0.205
ECR	2.381**	0.829	0.756	4.006
Eul/Ngl + Greens	2.329**	0.829	0.704	3.953
Proportional elec. system	−0.112	0.511	−1.151	0.926
seniority = junior	−0.270	0.483	−1.217	0.676

Pseudo R^2 (Nagelkerke) = 0.598
LR Chi^2 = 80.406
***$p < 0.001$; **$p < 0.005$; *$p < 0.05$
[a]ref.category

explanatory variables rather than to provide a comprehensive explanatory model.

If we look at Table 6.7, the data corroborate the expectation. Indeed, it shows that an MEP's type of Euroscepticism is strongly related to the role he or she plays. The more an MEP is opposed to European integration and the EU, the less likely he or she is to play the role of the Participant (reference category). An intergovernmentalist is also less likely than a soft Eurosceptic to play the role of Participant but still more likely to do so than a hard Eurosceptic. The relation between the roles and Euroscepticism is therefore relatively strong and statistically significant ($p = 0.000$ for hard Euroscepticism and 0.008 for intergovernementalism).

As far as the other individual-level elements are concerned, the analysis reveals that a Eurosceptic MEP in his/her first mandate seems less likely to choose the role of Participant but these relations do not reach statistical significance ($p = 0.576$). Similarly, MEPs from the fringes of the chamber (non-attached, ENF, I/D and EFDD) have a negative coefficient, meaning they are less likely to play the role of Participant. It is especially true for the non-attached who are, with MEPs from the radical right group ENF, the least likely to play the role of Participant.

On the contrary, members of the ECR group or Eurosceptics from the left (EULG/NGL) are the most likely to choose the role of Participant. Finally, the fact that a country has a proportional electoral system for national election is negatively related to the role of Participant but this variable fails to reach statistical significance (0.832).

Overall, the central hypothesis of this research can be considered as corroborated. The level and nature of opposition of MEPs towards the EU and the integration process are a key element to understand their strategies they develop. But their political affiliation also plays a role, which is quite logical: MEPs at the fringe of the chamber are also the most Eurosceptic and are less likely to be insiders (Pragmatists or Participants), contrary to their colleagues from radical left and the ECR group, which are more integrated as explained in the previous chapter.

5   Conclusion

In their study of political representation at the European level, Farrell and Scully (2007) showed that MEPs have clear but heterogeneous views of their role as representative. This variation can be explained, according to them, partially by broad and systematic variables such as the electoral system. But they noted that it is not easy to explain individual roles with broad and objective criteria and called for research on how MEPs understand and approach their role as individual representative. In a more recent study, they considered that there is a need to move beyond a macro perspective on institutional and aggregate outcomes towards a more micro-level analysis of individuals, which takes into account the attitudes of elected representatives (Scully and Farrell 2010, p. 37).

As an attempt to answer this call, this research concentrates on individual-level factors to explain the variance among the roles played by Eurosceptic MEPs. While the literature mostly focuses on the controversy between the impacts of political culture versus electoral system-related variables, it is argued here that attitudes and individual preferences, far from being secondary, should be placed at the heart of the analysis. The hypothesis at the core of this study is indeed that individual preferences regarding the integration process and the EU, together with the institutional context, are essential to understanding the way Eurosceptic MEPs conceive of and carry out their mandate.

The analysis confirms that the roles played by Eurosceptic MEPs depend not only on the rules of the game within the institution but also on their preferences regarding European integration and the EU. Indeed, it revealed that the formal and informal rules of the EP influence the room of manoeuvre for Eurosceptics. But it has also shown that the degree and the nature of their opposition to the European political system have an impact on the roles they play. The more an MEP is opposed to the integration process and the EU, the more likely he or she is to stay at the margins of EP's work (Absentee and Public Orator) whereas soft Eurosceptics are more likely to be involved in parliamentary work and become institutional insiders (Pragmatist and Participant). Of course, as noted by Beyers (1998, p. 2), arguing that "attitudes are important for understanding human behaviour is not the same as positing a deterministic relation between attitudes and behaviour". Actors' strategies are affected by many factors. MEPs' preferences towards Europe are not the only explanation for the roles they play and given the small size of the sample in this study, the results must be interpreted with caution. It is likely that other elements such as nationality, ideology, electoral system variables also affect the roles of Eurosceptics, as well as factors related to the personality of each individual which are very difficult to study systematically.

Nevertheless, the increased visibility of the EU in national political arenas since the Euro-crisis has triggered new resistance among public opinion and boosted the success of Eurosceptic parties at the 2014 EP elections. But beyond their shared Eurosceptic label, these parties have diverse stances on Europe: while some of them are hard Eurosceptics and would support their country's exit from the European project, most of them target specific aspects of the EU, its architecture or principles, such as the Euro or the free movement of people. Through an actor-centred perspective, the analysis has highlighted how important it is to consider the degree and nature of opposition to Europe displayed by MEPs to grasp how they view their mandate and behave in the parliament. More generally, it shows the need to take into account individual preferences regarding the political regime in order to understand the strategies of anti-system actors.

NOTES

1. It is beyond the scope of this study but it would be interesting to carry out an in-depth longitudinal analysis, including a wider variety of indicators, to examine the relation between seniority and the way Eurosceptic

MEPs conceive of and carry out their mandate. It would provide a better understanding of the potential institutional socialization of these anti-system actors.

2. For instance, one IND/DEM member was particularly active in his committee. He proposed many amendments, was rapporteur and was very proactive in policy-making in his policy area. His involvement was strongly criticized by his colleagues from the group, who were mostly Absentees and Public Orators. Indeed, they saw themselves as the only opposition in the EP and felt the activism of one member could threaten this identity of the group. They even questioned his level of Euroscepticism and asked him not to associate the group with his legislative initiative within his committee.

3. Another ordinal regression with all the independent variables can be found in annex.

4. A separate analysis was carried out which included the EU election ballot structure rather than the electoral system for domestic elections. No significant change could be detected. The same variables were significant ($R^2 = 0.542$).

REFERENCES

Bale, T., & Taggart, P. (2006). *First-Timers Yes, Virgins No: The Roles and Background of New MEPs*. SEI working papers no. 89.

Beauvallet, W., & Michon, S. (2010). L'institutionnalisation inachevée du Parlement européen. Hétérogénéité nationale, spécialisation du recrutement et autonomisation. *Politix, 23*(8), 147–172.

Beyers, J. (1998). Where does supranationalism come from? Ideas floating through the working groups of the council of the European Union. *EIOP Working Papers, 2*(9), 1–25.

Beyers, J. (2010). Conceptual and methodological challenges in the study of European socialization. *Journal of European Public Policy, 17*(6), 909–920.

Bowler, S., & Farrell, D. (1993). Legislator shirking and voter monitoring: Impacts of European parliament electoral systems upon legislator-voter relationships. *Journal of Common Market Studies, 31*(1), 45–69.

Bressanelli, E. (2012). National parties and group membership in the European Parliament: ideology or pragmatism? *Journal of European Public Policy, 19*(5), 737–754.

Crépon, S., Dézé, A., & Mayer, N. (2015). Introduction/Redécouvrir le Front National. In *Les fauxsemblants du Front national* (pp. 13–24). Presses de Sciences Po (PFNSP).

Deschouwer, K. (2008). "Comparing newly governing parties" dans K. Deschouwer, New Parties in government. In power for the first time, Londres, Routledge, pp. 1–16.

Farrell, D., & Scully, R. (2007). *Representing Europe's citizens? Electoral institutions and the failure of parliamentary representation.* Oxford: Oxford University Press.

Farrell, D., & Scully, R. (2010). The European parliament: One parliament, several modes of political representation on the ground? *Journal of European Public Policy, 17*(1), 36–54.

Georgakakis, D. (Ed.). (2012). *Le champ de l'Eurocratie. Une sociologie politique du personnel de l'UE.* Paris: Economica.

Hagger, M., & Wing, M. (1979). Legislative roles and clientele orientations in the European parliament. *Legislative Studies Quarterly, 4*(2), 165–196.

Hix, S., & Hagemann, S. (2009). Could changing the electoral rules fix European parliament elections? *Politique européenne,* (2), 37–52.

Katz, R. (1999). Role orientations in parliaments. In R. Katz & B. Wessels (Eds.), *The European Parliament, the National Parliaments, and European Integration* (pp. 61–85). Oxford, Oxford University Press.

Lewis, J. (2005). The Janus face of Brussels: Socialization and everyday decision making in the European Union. *International Organization, 599*(4), 937–971.

Mughan, A., Box-Steffensmeier, J., & Scully, R. (1997). Mapping legislative socialization. *European Journal of Political Research, 32*(1), 93–106.

Navarro, J. (2007). Comment le Parlement Européen socialise-t-il les députés européens? *Revue française de science politique, 57*(1), 94–97.

Navarro, J. (). *Les députés européens et leur rôle. Sociologie interprétative des pratiques parlementaires.* Brussels: Editions de l'Université de Bruxelles.

Startin, N. (2014). Contrasting fortunes, differing futures? The rise (and fall) of the Front National and the British National Party. *Modern & Contemporary France, 22*(3), 277–299.

Szczerbiak, A., & Taggart, P. (2002). The party politics of Euroscepticism in EU member and candidate states. *SEI Working Paper,* 51.

Szczerbiak, A., & Taggart, P. (2008). *Opposing Europe? The comparative party politics of Euroscepticism.* Oxford: Oxford University Press.

Wessels, B. (2005). Roles and orientations of members of parliament in the EU context: Congruence or difference? Europeanisation or not? *The Journal of Legislative Studies, 11*(3–4), 446–465.

Wessels, B., & Giebler, H. (2011). *Choosing a style of representation: The role of institutional and organizational incentives.* Presentation at the 6th ECPR General Conference, University of Iceland.

Whitaker, R., & Lynch, P. (2014). Understanding the formation and actions of Eurosceptic groups in the European parliament: Pragmatism, principles and publicity. *Government and Opposition, 49*(2), 232–263.

CHAPTER 7

General Conclusion: The Impact of Eurosceptic MEPs

The EU has reached a critical point. It is confronted with an accumulation of tensions triggered by the economic and financial crisis, the refugee crisis, the Brexit and an existential crisis not to mention the persistent legitimacy and democratic deficit. The integration process has entered a new phase, characterized by the rise of Euroscepticism and the unprecedented success of radical parties and the mainstreaming of anti-EU sentiments across the continent.

This context of crisis has increased the EU's visibility in national political arenas and has engendered a new wave of resistances among citizens and the (renewed) success of Eurosceptic parties. The 2014 EP elections attest to this trend with an upsurge in the support for radical and Eurosceptic parties. As noted by Grabow and Hartleb (2014: 7), "while Euroscepticism is not a new phenomenon, the scale and success of the opponents of the EU are striking, with right-wing and national populist parties leading the way". At the same time, Euroscepticism has not only become firmly embedded across Europe, it has also "come in from the cold" (Taggart and Szczerbiak 2013). No longer at the margins, it has entered the mainstream, and the current complex crisis has consolidated its position there. The success of fringe parties has led to a shift in mainstream parties' positions on Europe. Euroscepticism seems increasingly contagious as leaders of governmental parties are becoming

© The Author(s) 2018
N. Brack, *Opposing Europe in the European Parliament*,
Palgrave Studies in European Union Politics,
https://doi.org/10.1057/978-1-137-60201-5_7

more and more critical towards the EU (see Meijers 2017; Taggart and Szczerbiak 2013).

Against this backdrop, the study of Euroscepticism, its nature, causes and consequences remains crucial. As Mény remarked (2012, p. 162), "however excessive, contradictory, confusing and unpleasant are the messages, anti-EU populist rhetoric deserves our attention". While most research concentrate on the national level to uncover the nature and sources of parties' stances on Europe, this book focuses on the supranational level. The aim was to concentrate on Eurosceptic MEPs in order to analyze their strategies once elected. Indeed, Eurosceptic parties have usually been more successful at EP elections than during domestic polls, and they have used the supranational level to gain resources and legitimacy. But what do these elected representatives do in the EP? How do they see their job? To what extent and why do they behave differently? Based on the role theory, this study provides the first in-depth analysis of how and why Eurosceptics conceive and carry out their representative mandate in the EP. It proposed a typology of four roles—the Absentee, the Public Orator, the Pragmatists and the Participant—and showed that Eurosceptic MEPs carry out their mandate in different ways and have contrasting views of their job, duties and relations to citizens. The analysis also revealed that in order to understand the variation among the roles of this typology, two elements are essential: the institutional context in which they operate and MEPs' preferences regarding the EU and European integration.

The ambition is also to address, through the actor-centred approach adopted here, the issue of the democratic and legitimacy deficit of the EU in a fresh way. Indeed, by shifting the focus from an institutional to an individual level, the analysis of Eurosceptic MEPs could offer a reflection on the consequences of their presence for the EP and for the legitimacy of the EU. More generally, studying opposition to the EU within the supranational institutions can be useful to understand the key issue of the relation between conflict and legitimacy in democratic systems.

After summarizing the main findings of this research and proposing avenues for new research, the last part of the conclusion will provide food for thought regarding the implications of the presence of Eurosceptic MEPs. It is argued here that their presence and the roles they play, rather than endangering European integration, could be an asset for the affirmation of the EU as a democratic political system, open to conflict.

1 THE EUROPEAN PARLIAMENT AS A LABORATORY FOR THE ANALYSIS OF ANTI-SYSTEM ACTORS

1.1 *Which Strategies for Eurosceptic MEPs?*

Euroscepticism within the only directly elected European institution has comparatively been overlooked for many years. Whereas opposition to the EU has been at the heart of an extensive literature, research tends to concentrate on the national level in order to grasp the nature and the causes of Euroscepticism. As noted by scholars, it seems that Euroscepticism has regained primary political relevance as of 2010 as the financial and economic crisis, and then the migration crisis have provided fertile ground for the mobilization of (new) Eurosceptic, populist and radical parties (Conti 2016). But even now, the literature on Euroscepticism within the EU institutions remains limited.

This research aimed therefore to contribute filling this gap by concentrating on the EP and analyzing how Eurosceptics conceive and carry out their mandate, once elected at the supranational level. In other words, it sought to understand the strategies of elected representatives in a political system they strongly criticize or even oppose.

To do so, it relied on the motivational approach of role theory and on an inductive approach. The concept of role, defined as a dynamic configuration of objectives, characteristic attitudes and behaviours, was used to apprehend how Eurosceptics conceive and carry out their representative mandate in the EP. The analysis of more than 100 interviews with Eurosceptic MEPs, parliamentary assistants and EP civil servants, combined with observation of group meetings and the examination of the behaviour of the interviewed Eurosceptics allowed me to propose an original typology of four roles played by these actors: the Absentee, the Public Orator, the Pragmatist and the Participant.

The Absentee is characterized by two main elements: a comparatively low involvement in the assembly and a concentration of his/her activities at the national or local level. Such MEP derives little satisfaction from their European mandate. His/her weak involvement in the EP can be interpreted as an exit strategy from the work of the parliament, motivated by a total refusal to engage in the workings of the institution or by indifference towards the European mandate. While neglecting the parliament, absentees are very active at the national and local levels, where spend most of their time. This ideal-type of role is essentially motivated by activism—the promotion of Euroscepticism at home—but also by utilitarian and opportunistic considerations. Such MEP seeks to take advantage, financially and symbolically, of his/her mandate to promote his/her position, while not being involved in parliamentary work and preferring to claim proximity (true or not) to their constituents and fellow citizens through a strong activism at the national level.

Unlike the Absentee, the Public Orator chooses to be present in the EP in order to denounce and delegitimize the EU from the inside guided by a taste for anti-conformism and an attitude of frontal opposition, such MEP prioritizes two aspects of the representative mandate: public speaking and research and dissemination of negative information on European integration. The Public Orator sees himself/herself first and foremost as representatives in permanent opposition. But even though such MEP is relatively present in parliament, he/she is not very interested in the "traditional" aspects of parliamentary activities. Public Orators prefer to uphold their campaign of denunciation and maintain a balance between their presence within the system and their desire not to be integrated in the system they criticize. So, this role provides, to those who endorse it, the opportunity to develop an essentially negative strategy vis-à-vis the European polity: It means being present in the heart of the system to denounce it with no desire to reform it, while adopting a posture external to this system through non-compliance with its rules and norms.

The third role is the Pragmatist. While such MEP may share some characteristics with the Public Orator, the Pragmatist offers a completely different way of conceiving and carrying out the European mandate. MEPs playing this role develop a dual strategy whereby, on the one hand, they seek to achieve concrete results while, on the other hand, not compromising their Eurosceptic beliefs. In other words, as Eurosceptics, they see themselves as opposition actors, but also, as MEPs, they wish to emphasize the constructive nature of their opposition and their willingness to get involved to make a difference through their actions. Guided by a desire to be efficient, the Pragmatist is characterized by a greater investment in the EP's daily work, a tendency to follow the assembly's rules and a willingness to change, in a targeted and limited way, the system of which he/she are critical. They also emphasize their mission of representation, in the sense of "acting on behalf of" and believe they have a quasi-imperative mandate linking them to their constituents, fellow citizens or political party. Two subgroups could be distinguished, the first emphasizing its mission of control over legislation and seeing themselves as the watchdogs of European institutions; the second category is fundamentally guided by the defence of national or regional interests within the assembly as the parliament is used as a forum for the defence of specific interests which they cannot effectively defend at the national level.

The last role is the Participant. Like the Pragmatist, this strategy matches the posture of an insider, seeking change from within the system of which he/she is critical. Guided by a desire for influence, the Participant is characterized by his/her willingness to appear as an MEP like any other and adapt his/her behaviour to the rules of the game. Such MEPs do not see themselves as opposition players but rather as legislators. They invest the majority of their time in the chamber and its bodies. Unlike the Public Orators and the pragmatists, participants not only know and respect the formal and informal rules governing the operation of the EP but adjust their behaviour to them. In sum, they subscribe to the rules of political deliberation.

This typology shows that despite their common Eurosceptic position, there is a diversity in the ways Eurosceptics conceive of and carry out their European mandate. It confirms that MEPs still have heterogeneous behaviour and diverging attitudes regarding their job and their relations with voters (Costa and Navarro 2003, p. 132). It also attests that we should refrain from a simplistic or normative interpretation of the strategies of these anti-system actors. On the one hand, they do not all adopt an attitude of protest but exhibit diversified attitudes and behaviours, some being relatively well integrated in the parliamentary game. On the other hand, the analysis of the roles played by Eurosceptic MEPs reveals that like any elected representative, these actors interpret their mandate so as to match both their visions of the role of the MEP as well as the presumed expectations of their voters. Given the constraints they face and the lack of consensus on the best way to exercise he European mandate, they offer alternative ways of conceiving of and inhabiting the parliamentary function. These ways could differ from those of their colleagues, but they do not necessarily jeopardize the representative process at the European level, contrary to what their critics might say.[1]

1.2   Beyond the Case of Eurosceptic MEPs

The relevance of this typology goes beyond the case of Eurosceptic MEPs. First, although it has been developed on the basis of the attitudes, objectives and behaviours of Eurosceptics, the roles it contains may not be exclusive to these actors. It is indeed likely that other MEPs conceive and carry out their mandate in a similar way as the roles described here. If we look at the regular rankings of Votewatch, we can notice that a weak involvement in parliamentary activities or a comparatively low attendance is not restricted to Eurosceptics. Kauppi (2005) also noted that some MEPs, which he calls "tourists", are not much involved in the EP and prefer to focus on national or local activities. Similarly, some non-Eurosceptic MEPs concentrate on their speeches in plenary and seek publicity for their activities, a bit like Public Orators (Navarro 2009, p. 162–173). And others emphasize the defence and promotion of their voters' or their constituency's interests and try to politicize debates on EU issues at home, like Pragmatists do (Brack and Costa 2013). Hence, it would be interesting to reproduce this research to determine whether the typology can be useful to understand non-Eurosceptic MEPs' attitudes and behaviours and to examine, empirically, to what extent Eurosceptic MEPs differ from their non-Eurosceptic colleagues.

Second, the typology proposed here could also serve as basis to study anti-system actors in other parliamentary settings. The motivational approach argues that roles are the result of the interaction between the institutional context and individual preferences and are, therefore, embedded in a particular institution. But the particularistic nature of this approach could be countered by seeing the typology as basis to examine the strategies of contestation of individual actors within an institution (see for instance Hirschman 1970, 1978). The roles of Absentee and Public Orator correspond to an outsider position and can be interpreted as an exit strategy, from both the traditional parliamentary work as from the institution itself. They do not see themselves as being part of the parliament (Huitt 1961). The role of Absentee is the closest to an exit strategy: it's not a total exit since the actor participates in election and takes his/her seat but the role allows for a detachment from the institution, through a weak involvement in its activities and a focus on other territorial levels. The Public Orator does not seek either to integrate or to change the system he/she criticizes, stays aside and is not interested in parliamentary work. Such actor claims his/her opposition to the system from within the institution, notably by refusing to respect its rules and to accept the risk of participating in the deliberation. The roles of Pragmatist and Participant can be conceived as an insider position and more like a voice option. Their dissatisfaction with the European political system is expressed through the mobilization of the various parliamentary tools at their disposal to change the source of their discontent. The Pragmatist gets involved in the chamber in the hope of influencing or at least of controlling, in a limited way, some European public policies, while maintaining a posture of opposition. The Participant accepts the rules of the parliamentary game and can compromise on his/her Eurosceptic position in order to have some impact on the legislative process.

While several democracies, inside and outside the EU, are facing contestation from movements and parties against their institutional and constitutional structure, this typology could serve as basis to future studies on anti-system actors in national parliamentary assemblies. Belgium, Canada, Spain and the UK in particular could be interesting cases, where political parties ask for a deep reform of the State. An avenue for future research could hence be to determine to what extent the patterns of behaviours, objectives and attitudes highlighted here could be identified within other national parliament and allow to grasp the strategies developed by these anti-system parties.

2   EXPLAINING MEPs' ROLE CHOICE: THE INTERACTION BETWEEN INSTITUTIONAL CONTEXT AND INDIVIDUAL PREFERENCES

One of the main challenges of role theory is to explain the variation among roles and why people play one role rather than another. Drawing on the insights of the motivational approach, the central hypothesis of this book assumes that the roles played by Eurosceptic depend on the interaction between institutional and individual factors. Two elements in particular were examined: the impact of the EP formal and informal rules on the one hand and of the individual preferences regarding the integration and the EU on the other hand. The main findings will be briefly summarized before assessing how the EP has dealt with the persistence of Eurosceptic members.

2.1   *The Influence of the Institutional Context*

According to new institutionalism, the institutional context is a key element in explaining the behaviour and attitudes of elected representatives.

The rules of the institution act as a source of constraints and of opportunities for its members and, at the same time, frame the repertoire of strategies they can have (Strøm 1997, p. 163).

The systematic analysis of the formal and informal rules of the EP revealed that the institutional context influences the roles played by Eurosceptics. It steers individual member's choices in certain directions, by encouraging and discouraging certain kinds of behaviour. It does not mean that the institutional context dominates actors' behaviour or change their core attitudes and beliefs. But it affects their perceptions of the institutional reality and their strategies by delimitating appropriate behaviour (Beyers 1998).

More precisely, the rules of the game have evolved dramatically over the last 30 years. And although all MEPs are subject to the rules of procedure, they are crucial to understanding the room for manoeuvre of Eurosceptic members. The institutional context impacts the range of roles available to Eurosceptic MEPs by influencing their ability to achieve their objectives. Eurosceptic MEPs belong to the fringes and the formal and informal rules tend to give them incentives to participate and integrate the EP's structure or otherwise to remain permanently marginalized. If the institutional context alone is not enough to explain the variation in the roles played by Eurosceptic MEPs, it nevertheless contributes to a better understanding of the typology of roles.

More generally, these findings give a better idea as to how the EP has accommodated to the persistent presence of an anti-system opposition. The efficiency and legitimacy of its deliberation depend notably on the ability and willingness of its members to demonstrate that they can deal with the EP's powers. But, as it has been shown, there is a minority of Eurosceptics whose aim is to disrupt parliamentary proceedings and to delegitimize the institution. In order to preserve its efficiency and its legitimacy, especially in its relations with the other European institutions, the EP has constantly rationalized the way it works through various reforms of its rules of procedure. These reforms have changed the distribution of power among actors in the chamber and led to a specialization of its members as well as to a division of labour among various types of actors within the EP. They have also resulted in an empowerment of the political groups at the expenses of individual members and to a stricter regulation of MEPs' behaviour, reducing thereby Eurosceptics' ability to be a nuisance, especially Public Orators. Due to these evolutions, the presence of an anti-system opposition cannot fundamentally jeopardize the legitimacy or the efficiency of the EP's functioning, because these actors have no other choice than to use the existing institutional tools to express their opposition. Due to the constraints and resources coming from the institutional context, Eurosceptics can choose between (limited) involvement in the work of the assembly, a structurally marginalized position allowing them to denounce the so-called consensual functioning of the EP or pursue a strategy of empty chair.

2.2   *The Key Role of Individual Preferences*

In spite of some recent and inspiring research on political representation at the supranational level, there is still a lot we should know about MEPs, their behaviour, their attitudes towards the EP and towards the integration process (Farrell and Scully 2007; Priestley 2008; see also Whitaker et al. 2017). If the literature highlights the influence of these attitudes on how MEPs' role orientations and behaviour, many scholars adopt a macro-level approach and consider individual preference as "an explanatory complement" to other factors, considered more central, such as the electoral system and political culture.

Here MEPs' preferences regarding the EU and European integration were at the heart of its explanatory model. The analysis showed that if the role depends on several variables, among which political affiliation, the degree and nature of an MEP's opposition to Europe significantly influences his/her choice of a role. The more an MEP is hostile towards the integration process /the EU, the more likely he/she is to play the role of Absentee or Public Orator whereas a soft Eurosceptic is more likely to play the role of Participant.

These results corroborate the central hypothesis: the interaction between the formal and informal rules of the EP and the MEPs' preferences regarding European integration, and the EU explains to a large extent the roles Eurosceptics play. More generally, these results demonstrate that an actor-centred perspective is fruitful to understand anti-system actors in parliamentary settings. It allows to reveal the impact of the institutional context on this kind of elected representatives and to emphasize how important it is to take into account the degree and nature of their opposition to the system in which they operate in order to comprehend the way they conceive and carry out the representative mandate.

The research strategy developed here, combining a wide variety of data, as well as inductive and deductive approaches, is demanding and time-consuming. But the comprehensive nature of the explanatory model developed here, and the choice of an actor-centred perspective allows to provide an in-depth understanding of the complexity and multidimensionality of the European mandate and to take into consideration the subjective dimension of the representative process.

3   The Implications of the Presence of Eurosceptics MEPs

Until recently, the impact of Euroscepticism had been rather indirect. Eurosceptics have been acted as agenda-setters and have partially influenced the terms of the debate on European integration. They have raised the key issue of legitimacy at the EU level and of the relationship between the integration process and national democracies (Leconte 2010, p. 13). But their influence on the decision-making has been limited. It remains so today at the EU level as Eurosceptic MEPs remain too poorly organized and heterogeneous to have a significant influence deliberation of the EP or have blackmail potential on the European decision-making process.

That does not mean that Eurosceptics do not have any impact at all. European elections have strengthened these parties at home. Political parties like the French FN, UKIP or even Alternative for Germany were at first mainly focused on EU elections. They have been developing a strong anti-EU discourse, and the electoral rules have allowed them to get representation in the EP, which was not always possible in general elections. They have also benefited from the fact that EU elections are "second order" and thus favourable to anti-system parties. Progressively, they have become embedded at the local and national levels and now play an increasing role in politics in some countries. Their position in the EP has provided them with resources (positions, staff, access to media, etc.) and increased legitimacy (Startin 2010; Reungoat 2015). These parties have managed to expand their electoral basis and to put governments and other national parties under pressure to address European integration. Indeed, with their electoral success, they put pressure on mainstream parties to shift their positions on EU issues. Eurosceptic parties have been trying to change the terms of the national competition. Not only have they forced others to position themselves, even though mainstream parties are internally divided (van de Wardt 2015) but they have also had a contagious effect on other parties. And as noted by Kriesi (2016), the gains made by Eurosceptics during elections, even at the national level, will make their influence increasingly felt at the intergovernmental level. Moreover, while the solutions put forward to past crisis were either more Europe or the status quo, the Brexit made a visible difference (Young 2016). Now, less Europe or even no Europe has emerged as a real option, and it can be considered as a first major victory for Euroscepticism.

The presence of Eurosceptics at the core of the EU institutions is not without consequences either. The presence of such dissenting voices has an impact on the EP's representativeness as well as on the democratic legitimacy of the EU. It is argued that their presence should not systematically be seen as an obstacle to European integration but also as an asset for the EU's legitimacy.

3.1   Consequences for the European Parliament: Eurosceptics as a Potential Asset for the Institution's Representativeness

While European citizens are increasingly willing to express dissatisfaction with the EU, the EP as the only directly elected institutions has failed to build effective links between the people and the EU (Farrell and Scully 2007). There are segments of the population who do not share the same view as their representatives on EU issues, and there is a lack of congruence on the EU dimension between voters and MEPs (Mattila and Raunio 2012; Thomassen 2012). In other words, the positions of Eurosceptic voters are almost totally ignored.

In that respect, the presence and the roles of Eurosceptic MEPs could help enhance the linkage between citizens and EU institutions. Indeed, these dissenting voices provide a channel for the expression of oppositions found in some segments of the population that would otherwise remain unrepresented. They allow citizens' dissatisfaction to be expressed inside the EP and, hence, make an opposition not only to but also in the EU possible. Contradicting the widely held idea of European elites entirely devoted to furthering the integration process, the presence and strategies of Eurosceptic MEPs contribute to increase the EP's representativeness as an institution open to society in its diversity. While challenging the legitimacy of the EP's deliberation, either through an empty-chair strategy (Absentee) or through a posture of vocal opposition (Public Orator), Eurosceptics contribute to the legitimacy of the institution through their participation in EP elections. Indeed, by participating in election (rather than resorting to boycott as Sinn Fein did in the British context), and entering the institution, they help integrate the most Eurosceptic segment of the population within the system and contribute to the plural and democratic nature of the institution, legitimizing thereby indirectly its deliberation. Moreover, as this research has shown, a majority of the Eurosceptics do not remain in an outsider position. Pragmatists and Participants are involved in the daily work of the institution. They recognize its legitimacy and its decision-making process. Complying with the rules and practices of the institution, they integrate with the system they criticize without being able to significantly influence the EU's decision-making on sensitive issues. Similarly to the "function tribunitienne" that the French Communist Party assumed (Lavau 1968; see also Hamel et al. 1975) these Eurosceptics contribute in a crucial manner to legitimizing the EP.

The presence of an anti-systemic opposition, even in its most conflictual form, could be an asset for the representativeness of the EP and could strengthen the role of the EP as an arena for political conflict. However, that would require that these oppositions are not only represented in the chamber but also engaged with, and that a debate takes place in which citizens can identify themselves. For now, the status of opposition in the EP is still indefinite: Eurosceptics are ideologically divided and split across different political groups but more importantly, they face strong institutional constraints. To deal with the filibustering and delaying tactics, as well as the outrageous behaviour of some Eurosceptics, there have been frequent reforms of the rules of procedure, and the individual freedom of elected representatives has been gradually reduced. This adaptation of the institution to the presence of dissenting voices raises questions as to the status of political opposition in the chamber but more generally, to the role of the EP as arena for debate and conflict. The evolution of the rules generates a tension between the need for efficiency, in order for the EP's voice to be heard in the decision-making process, on the one hand, and the respect of pluralism and of MEPs' individual freedom, on the other hand. This tension refers to the more general debate between two visions of democracy in the EU: democracy through parliament or democracy in parliament. The first vision entails a democratization of the European lawmaking process through an empowerment of the EP as the democratically elected institution. It requires the institution to be efficient, to formulate clear, coherent and moderate position in order to maximize its influence in the inter-institutional negotiations. The second implies a free, spontaneous and public parliamentary deliberation and requires the respect of pluralism and of representativeness (Costa 2010). So far, MEPs seem to have given priority to the first vision at the expense of the second, and they could ensure the empowerment of their institution (see also Kohler 2013). The EP became less and less a talking shop and is now an influential legislative assembly.

But it has also led to an increasingly bureaucratic functioning of the assembly. If the rationalization of the EP's functioning has contributed to consolidate its position in the institutional triangle, it has been at the expenses of the representative function of the chamber. The emphasis has been much more on efficiency than on the function of symbolic representation of the parliament. As a result, the EP is not fulfilling its task as public arena for debate and of political conflict, which reduces its input legitimacy stemming from the principle of representation. It is not surprising to see that the empowerment of the EP has been inversely proportional to the attention it generates among citizens (Rozenberg 2009). It was expected that the EP contributes to solve the democratic and legitimacy deficit of the EU. But its direct election and its empowerment do not seem to do the trick while the way it works does not contribute to make parliamentary debates and what is at stake understandable for citizens. The increased number of Eurosceptic MEPs since 2014 could have triggered a change in that aspect and their presence could then be a real asset for parliamentary democracy at the supranational level. But so far, it does not seem to be the case as the "grand coalition" is still in place and new reforms of the EP rules have been put in place to ensure that Eurosceptics do not gain any influence.

3.2 Eurosceptic MEPs and the Politicization of Europe

In addition to increasing the EP's representativeness, the presence of dissenting voices at the heart of the EU could be a resource for the legitimization challenges of the European polity. The EU relies on largely consensual and depoliticized interactions, leading some scholars to categorize it as leaning towards a "consociational" political system (Bogaards 2002; Costa and Magnette 2003). As noted by Abélès (1996: 63), "political practices at the European level involve comprehension (in the etymological sense of taking together) rather than confrontation".

EU institutions tend to emphasize the technical rather than the political aspects of politics, in order to facilitate reaching compromise and overcoming both political and national divisions. This "technicisation" of issues, understood as the reduction of ideological and intergovernmental conflicts through the use of technical or consensual arguments (Lascoumes 2009), is essential in building alliances. But it also results in a depoliticization of the debates and a lack of clarity for citizens to understand what is at stake. This logic of conflict avoidance fuels the EU's legitimacy deficit as citizens perceive its institutions as remote, technocratic and cut-off from their daily concerns. The situation is further reinforced by the relative weakness of its democratic institutions and more particularly, by the lack of an institutionalized site for the expression of opposition. A political community exists only insofar as the opposition is present within the political system (Zellentin 1967). But the EU seems to have missed the third milestone on the path towards fully democratic institutions (Dahl 1966, 1971), namely the establishment of the right of an organized opposition within the system to call to vote against the government. The lack of electoral accountability fuels discontent among voters as they cannot express their discontent to EU policies or actors, other than voting for radical parties. As a result, classical opposition tends to turn into principled opposition to the EU, i.e. Euroscepticism (Mair 2007), while the lack of politics at the EU level leads to indifference and apathy among citizens, as evidenced by the low turnout during EP elections.

The presence of Eurosceptics in the EP could be seen as an asset in that respect. It contributes to the politicization of Europe, understood as increasing controversiality of joint decision-making, greater partisan conflict on European issues and the widening of the audience (De Wilde 2011; Schmitter 1969; Zürn 2016). Eurosceptic actors have been the main drivers of politicization of European integration (Grande and Kriesi 2016; Hooghe and Marks 2009), notably by posing fundamental questions related to the EU responsiveness to societal demands and increasing democratic awareness and critical capacity of citizens.

This politicization has not led to deeper integration through more authority transfers as expected by the neofunctionalists. On the contrary, it has resulted in a constraining dissensus (Hooghe and Marks 2009). While it could appear critical for the European project in the short term, especially in a context of crisis, that does not necessarily mean that politicization will have a constraining effect on the integration process (De

Wilde et al. 2016). Quite the contrary, its effect can be beneficial for the EU and its democratic nature: politicization contributes to the articulation of conflicts, and conflict is a key ingredient of democratic politics (Schattschneider 1975; see also Schmidt 2006). As noted by Magnette and Papdopoulos (2008, p. 14), "the politicization of the EU should be seen as a value in itself and not merely as a positive or negative instrument for European integration".

Eurosceptic MEPs are key actors in triggering and politicizing debates on EU issues, both at the national and supranational levels. And unlike pro-EU actors, Eurosceptics bring to European politics the "gift of plain speaking" (Duff 2013, p. 152), making dividing lines and EU issues more understandable for citizens. Through the politicization of these issues, they contribute to the emergence of a debate and of a more political and confrontational style in a consensual and technocratic polity. They contribute to expanding the scope of conflict within the political system, by expanding the audience of the debates from a closed, elite-dominated arena to wider publics (Statham and Trenz 2012). This could help the EU to switch from a negotiating democracy to a debate democracy since this increased contestation through politicization is a core element of a consolidated and "normal" political system (De Wilde and Zürn 2012). Their presence might therefore be an asset for the affirmation of the EU as a democratic political system, open to conflict and help alleviate its democratic deficit.

However, one of the assumptions is that for the politicization to have positive effect on the integration process, it requires the supporter of the European project to take the opportunity to articulate their views and mobilize citizens (Habermas 2012; Hix 2006; Kriesi 2016). So far, mainstream parties have mostly de-emphasized EU issues: They are internally divided and have no interest in putting those issues on the agenda (Grande et al. 2016; Kriesi 2016). They avoid talking about Europe or even obscure their positions, which hampers a fully-fledged debate on European integration (Adam et al. 2016). In the EP, this trend is reflected by the tendency of the pro-EU political groups to vote together and form a grand coalition, blurring the policy differences between right and left and therefore contributing to the de-politicizing the policy-making process. As showed by a recent survey (Votewatch 2015), the increased presence of Eurosceptics has altered the dynamics of the parliament during the first half of the 8th legislature, by forcing the EPP and S&D to dilute their differences. This grand coalition has come under threat in 2017 with the election of the new president of the EP where the EPP disregarded their gentlemen agreement with the other largest group, the S&D. Only time will tell if a new dynamic will emerge in the chamber, in which meaningful debates can take place on the arguments put forward by Eurosceptics. But so far, pro-integration actors have favoured a non-partisan approach to the EU functioning, which constitutes a strong challenge to the legitimization of the European polity.

More globally, the results of the 2014 EP elections and the Brexit referendum could be interpreted as a signal or even a warning for (EU) elites. With the victory of pro-EU candidates and parties at the French and Dutch elections in 2017, European elites could heave a sigh of relief. But the scores of Eurosceptic and radical parties were significant, and the concerns of their voters are not going to disappear just because a pro-EU government could be formed. There is a need of debate on the EU's reform, direction and *raison d'être*. The current context of crisis exacerbates the EU's legitimacy deficit and stresses even more the need for a debate on the nature and purpose of the European project. In that respect, conflicts, opposition and a plurality of views are at the heart of a democratic regime (Nicolaïdis and Pelabay 2007, 2008). It could be damaging for the EU to persist in ignoring the Eurosceptics. As a political system which claims to be open, transparent and democratic, "the greatest danger is not the election of so many Eurosceptics to the EP but the risk that the parliament and the Union can continue to function as if nothing has happened. (…) (The Eurosceptics) form a legitimate part of the body politic and deserve as much attention as any other section of society" (Usherwood 2014). The existence of an anti-system opposition within the chamber is not likely to undermine the effectiveness of the decision-making process because this opposition has little choice but acting within the institutional arrangements. But in the absence of a dialogue with the EU's critics, the EP cannot yet be considered as a proper institutionalized site where opposition is engaged with. And the EU does not appear to be open to criticism and conflict. Rather than endangering European integration, the presence of Eurosceptics in the EP could be turned into an asset for the EU's legitimacy. They provide a channel for the expression of opposition of segments of public opinion. It attests to the democratic nature of the EU, which cannot be presented like a bureaucratic Leviathan exclusively composed of federalists. As such, they contribute to increasing the EP's representativeness as well as to the politicization of European issues. A debate seems to have emerged with the publication of the Commission White Paper on the future of Europe in March 2017. Only time will tell whether this debate will include and engage with dissenting voices throughout the continent. And whether this could lead to a normalization of the EU from a conflict-avoiding system to a more democratic and mature polity, which could, paradoxically, deprive Eurosceptics from their main arguments.

NOTE

1. For instance, Guy Verhofstadt, the leader of the ALDE group, denounce the way N. Farage carries out his mandate: "Well, colleagues, what I think is the biggest waste of money in the European Union today is the salary we are all paying to Mr Farage—that is the biggest waste of money! Mr Farage, let us be honest about it. You are a member of the Committee on Fisheries, for example, and you are never there, never! In 2011, no attendance. In 2012, no attendance. It is fantastic what you are doing. You come here saying that the salaries that are paid are a scandal, and you pay yourself a salary without doing any work in your own committee. (…)You can laugh. I hope that maybe this can be sent out on the BBC this evening, and on all the other private television channels in Britain, showing how you are in fact cheating your own citizens here, all the time, three years in a row already. See the debate on the "preparations for the European Council meeting with particular reference to the Multiannual Financial Framework", 21 November 2012.

REFERENCES

Abélès, M. (1996). *En attente d'Europe: débat avec Jean-Louis Bourlanges.* Paris: Hachette.

Beyers, J. (1998). Where does supranationalism come from? Ideas floating through the working groups of the Council of the European Union. *EIOP working papers, 2*(9), 1–25.

Bogaards, M. (2002). Consociational interpretations of the European Union. *European Union Politics, 3*(2), 357–381.

Conti, N. (2016). The Italian political elites and Europe: Big move, small change? *International Political Science Review*, online first. http://journals.sagepub.com/doi/abs/10.1177/0192512116641803.

Costa, O., & Magnette, P. (2003). The European Union as a consociation? A methodological assessment. *West European Politics, 26*(3), 1–18.

190   N. BRACK

Dahl, R. (1966). *Political oppositions in western democracies.* New Haven: Yale University Press.

Dahl, R. A. (1971). *Polyarchies: Participation and opposition.* New Haven: Yale University Press.

De Wilde, P. (2011). No polity for old politics? A framework for analyzing the politicization of European integration. *Journal of European Integration, 33*(5), 559–575.

De Wilde, P., & Zürn, M. (2012). Can the politicization of European integration be reversed? *Journal of Common Market Studies, 50*(S1), 137–153.

Farrell, D., & Scully, R. (2007). *Representing Europe's citizens? Electoral institutions and the failure of parliamentary representation.* Oxford: Oxford University Press.

Grabow, K., & Hartleb, F. (2014). *Europa-No, thanks?: Study on the rise of right-wing and national populist parties in Europe.* Bonn: Konrad-Adenauer-Stiftung.

Grande, E., & Hutter, S. (2016). Beyond authority transfer: Explaining the politicization of Europe. *West European Politics, 39*(1), 23–43.

Grande, E., & Kriesi, H. (2016). Conclusions: The postfunctionalists were (almost) right. In S. Hutter, E. Grande, & H. Kriesi (Eds.), *Politicising Europe* (pp. 279–300). Cambridge: Cambridge University Press.

Habermas, J. (2012). *The crisis of the European Union: A response.* London: Polity.

Hamel, J., & Thériault, Y. (1975). La fonction tribunitienne et la députation créditiste à l'Assemblée nationale du Québec: 1970–1973. *Canadian Journal of Political Science, 8*(1), 3–21.

Hirschman, A. O. (1970). *Exit, voice and Loyalty: Responses to decline in firms, organizations and states.* Cambridge: Harvard University Press.

Hirschman, A. O. (1978). Exit, voice and the states. *World Politics, 31*(1), 90–107.

Hix, S. (2006). La politisation de l'Union: remède ou poison? Paris: Notre Europe.

Hooghe, L., & Marks, G. (1999). The making of polity: The struggle over European integration. In M. Kitschelt, P. Lange, G. Marks, & J.-D. Stephens (Eds.), *Continuity and change in the contemporary capitalism* (pp. 70–99). Cambrigde: Cambirdge University Press.

Hooghe, L., & Marks, G. (2009). A Post-functionalist theory of European integration: From permissive consensus to constraining dissensus. *British Journal of Political Science, 39*(1), 1–23.

Huitt, R. (1961). The outsider in the Senate: An alternative role. *The American Political Science Review, 55*(3), 566–575.

Kauppi, N. (2005). *Political power in the European Parliament.* Manchester: Manchester University Press.

Kriesi, H. (2016). The politicization of European integration. *Journal of Common Market Studies, 54*(S1), 32–47.

Lascoumes, P. (2009). Les compromise parlementaires, combinaisons de sur-politisation et de sous-politisation. *Revue française de science politique, 59*(3), 455–478.

Lavau, G. (1968). A la recherche d'un cadre théorique pour l'étude du Parti communiste français. *Revue française de science politique, 18*(3), 445–466.

Leconte, C. (2010). *Understanding Euroscepticism*. Palgrave MacMillan: Basingstoke.

Magnette, P., & Papadopoulos, Y. (2008). *On the politicization of the European Consociation: A middle-way between Hix and Bartolini* (p. C0801). Eurogov: European governance papers.

Mair, P. (2007). Political opposition and the European Union. *Government and Opposition, 42*(1), 1–17.

Mattila, M., & Raunio, T. (2012). Drifting further apart: National parties and their electorates on the EU dimension. *West European Politics, 35*(3), 589–606.

Meijers, M. J. (2017). Contagious Euroscepticism: The impact of Eurosceptic support on mainstream party positions on European integration. *Party Politics, 23*(4), 413–423.

Mény, Y. (2012). Conclusion: A voyage to the unknown. *Journal of Common Market Studies, 50*(S1), 154–164.

Navarro, J. (2009). *Les députés européens et leur rôle. Sociologie interprétative des pratiques parlementaires*, Brussels: Editions de l'Université de Bruxelles.

Nicolaïdis, K., & Pelabay, J. (2007). Comment raconter l'Europe tout en prenant la diversité narrative au sérieux? *Raison publique, 7*, 63–83.

Nicolaïdis, K., & Pelabay, J. (2008). One union, one story? In Praise of Europe's narrative diversity. In A. Warleigh-Lack (Ed.), *Reflections on European Integration*. London: Palgrave.

Priestley, J. (2008). *Six battles that shaped Europe's parliament*. London: John Harper Publishing.

Rozenberg, O. (2009). L'influence du Parlement européen et l'indifférence de ses électeurs: une corrélation fallacieuse? *Politique européenne, 28*(2), 7–36.

Schattschneider, E. (1975). *The semi-sovereign people: A realist's view of democracy in America*. Hinsdale: The Dryden Press.

Schmitter, P. (1969). Three neo-functional hypothesis about international integration. *International Organization, 23*(1), 161–166.

Startin, N. (2010). Where to for the radical right in the European Parliament? The rise and fall of transnational political cooperation. *Perspectives on European Politics and Society, 11*(4), 429–449.

Strøm, K. (1997). Rules, reasons and routines: Legislative roles in parliamentary democracies. In W. C. Müller & T. Saalfeld (Eds.), *Members of parliament in Western Europe: Roles and behaviour* (pp. 155–174). London: Frank Cass.

Taggart, P., & Szczerbiak, A. (2013). Coming in from the Cold? Euroscepticism, government participation and party positions on Europe. *Journal of Common Market Studies, 51*(1), 17–37.

Thomassen, J. (2012). The blind corner of political representation. *Representation, 48*(1), 13–27.

Usherwood, S. (2014). "The Eurosceptic paradox", EPERN, Available at https://epern.wordpress.com/2.014/06/09/the-eurosceptic-paradox/.

Whitaker, R., Hix, S., & Zapryanova, G. (2017). Understanding members of the European Parliament: Four waves of the European Parliament Research Group MEP survey. *European Union Politics*, Forthcoming, doi:10.1177/1465116516687399.

Young, A. R. (2016). An inflection point in European Union studies? *Journal of European Public Policy, 23*(8), 1109–1117.

Zellentin, G. (1967). Form and function of the opposition in the European communities. *Government and Opposition, 2*(3), 416–435.

Zürn, M. (2016). Opening up Europe: Next steps in politicisation research. *West European Politics, 39*(1), 164–182.

Appendix 1: Operationalization of the Concept of Role

The operationalization of the concept of role can be summarized in the form of the following table:

Dimensions	Indicators	
	Attitudes (interview data)	Behaviours
Focus of representation	Who do you represent first and foremost in the EP?	Proportion of written questions with a European, regional, national or local focus or relating to problems of their electorate or with no particular focus
	What does it mean for you to be a good representative?	
	How much time per month do you spend in your district?	
	How would you qualify your relationship with the citizens?	
Perception of role	Thinking about your broad role as MEP, what are the most important duties and responsibilities involved?	

(continued)

Dimensions	Indicators	
	Attitudes (interview data)	Behaviours
	How important is your work as MEP to the functioning of the society as a whole?	
Priorities	What are the activities you try to never miss? Why? How did you choose the parliamentary committees in which you seat? How much time do you spend working in and for the committees a month?	Number of reports, questions, opinions, written declarations, speeches in plenary
	What parliamentary tools do you most often use (questions, speeches, amendments, etc.)? Why?	Responsibility within the EP and its bodies (including within the groups)
	What are your priorities for this parliamentary term?	Attendance in plenary
		Voting behaviour in one year: proportion of negative votes, proportion of votes in the EP minority/analysis of voting themes (vote differentiated by policy area)
Motivation/gratification	Why did you decide to become a politician?	Respect for rules of the institution
	Why did you decide to stand as candidate for the European elections?	
	Thinking about your political activity, what do you find personally most satisfying about it?	
	What would you miss most if you left politics?	
	What would you like to do 10 years from now?	

Appendix 2: Ordered Logit Model for the Typology of Roles, all Independent Variables

	Estimate	S.E.	95% Confidence interval	
			Lower bound	Upper bound
Hard Euroscepticism	−5880***	1282	−8392	−3367
Intergovernmentalism	−1690*	698	−3058	−322
Soft Euroscepticism	0[a]			
Gender = male	128	626	−1099	1356
Seniority = junior	−335	620	−1551	881
Political experience = none	−444	582	−1584	696
Non attached	−1173	1393	−3903	1558
ENF	−1907	1668	−5177	1362
I/D + EFD(D)	−1495	1001	−3.457	0.466
ECR	−256	0.931	−2082	1569
Eul/Ngl + Greens	256	0.931	−1.569	2.082
Proportional elec. system (national)	634	3827	−6867	8135
UK	2425	4141	−10.541	5691
Belgium	−4.657	4.289	−3749	13.063
Netherlands	−4.448	4.144	−3673	12.570
France	−1.466	1.159	−0.805	3.737
Sweden	−2.192	4.032	−5.711	10.095
Italy	0.167	3.879	−7436	6993
Portugal	793	4259	−7555	9142
Greece	−1.562	4244	−6755	9880
Cyprus	−2202	4556	−6746	11.151
Germany	061	4062	−7900	8022
Finland	−3364	4299	−5062	11.791
Denmark	−1885	4082	−6115	9885

(continued)

© The Editor(s) (if applicable) and The Author(s) 2018
N. Brack, *Opposing Europe in the European Parliament*,
Palgrave Studies in European Union Politics,
https://doi.org/10.1057/978-1-137-60201-5

	Estimate	S.E.	95% Confidence interval	
			Lower bound	Upper bound
Poland	−2425	4141	−5691	10.541
Czech Rep.	287	4045	−8215	7642
Ireland	1233	2813	−4281	6747
Austria	−3339	4269	−5028	11.706
Croatia	−3173	4704	−6048	12.393
Hungary	−0.491	2377	−5149	4167
Spain	−1.295	4.942	−8.392	10.981

Pseudo R^2 (Nagelkerke) = 0.692
LR Chi^2 = 101.659
***$p < 0.001$; **$p < 0.005$; *$p < 0.05$
[a]ref. category

Interviews List

Eurosceptic MEPs

1. MEP 1, NL, interview in Dutch, in Brussels, 12 September 2009
2. MEP 2, UK, interviewed in Brussels, 23 July 2009
3. MEP 3, NL, interviewed in Dutch, in Brussels, 28 October 2009
4. MEP 4, UK, interviewed in Brussels, 7 October 2009
5. MEP 5, UK, interviewed in Brussels, 23 February 2011
6. MEP 6, GR, interviewed in Brussels, 8 December 2010
7. MEP 7, UK, interviewed in Strasbourg, 15 July 2009
8. MEP 8, UK, interviewed in Brussels, 28 January 2010
9. MEP 9, FR, interviewed in Brussels, 26 January 2010
10. MEP 10, UK, interviewed in Brussels, 23 March 2006 and 9 December 2009
11. MEP 11 UK, interviewed in Brussels, 14 October 2009
12. MEP 12, BE, interviewed in Brussels, 1 September 2009 and 14 February 2014
13. MEP 13, UK, interviewed in Brussels, 3 February 2010
14. MEP 14, DE, interviewed in Brussels, 9 June 2010
15. MEP 15, UK, interviewed in Brussels, 21 March 2006
16. MEP 16, DK, interviewed in Brussels, 9 July 2009
17. MEP 17, UK, interviewed in Brussels, 30 March 2011
18. MEP 18, UK, interviewed in Brussels, 22 March 2010
19. MEP 19, CZ, interviewed in Brussels, 12 April 2011
20. MEP 20, NL, interviewed in Brussels, 29 October 2009

© The Editor(s) (if applicable) and The Author(s) 2018
N. Brack, *Opposing Europe in the European Parliament*,
Palgrave Studies in European Union Politics,
https://doi.org/10.1057/978-1-137-60201-5

21. MEP 21, FR, interviewed in Brussels, 5 May 2010
22. MEP 22, UK, interviewed in Strasbourg, 15 July 2009
23. MEP 23, SE, interviewed in Brussels, 21 March 2006
24. MEP 24, PL, interviewed in Brussels, 12 January 2010
25. MEP 25, PT, interviewed in Brussels, 3 March 2010
26. MEP 26, CY, interviewed in Brussels, 9 December 2009
27. MEP 27, IRL, interviewed in Brussels, 3 February 2010
28. MEP 28, UK, interviewed in Brussels, 26 August 2009
29. MEP 29, SE, interviewed in Brussels, 18 March 2010
30. MEP 30, FR, interviewed in Brussels, 6 October 2010
31. MEP 31, PT, interviewed in Brussels, 26 January 2010
32. MEP 32, SE, interviewed in Brussels, 23 November 2011
33. MEP 33, DE, interviewed in Brussels, 9 June 2010
34. MEP 34, SE, phone interview, 5 March 2010
35. MEP 35, CZ, interviewed in Brussels, 17 March 2010
36. MEP 36, UK, interviewed in Brussels, 3 February 2010
37. MEP 37, AT, phone interview, 2 February 2010
38. MEP 38, PT, interviewed in Brussels, 11 June 2010
39. MEP 39, NL, interviewed in Brussels, 30 November 2010
40. MEP 40, UK, interviewed in Brussels, 20 March 2006 and 2 July 2009
41. MEP 41, IT, interviewed in Brussels, 23 June 2010
42. MEP 42, CZ, interviewed in Brussels, 9 June 2010
43. MEP 43, IT, interviewed in Brussels, 13 April 2010
44. MEP 44, FR, interviewed in Brussels, 2 April 2009
45. MEP 45, DE, interviewed in Brussels, 28 January 2010
46. MEP 46, FI, interviewed in Brussels, 16 March 2011
47. MEP 47, IRL, phone interview, 7 August 2009
48. MEP 48, IT, interviewed in Brussels, 17 March 2011
49. MEP 49, SE, interviewed in Brussels, 28 April 2009
50. MEP 50, DK, interviewed in Brussels, 2 February 2010
51. MEP 51, IT, interviewed in Brussels, 3 June 2010
52. MEP 52, UK, interviewed in Brussels, 16 March 2010
53. MEP 53, CY, interviewed in Brussels, 11 November 2009
54. MEP 54, UK, phone interview, 15 April 2006
55. MEP 55, PL, phone interview, 7 April 2010
56. MEP 56, FR, phone interview, 20 August 2010
57. MEP 57, UK, interviewed in Brussels, 7 July 2009
58. MEP 58, BE, interviewed in Brussels, 28 January 2010

59. MEP 59, SE, interviewed in Brussels, 1 December 2010
60. MEP 60, UK, interviewed in Brussels, 30 June 2009
61. MEP 61, CZ, interviewed in Brussels, 2 June 2010
62. MEP 62, DE, interviewed in Brussels, 15 March 2010
63. MEP 63, CZ, interviewed in Brussels, 18 April 2006
64. MEP 64, UK, interviewed in Brussels, 18 January 2012
65. MEP 65, UK, interviewed in Brussels, 15 September 2009
66. MEP 66, DE, interviewed in Brussels, 15 October 2015
67. MEP 67, UK, interviewed in Brussels, 16 September 2015
68. MEP 68, HU, interviewed in Brussels, 16 June 2015
69. MEP 69, UK, interviewed in Brussels, 10 November 2015
70. MEP 70, DK, interviewed in Brussels, 12 January 2016
71. MEP 71, IT, interviewed in Brussels, 11 November 2015
72. MEP 72, UK, interviewed in Brussels, 19 April 2016
73. MEP 73, GR, interviewed in Brussels, 26 February 2015
74. MEP 74, IT, interviewed in Brussels, 17 March 2015
75. MEP 75, FI, interviewed in Brussels, 30 March 2015
76. MEP 76, CZ, interviewed in Brussels, 15 April 2015
77. MEP 77, FR, interviewed in Brussels, 25 February 2015
78. MEP 78, FR, interviewed in Brussels, 25 February 2015
79. MEP 79, FR, interviewed in Brussels, 25 February 2015
80. MEP 80, FR, interviewed in Brussels, 25 February 2015
81. MEP 81, FR, interviewed in Brussels, 5 May 2015
82. MEP 82, DE, interviewed in Brussels, 5 May 2015
83. MEP 83, DE, interviewed in Brussels, 16 September 2015
84. MEP 84, IT, interviewed in Brussels, 16 September 2015
85. MEP 85, FR, interviewed in Brussels, 27 May 2015
86. MEP 86, DE, interviewed in Brussels, 7 May 2015
87. MEP 87, FI, interviewed in Strasbourg, 2 July 2014
88. MEP 88, ES, interviewed in Brussels, 28 January 2016
89. MEP 89, IT, interviewed in Brussels, 2 December 2015
90. MEP 90, IT, interviewed in Brussels, 2 December 2015
91. MEP 91, IT, interviewed in Brussels, 20 January 2016
92. MEP 92, PL, phone interview, 20 April 2016
93. MEP 93, HR, interviewed in Brussels, 21 March 2016
94. MEP 94, AT, interviewed in Brussels, 10 November 2010
95. MEP 95, IT, interviewed in Brussels, 12 January 2015
96. MEP 96, UK, interviewed in Brussels, 25 September 2014
97. MEP 97, SE, interviewed in Strasbourg, 3 July 2014

98. MEP 98, UK, interviewed in Strasbourg, 15 July 2009
99. MEP 99, FR, interviewed in Brussels, 4 May 2011
100. MEP 100, PL, phone interview, 13 May 2010
101. MEP 101, UK, phone interview, 15 September 2011.

Non Eurosceptic MEPs

1. MEP 102, ALDE, BE, phone interview, 7 April 2006
2. MEP 103, S&D, FR, interviewed in Brussels, 9 November 2009
3. MEP 104, S&D, FR, interviewed in Strasbourg, 16 July 2009
4. MEP 105, S&D, FR, interviewed in Brussels, 24 February 2010
5. MEP 106, EPP, LU, interviewed in Brussels, 27 January 2010
6. MEP 107, EPP, ES, interviewed in Brussels, 3 February 2010
7. MEP 108, EPP, PL, interviewed in Brussels, 7 April 2010
8. MEP 109, EPP, FI, interviewed in Brussels, 13 July 2010
9. MEP 110, EPP, RO, interviewed in Brussels, 17 March 2010.

Civil Servants

1. Interview CPE #1, Brussels, 23 June 2010
2. Interview CPE #2, Brussels, 29 January 2010
3. Interview CPE #3, Brussels, 25 February 2010
4. Interview CPE #4, Brussels, 23 November 2011
5. Interview CPE #5, Brussels, 12 April 2006
6. Interview CPE #6, Brussels, 8 June 2010
7. Interview CPE #7, Brussels, 18 March 2014
8. Interview CPE#8, Brussels, 10 January 2017.

Parliamentary Assistants

1. Interview A # 1, Brussels, 12 March 2010
2. Interview A #2, Brussels, 29 April 2010
3. Interview A #3, phone interview, 29 March 2006
4. Interview A #4, Brussels, 12 February 2010
5. Interview A #5, Brussels, 25 March 2011
6. Interview A #6, Brussels, 18 January 2010
7. Interview A #7, Brussels, 21 March 2006
8. Interview A #8, Strasbourg, 15 July 2009

9. Interview A #9, Brussels, 12 October 2010
10. Interview A #10, Brussels, 8 April 2011
11. Interview A #11, Brussels, 9 April 2010
12. Interview A #12, Brussels, 12 November 2009
13. Interview A #13, Brussels, 8 February 2010
14. Interview A #14, Brussels, 5 March 2010
15. Interview A #15, Brussels, 18 March 2015.

BIBLIOGRAPHY

Albertazzi, D., & McDonnell, D. (2007). *Twenty-first century populism: The spectre of Western European democracy.* London: Palgrave.

Andersen, S., & Eliassen, A. K. (1996). *The European Union: How democratic is it?* London: Sage.

Armingeon, K., & Guthmann, K. (2014). Democracy in crisis? The declining support for national democracy in European countries 2007–2011. *European Journal of Political Research, 53*(3), 423–442.

Aspinwall, M. (2002). Preferring Europe: Ideology and national preferences on European integration. *European Union Politics, 3*(2), 81–111.

Baker, D., & Seawright, D. (1998). *Britain for and against Europe: British politics and the question of European integration.* Oxford: Clarendon Press.

Bartolini, S. (2000). *The political mobilization of the European left, 1860–1980: The Class Cleavage.* Cambridge: Cambridge University Press.

Bartolini, S. (2005). *Restructuring Europe: Centre formation, system building, and political structuring between the nation state and the European Union.* Oxford: Oxford University Press.

Batory, A. (2002). Attitudes to Europe: Ideology, strategy and the issue of European Union membership in hungarian party politics. *Party Politics, 8*(5), 525–539.

Beauvallet, W. (2003). Institutionnalisation et professionnalisation de l'Europe politique: le cas des eurodéputés français. *Politique européenne, 9,* 99–122.

Beauvallet, W., & Michon, S. (2006). From notables to specialists: European parliamentarians and the construction of new political roles. *Etudes Européennes,* 1–15.

Beauvallet, W., & Michon, S. (2012). Faire carrière au Parlement européen. Activation de dispositions et socialisation institutionnelle. In D. Georgakakis

© The Editor(s) (if applicable) and The Author(s) 2018
N. Brack, *Opposing Europe in the European Parliament,*
Palgrave Studies in European Union Politics,
https://doi.org/10.1057/978-1-137-60201-5

(Ed.), *Le champ de l'Eurocratie. Une sociologie politique du personnel de l'UE* (pp. 13–43). Paris: Economica.

Belot, C. (2002). Les logiques sociologiques de soutien au processus d'intégration européenne: éléments d'interprétation. *Revue Internationale de Politique Comparée, 9*(1), 11–29.

Berry, J. (2002). Validity and reliability issues in elite interviewing. *PS Online, 35,* 679–682.

Bouillaud, C. (2005). L'euroscepticisme partisan lors des élections européennes de juin 2004. Un premier essai d'estimation et d'explication. In P. Delwit & P. Poirier (Eds.), *Parlement puissant, électeurs absents? Les élections de juin 2004* (pp. 219–251). Brussels: Editions de l'Université de Bruxelles.

Brady, H. E., & Collier, D. (2004). *Rethinking social inquiry.* Boulder: Rowman and Littlefield.

Cain, B. E., Ferejohn, J. A., & Fiorina, M. P. (1987). *The personal vote: Constituency service and electoral independence.* Cambridge: Harvard University Press.

Carrubba, C. J. (2001). The electoral connection in European Union politics. *Journal of Politics, 63*(1), 141–158.

Cayrol, R., Parodi, J. L., & Ysmal, C. (1971). L'image de la fonction parlementaire chez les députés français. *Revue française de science politique, 21,* 1173–1206.

Checkel, J. T. (2003). Going native in Europe? Theorizing social interaction in European institutions. *Comparative Political Studies, 36*(1–2), 209–231.

Clements, B., Nanou, K., & Verney, S. (2014). 'We no longer love you, but we don't want to leave you': The Eurozone crisis and popular Euroscepticism in Greece. *Journal of European Integration, 36*(3), 247–265.

Coenen-Huther, J. (2003). Le type idéal comme instrument de la recherche sociologique. *Revue française de sociologie, 44*(3), 531–547.

Collier, D., & Elman, C. (2010). Qualitative and multi-method research: Organizations, publication, and reflections on integration. In J. M. Box-Steffensmeier, H. E. Brady, & D. Collier (Eds.), *The oxford handbook of political methodology* (pp. 779–795). Oxford: Oxford University Press.

Conti, N. (2003). Party attitudes to European integration: A longitudinal analysis of the italian case. *SEI working paper, 70,* 15–18.

Conti, N. (2007). Domestic parties and European integration: The problem of party attitudes to the EU, and the Europeanisation of parties. *European Political Science, 6,* 192–207.

Conti, N., & Memoli, V. (2012). The multifaceted nature of party based Euroscepticism. *Acta Politica, 47*(2), 91–112.

Curtis, A., & Jupille, J. (2011). The European Union. In G. T. Kurian (Ed.), *The encyclopedia of political science.* Washington, DC: CQ Press.

Dahl, R. (1965). Reflections on opposition in western democracies. *Government and Opposition, 1*(1), 7–24.

Dahl, R. A. (1973). *Regimes and oppositions*. New Haven: Yale University Press.

Déloye, Y. (2008). En guise de conclusion: ce que résister veut dire ou les paradoxes d'une construction européenne face aux contingences historiques et aux logiques politiques nationales. *Revue internationale de politique comparée, 15*(4), 679–685.

De Wilde, P. (2009). Welcome sceptics! *Hamburg Review of Social Sciences, 4*(2), 59–73.

De Wilde, P., Leupold, A., & Schmidtke, H. (2016). Introduction: The differentiated politicisation of European governance. *West European Politics, 39*(1), 3–22.

Dexter, L. (1970). *Elite and specialised interviewing*. Evanston: Northwestern University Press.

Faas, T. (2004). To defect or not to defect? National, institutional and party group pressures on MEPs and their consequences for party cohesion in the European parliament. *European Journal of Political Research, 42*(6), 841–866.

Forster, A. (2002). *Euroscepticism in contemporary British politics*. London: Routledge.

Franklin, M., & Scarrow, S. (1999). Making Europeans? The socialisation power of the European parliament. In R. Katz & W. Wessels (Eds.), *The European parliament, the national parliaments and European integration* (pp. 45–60). Oxford: Oxford University Press.

Gabel, M. (1998). *Interests and integration: Market liberalization, public opinion and European Union*. Ann Arbor: University of Michigan Press.

Gabel, M. (1998). Public support for European integration: An empirical test of five theories. *The Journal of Politics, 60*(2), 333–354.

Gaffney, J. (1996). *Political parties and the European union*. London: Routledge.

Haas, E. (1958). *The uniting of Europe: Political, social and economic forces*. Stanford: Stanford University Press.

Halikiopoulou, D., Nanou, K., & Vasilopoulou, S. (2012). The paradox of nationalism: The common denominator of radical left and radical right Euroscepticism. *European Journal of Political Research, 51*(4), 504–539.

Hall, P. A., & Taylor, R. C. (1996). Political science and the three new institutionalisms. *Political studies, 44*(5), 936–957.

Harmsen, R., & Spiering, M. (2004). *Euroscepticism: Party politics, national identity and European integration*. Amsterdam: Rodopi.

Hartleb, F. (2012). European project in danger? Understanding precisely the phenomena Euroscepticism, populism in times of crisis. *Review of European Studies, 4*(5), 45–63.

Hetshusen, V., Young, G., & Wood, D. M. (2005). Electoral context and MP constituency focus in Australia, Canada, Ireland, New Zealand and United Kingdom. *American Journal of Political Science, 49*(1), 32–45.

Hix, S. (1999). Dimensions and alignments in European union politics: Cognitive constraints and partisan responses. *European Journal of Political Research, 35*(2), 69–106.

Hix, S. (2001). Legislative behaviour and party competition in the European parliament: An application of nominate to the EU. *Journal of Common Market Studies, 39*(4), 663–688.

Hix, S., Raunio, T., & Scully, R. (2003). Fifty years on: Research on the European parliament. *Journal of Common Market Studies, 41*(2), 191–202.

Hix, S., Kreppel, A., & Noury, A. (2003). The party system in the European parliament: Collusive or competitive? *Journal of Common Market Studies, 41*(2), 309–331.

Hix, S., Noury, A., & Roland, G. (2005). Power to the parties: Cohesion and competition in the European parliament: 1979–2001. *British Journal of Political Science, 35*(2), 209–234.

Hooghe, L. (2005). Several roads lead to international norms, but few via international socialization: A case study of the European commission. *International Organization, 59*, 861–898.

Hooghe, L. (2007). What drives Euroskepticism? Party-public cueing, ideology and strategic opportunity. *European Union Politics, 8*(5), 5–12.

Hooghe, L., & Marks, G. (2008). European Union? *West European Politics, 31*(1/2), 108–129.

Høyland, B. (2010). Procedural and party effects in European parliament roll-call votes. *European Union Politics, 4*(4), 597–613.

Hug, S. (2006). Selection effect in Roll-call votes. *Centre for Comparative and International Studies Working Paper*. Zürich Swiss Federal Institute of Technology, 15.

Hutter, S., Grande, E., & Kriesi, H. (2016). *Politicising Europe: Integration and mass politics*. Cambridge: Cambridge University Press.

Jewell, M. E. (1983). Legislator-constituency relations and the representative process. *Legislative Studies Quarterly, 8*, 303–337.

Kerrouche, E. (2004). Appréhender le rôle des parlementaires: études comparatives des recherches menées et perspectives. In O. Costa, E. Kerrouche, & P. Magnette (Eds.), *Vers un renouveau du parlementarisme en Europe?* (pp. 35–55). Brussels: Editions de l'Université libre de Bruxelles.

King, G., Keohane, R., & Verba, S. (1994). *Designing social inquiry: Scientific inference in qualitative research*. Princeton: Princeton University Press.

Kircheimer, O. (1957). The waning of opposition in parliamentary regimes. *Social Research, 24*(1), 127–156.

Kriesi, H., Grande, E., Lachat, R., Dolezal, M., Bornschier, S., & Frey, T. (2008). *Globalization and the transformation of the national political space, six countries compared*. Cambridge: Cambridge University Press.

Laffan, B. (2014). Testing times: The growing primacy of responsibility in the Euro area. *West European Politics, 37*(2), 270–287.

Lavau, G. (1981). *A quoi sert le Parti communiste français?* Paris: Fayard.

Leca, J. (1992). Représentation. In O. Duhamel & Y. Meny (Eds.), *Dictionnaire constitutionnel* (pp. 914–917). Paris: Presses Universitaires de France.

Lewis, J. (1998). Is the 'Hard Bagaining' image of the council misleading? The committee of permanent representatives and the local elections directive. *Journal of Common Market Studies, 36*(4), 479–504.

Lindstädt, R., Slapin, J. B., & Wielen, R. J. V. (2012). Adaptive behaviour in the European parliament: Learning to balance competing demands. *European Union Politics, 13*(4), 465–486.

Lipset, S. M., & Rokkan, S. (1967). *Party systems and voter alignments: Cross-national perspectives.* New York: Free Press.

Lubbers, M., & Scheepers, P. (2005). Political versus instrumental Euroscepticism: Mapping skepticism in European countries and regions. *European Union Politics, 2*(6), 223–242.

Mair, P. (2006). Polity-scepticism, party failings and the challenge to European democracy. *Uhlenbeck Lecture 24.* Wassenaar: NIAS.

March, J. G., & Olsen, J. P. (1996). Institutional perspectives on political institutions. *Governance, 9*(3), 247–264.

Marks, G., & Steenbergen, M. (2002). Understanding political contestation in the European Union. *Comparative Political Studies, 35*(2), 879–892.

Marks, G., & Steenbergen, M. (2004). *European integration and political conflict.* Cambridge: Cambridge University Press.

Marks, G., Hooghe, L., Nelson, M., & Edwards, E. (2006). Party competition and European integration in the East and West: Different structure, same causality. *Comparative Political Studies, 39*(2), 433–459.

Marquand, D. (1979). *Parliament for Europe.* London: Jonathan Cape.

Marsh, M., & Norris, P. (1997). Political representation in the European parliament. *European Journal of Political Research, 32*(2), 153–164.

Mayhew, D. R. (1974). *Congress—The electoral connection.* New Haven: Yale University Press.

McLarren, L. (2004). Opposition to European integration and fear of loss of national identity: Debunking a basic assumption regarding hostility to the integration project. *European Journal of Political research, 43*(6), 283–306.

Miller, W. E., & Stokes, D. E. (1963). Constituency influence in congress. *American Political Science Review, 57*(1), 45–56.

Milner, S. (2000). Introduction: A healthy Euroscepticism. *Journal of European Integration, 22*(1), 1–14.

Müller, W. C., & Saalfeld, T. (1997). *Members of parliament in Western Europe: Roles and behaviour.* London: Frank Cass.

Mülböck, M. (2012). National versus European: Party control over members of the European parliament. *West European Politics, 35*(3), 607–631.

Neumayer, L. (2005). De l'euroréalisme au souverainisme? Le discours eurosceptique dans trois nouveaux Etats membres de l'UE. In P. Delwit & P. Poirier (Eds.), *Parlement puissant, électeurs absents? Les élections européennes de juin 2004* (pp. 251–271). Brussels: Editions de l'Université de Bruxelles.

Nicolaïdis, K. (2013). European demoicracy and its crisis. *Journal of Common Market Studies, 51*(2), 351–369.

Nicoli, F. (2016). Hard-line Euroscepticism and the Eurocrisis. Evidence from a panel study of 108 elections across Europe. *Journal of Common Market Studies, forthcoming.*

Norton, P., & Wood, D. (1990). Constituency service by members of parliament: Does it contribute to a personal vote? *Parliamentary Affairs, 43*(2), 196–208.

Norton, P. (2001). Playing by the rules: The constraining hand of parliamentary procedure. *Journal of Legislative Studies, 7*(3), 13–33.

Pisany Ferry, J. (2013). *The Eurocrisis and its aftermath.* Oxford: Oxford University Press.

Przeworski, A., Stokes, S., & Manin, B. (1999). *Democracy, accountability, and representation.* Cambridge: Cambridge University Press.

Raunio, T. (2000). Losing independence or finally gaining recognition? Contacts between MEPs and National Parties. *Party Politics, 6*(2), 211–233.

Rittberger, B. (2007). *Building Europe's parliament: Democratic representation beyond the nation state.* Oxford: Oxford University Press.

Ray, L. (2007). Mainstream Euroskepticism: Trend or Oxymoron? *Acta Politica, 42*(2/3), 153–172.

Richards, D. (1996). Elite interviewing: Approaches and pitfalls. *Politics, 16*(3), 199–204.

Rosenthal, H., & Voeten, E. (2004). Analyzing roll calls with perfect spatial voting: France 1946–1958. *American Journal of Political Science, 48*(3), 620–632.

Schattschneider, E. (1957). Intensity, visibility, direction and scope. *American Political Sience Review, 51,* 933–942.

Schmidt, V. (2007). *The EU and National polities.* Oxford: Oxford University Press.

Schmitt, H., & Thomassen, J. (1999). *Political representation and legitimacy in the European Union.* Oxford: Oxford University Press.

Searing, D. (1986). A theory of political socialization: Institutional support and deradicalization in Britain. *British Journal of Political Science, 16*(3), 341–376.

Silverman, D. (2006). *Interpreting qualitative data: A guide to the principles of qualitative research.* London: Sage.

Slapin, J. B., & Proksh, S.-O. (2010). Look who's talking: Parliamentary debate in the European Union. *European Union Politics, 11*(3), 333–357.

Smith, A. (1999). L'espace politique européen, une vue trop aérienne. *Critique internationale, 2,* 168–180.

Szczerbiak, A., & Taggart, P. (2003). Theorizing party-based Euroscepticism: Problems of definition, measurement and causality. *SEI Working Paper, 36.*

Usherwoord, S. (2004). Bruges as a lodestone of British opposition to the European Union. *Collegium, 39,* 5–16.

Van de Wardt, M. (2014). Putting a Damper on: Do parties de-emphasize issues in response to internal divisions among their supporters? *Party Politics*, 20(3), 330–340.

Vasilopoulou, S. (2009). Varieties of Euroscepticism: The case of the European extreme right. *Journal of Contemporary European Research*, 5(1), 223–244.

Verschueren, N. (2009). Réactions syndicales aux premières heures de l'intégration européenne. In A. Crespy & M. Petithomme (Eds.), *L'Europe sous tensions. Appropriation et contestation de l'intégration européenne* (pp. 197–214). Paris: L'Harmattan.

Wessels, B. (1999). Whom to represent? Role orientations of legislators in Europe. In H. Schmitt & J. Thomassen (Eds.), *Political representation and legitimacy in the European Union* (pp. 209–234). Oxford: Oxford University Press.

Wessels, B. (2007). Discontent and European identity: Three types of Euroscepticism. *Acta Politica*, 42(2/3), 287–306.

Whitaker, R. (2005). National parties in the European parliament: An influence in the committee system? *European Union Politics*, 6(1), 5–28.

Wodak, R. (2009). The discourse of politics in action. *Politics as usual*. Basingstoke: Palgrave McMillan.

Wood, D. M., & Yoon, J. B. (1998). Role orientations of junior MPs: A test of Searing's categories with emphasis on constituency activities. *Journal of Legislative studies*, 4(3), 51–71.

INDEX

© The Editor(s) (if applicable) and The Author(s) 2018
N. Brack, *Opposing Europe in the European Parliament*,
Palgrave Studies in European Union Politics,
https://doi.org/10.1057/978-1-137-60201-5

CPI Antony Rowe
Chippenham, UK
2018-03-06 21:22